Doghiker

The dog enters thoroughly into the spirit of the enterprise; he is not indifferent or preoccupied; he is constantly sniffing adventure, laps at every spring, looks upon every field and wood as a new world to be explored, is ever on some fresh trail, knows something important will happen a little farther on, gazes with the true wonder-seeing eyes, whatever the spot or whatever the road finds it good to be there, -- in short, is just that happy, delicious, excursive vagabond that touches one at so many points, and whose human prototype in a companion robs miles and leagues of half their power to fatigue.

—John Burroughs,
"The Exhilarations of the Road," *Winter Sunshine*

DOGHIKER

*Great Hikes with Dogs
from the Adirondacks through the Catskills*

Alan Via

Cartography by Liz Cruz

excelsior editions

Photographic credits
front cover: *Winter,* Deb Osterhoudt
Rev—Pilot Knob, Mike Arthur
Take a Look at this—Hopkins view, Rob Osterhoudt
back cover: *Enjoying the view from Buck Mt.,* Aldo DiVirgilo
page i: *Bookah on Acra Point,* Joanne Hihn
page ii: *Bookah running thru flowers on Cave Mt.,* Alan Via
page v: *Bookah in ferns,* Moonray Schepart
Toby, Lillian Browne

book and cover design, Laurie Searl

Published by
State University of New York Press, Albany

Excelsior Editions is an imprint of State University of New York Press
For information, contact
State University of New York Press, Albany, NY
www.sunypress.edu

Library of Congress Cataloging-in-Publication Data

Names: Via, Alan, [Date–], author.
Title: Doghiker : great hikes with dogs from the Adirondacks through the
Catskills / Alan Via.
Description: Albany : Excelsior Editions, an imprint of State University of
New York Press, 2020. | Includes index. |
Identifiers: LCCN 2019040020 | ISBN 9781438478388 (paperback) |
ISBN 9781438478371 (ebook)
Subjects: LCSH: Hiking with dogs. | Hiking with dogs—New York
(State)—Adirondack Mountains—Guidebooks. | Hiking with dogs—New York
(State)—Catskill Mountains—Guidebooks. | Dogs—Training. | Adirondack
Mountains (N.Y.)—Guidebooks. | Catskill Mountains (N.Y.)—Guidebooks.
Classification: LCC SF427.455 .V53 2020 | DDC 796.5109747/1—dc23
LC record available at https://lccn.loc.gov/2019040020

10 9 8 7 6 5 4 3 2 1

Dedicated to our beloved Bookah (10/31/2004–10/28/2013), friend and partner.
She began this adventure and her spirt still haunts my summits.
And for Toby who follows in Boo's pawprints.

One way to get down the Cornell Crack.
—Joanne Hihn

Contents

Foreword

If you live with dogs, you'll never run out of things to write about.

—Sharon DeLarose

One might ask, "Do we really need a guide that encourages people to take their dogs hiking?" You may even feel that dogs don't belong on hiking trails. So why this book?

It's not my intent to recruit, encourage, or otherwise get more dogs hiking. Even if you firmly believe dogs belong at home, you'll discover my aim is to encourage good behavior rather than wishing away potential problems. Getting dog owners to think about positive trail behavior benefits everyone. I believe a better outcome results from encouraging responsible dog ownership and training rather than deploring bad trail behavior. My hope is that *Doghiker* encourages positive environmental impact and the enjoyment of those with whom doghikers share trails.

A recent survey shows dog ownership in America is at its highest-ever level with over seventy million canines and 63 percent of households containing at least one dog. According to the American Pet Products Association, Americans spent over $72 billion on pets in 2018, with more than $30 billion of that for pet food. Combine these statistics with an active population wanting to be fit and outdoors with their dogs, and it's an easy leap to see why we're seeing more dogs on trails. One of the most frequent inquiries hiking clubs and trip leaders receive is, "Where can we take our dog?" It was one of the most common questions asked at a recent outdoors expo.

I'm often asked what makes a good dog hike. Dogs don't care if the views are great, the trails are lined with wildflowers and interesting sights, or whether the photography may be stunning. Dogs love being outdoors with their people. If there are places for them to sniff and explore along a trail, any dog will be happy. I believe the most important factor for a good dog hike is that it needs to be fun, interesting, and engaging for dog owners. In my view, any hike has the potential to be a great dog hike if the human hikers are really enjoying it.

Doghiker differs from other guides in a number of ways. It covers the Adirondacks, the Catskills, and areas in-between. It's also a great standalone guide for hikers without dogs. I saw little point is selecting hikes people wouldn't really enjoy. You'll quickly realize *Doghiker* is not the typical trailhead-to-destination hiking guide. I've tried to put myself in your boots (and paws), pointing out terrain features and those of the surrounding forest. You'll read about wildflowers, fern glades, bird and animal life, as well as the best places for photography and views. Hikes were selected for interest, variety, geographic diversity, range of difficulty, and enjoyment.

The peak finder map locates each hike and a chart provides individual details. Each hike has a custom topographic map designed specifically for it. The maps show trailheads, surrounding roads, side trails, water features, and places of note. Each hike description begins with a paragraph outlining the highlights of the hike and what to expect. Directions, including GPS coordinates for intersections and trailheads, are provided to make it easy to locate the trailheads. Trail

Leo relaxing on the summit
—Alan Via

mileage, elevation gain, trail conditions, canine hydration opportunities, and potential dog hazards are all provided, as well as a difficulty rating for each hike, whether leashes are necessary, view ratings, and the best time of year to hike that trail. The summaries make it easy to select hikes suitable for you and your doghiker.

Doghiker provides more than a where-to-go with maps. There are chapters on dog selection, training, conditioning, and equipment. Others have information on canine first aid, nutrition, and how to keep your dog safe and happy on and off the trail. Even experienced dog owners should discover useful tips.

My family has enjoyed active dogs over a lifetime. Our pooches came in all sizes and types. They were mutts, a hound, two springers, a setter, and two labs. Our hiker dogs, Bookah and Toby, were the book's col*LAB*orators. I've had the chance to observe my dogs and those of others over the years. Some are excellent hikers, with great demeanor and woods courtesy. Others demonstrate they've received little training, giving all doghikers a bad name. You'll notice I'm as concerned with the enjoyment of dog-less hikers as those who hike with canine companions. With so many people sharing the mountains, the days of "love me, love my dog" are long past. I'd like to

Author making trail notes
—Joanne Hihn

think this guide, in addition to showing readers where to go, reminds them that we are all ambassadors for the dog hiking community.

Please pick up and carry out waste, and leash dogs on summits and sensitive terrain or when encountering hikers. Try to look through the eyes of others to see the impression you and your dog are making. Researching and hiking each of these mountains with my dogs, Bookah and Toby, has been pure enjoyment. I (we) hope you enjoy these trails as much as we have. Stroll through the pages and discover wonderful places to hike.

A final note for readers: Hiking, documenting and keeping up on the seventy-seven hikes contained herein has been a labor of love. Trail maintainers are always making small changes and improvements. I've done my best to keep up with trail modifications, but you may experience a few changes that have occurred as the manuscript was in process or after publication.

Doghiker Gryffin.
—Tim Lucia

Acknowledgments

For Annabelle

She was not a perfectly trained dog—
she was a perfect family pet.
Full stomach, love, and affection
Was all she asked for.
She filled our lives with much more.

—Matt Via

My name is on the cover, but *Doghiker* was a collaborative effort with others who helped and supported the project in so many ways.

It's a much better "read" thanks to Barbara Via's critical eye. Her picky review of drafts wore out red pencils and turned margins into an editorial red tide. Barbara's nose for nonsense salvaged many a paragraph. She cherished Bookah and loves hiking with Toby.

Michael Cooper's critical comments, skillful advice, review of the manuscript, and generosity was crucial in so many ways. I'll always be grateful for his invaluable assistance.

It isn't an exaggeration to say that *Doghiker* may have never made it to print without Liz Cruz. She's the talented cartographer who created each of the gorgeous maps. Liz designed the prototype of the book and has been my sounding board through every phase of *Doghiker.*

Imagine my delight when learning Lisa Metzger would copy-edit *Doghiker.* Her vast experience editing hiking guidebooks made this talented professional uniquely qualified to make sense of my hiker-inflected language, terms, and slang. Lisa diplomatically used the phrase, "Did you mean to say this, Alan?" at the beginning of so many of her questions that I often laughed out loud. Thanks, Lisa for making *Doghiker* so much more readable.

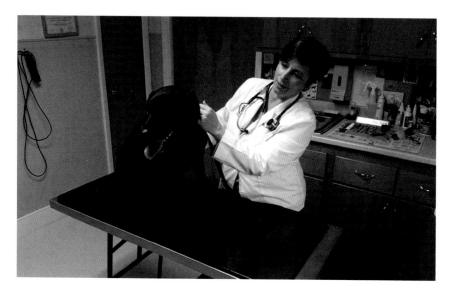

Dr Jennifer Bull—Toby's annual checkup
—Alan Via

Jennifer Bull, DVM, Delmar Animal Hospital, collaborated on sections relating to safety, protection, first aid, medical treatment, training, conditioning, and much more. Her invaluable advice and insights strengthen all aspects of the book.

Doctor Bull and her staff took care of Bookah, and Toby is under her expert care.

Thank you—

Michael Kudish, professor emeritus of botany, who has been an accomplice on many Catskill hikes and bushwhacks.

Ralph Ryndak, Mike Cantwell, and Ann Roberti, who provided background information on some of the hike descriptions. I learn something every time I'm in the woods with them.

Audrey, Pat, and Maria Sallese, and Marge Fisher, who brighten any day on the trail. They've put up with dogs' shenanigans for years, never concerned with the mess left in their wakes.

Michele Rawlins, who is a friend, hiker, and dog walking partner. Her dog, Layla, is Toby's sister and Michele's contagious enthusiasm makes every outing more enjoyable.

Dick and Joanne Hihn, who spent more time with Bookah on hikes and in cars than anyone. She loved cuddling with "Aunt Joanne" to and from hikes. Dick and Jo joined me on almost all of their bush-whacking adventures.

Becky Steiner, who has been a friend and dog walking partner for years. I've enjoyed the countless miles and conversations and am appreciative of her assistance with Bookah and Toby.

Doug and Marlene Sluiter's post hike hospitality always included Bookah biscuits. I'm indebted to Doug for the "homework" obtaining hiking permissions from his Delaware County friends and neighbors and for all the great bushwhacks we've done together.

Sandy and Bill Allen, who raise exceptional Labrador retrievers at YBR Labs and Farm. Barbara and I are grateful they brought Bookah and Toby into our lives. Sandy's advice has been immeasurably important over the years.

Thanks to friend, hiker, and artist Eileen Catasus-Chapman, for the gorgeous artwork and her trail companionship.

Thanks also to Jim "Ledgehound" Hopson. Not only for all the great hikes and bushwhacks we've done, but for the support and friendship when I needed to get back out in the woods after Bookah's passing.

I'd like to extend special appreciation to the Mohawk Hudson Land Conservancy for the land they've saved for future generations and for some of the most dog-friendly hikes in *Doghiker*. This wonderful organization deserves your support.

Mike Arthur and his dog, Rev, are accomplished Adirondack hikers and bushwhackers. I always look forward to Mike's trip reports and photography in his excellent blog, *Off on Adventure.*

George Senft's blog, *Grog's Hiking Adventures,* is a must-read for great places to hike. George's trip reports with his doghikers, Howie and Benny, are a pleasure to read.

Thank you to dog trainer-extraordinaire, Jody Diehl, for the great starts you gave Bookah and Toby and to Sabrina Lafave-Saletnik for her insights on dog training

Thank you to the photographers and artists who generously contributed their work to *Doghiker*. Their names are with each of their wonderful contributions.

With almost certain knowledge I've forgotten some . . . many thanks for the miles and smiles to friends Ralph Ryndak, Maddy Hand, Doug Sluiter, Rob Stewart, Bill Chriswell, Moonray Schepart, Tony Versandi, Jay Hui, Mike and Alexis Cantwell, Linda Richards Van Steenburg, Nick Minglis, Brian and Cindy Yourdon.

Book designer, Laurie Searl, editor Amanda Lanne-Camilli, and the extraordinary team at SUNY Press did a spectacular job transforming my vision into *Doghiker*.

Many thanks to Fred LeBrun and Neal Burdick, who have both inspired me to be a better writer. And thanks also to Neal for the excellent index.

Here's to the dogs who've shared their lives and trails with us: Bookah, Toby, Annabelle, Ivan, Janie Gizmo, Leo, Layla, Cooper, Sunny, Gio, Shiloh, Buckley, Oscar, Ruben, Touché, Deni, and Callie. And, way back, Patches, Jake, and Penny.

A very special dedication goes to my lifetime friend and hiking companion, Carlo Chizzolin, who left us while *Doghiker* was being written. Carlo and I enjoyed hiking, backpacking, and bushwhacking adventures throughout the Adirondacks, Catskills, Vermont, and New Hampshire mountains over the decades. His knowledge and gentle spirit were an inspiration to everyone he met.

Janie Gizmo — A tired dog is a good dog.
—Matt Via

Don't Worry, He Won't Bite

Qui me amat, amat et canem meum.
(Who loves me, loves my dog too.)

—Bernard of Clairvaux

How often have we been reassured, "Don't worry, he won't bite"? I'm sure you sometimes wonder whether the unleashed, galumphing beast running toward you is aggressive, protecting its owner, or just being exuberantly friendly. Hikers with children, the allergic, or the intimidated shouldn't have to defend their summit lunches or be troubled by an uncontrolled dog anywhere on a hike.

A small hiking group I was once leading ran into two large, snarling dogs on the summit of Santanoni Peak in the Adirondacks. The dogs were clearly threatening while the unconcerned owners were eating lunch, ignoring our discomfort. On a trailed hike in the Catskills, a friend and I had our backs to a large tree while a mastiff-sized dog had us trapped. I kept the dog at bay with hiking poles while the owners casually strolled up the trail, invoking the title of this chapter. They were not the least concerned or apologetic about our predicament. Another hiking friend was attacked on a trail by a large dog, escaping with torn pants but without injury. It was all the two owners could do to keep the dog away and my friend is now wary any time a dog comes running toward him on a trail.

These may seem like extreme examples, but this sort of behavior happens with enough frequency that people who hike with dogs should consider how others may view their doghikers.

Dog owners need to remember that not everyone loves their adorable doofus. They should assume other hikers won't want the muddy paw prints their dog deposits on strangers while the owner tells them that the dog is just being friendly. I revel in my dog's outdoors enthusiasm, but cringe when I see a dog lavishing unwelcome attention on others.

You might wonder why I'm leading off a dog hiking book with the reasons why so many people object to sharing trails with dogs. Your right to take a dog into the woods comes with a responsibility to keep the dog under your control, on leash, or sitting by your side as you greet others. Let's all be ambassadors for good dog behavior.

Bookah on 'stay'—Slide Mt.
—Joanne Hihn

Getting Your Dog

There is no psychiatrist in the world like a puppy licking your face.

—Ben Williams

Let's get the big question out of the way: rescue or responsible breeder?

Rescues make wonderful and successful hikers and their adopters perform a needed and unrivalled service. Many of my hiker friends have rescues that are great hiking dogs. When looking for our first doghiker, we researched rescues and got in touch with a Labrador retriever rescue center. During a series of conversations, we learned a great deal, but the key question they kept returning to was, what did we expect from a dog?

They were convinced we could get a great puppy and wonderful pet, but also noted that large breed dogs like labs sometimes develop joint problems that manifest when they mature. It is especially common with labs, shepherds, goldens, or other large breed types. Determining the level of risk for an individual dog is more difficult when the health and background of the parents are unknowns.

Learning how important it was for us to minimize potential problems, they directed us to a wonderful breeder whose dogs are bred for temperament and athleticism, and screened for genetic problems. Any dog can develop health issues, of course, and there's never a guarantee they won't. The breeder we chose screens parents and grandparents for breed-specific diseases, testing for hip issues with PennHIP and OFA radiographs. Readers with great rescue dogs may disagree, but this was the right choice for us. You need to evaluate how important these issues are for you.

If looking for a rescue, try to obtain as much information about the dog's history and circumstances as is available. Let the rescue organization be aware you're looking for an active, outdoors dog. Do they know anything about the parents, dog, or puppy? Was it treated

Shiloh and Bill enjoying the view from Wittenberg.
—Eileen Catasus Chapman

well and was there an absence of health issues when they received the dog? Whatever your decision, take your time to make the right one as you'll be bringing a dog into your life for many years.

Consider what Jon Katz, author of many dog books, has to say: "Get the dog that will make you happy, get a dog you can make happy. Get the dog you want, not the dog other people tell you that you should want. Give the dog the best life you can for as long as you can. . . . Do your homework, take it seriously. It is serious."

Other Considerations

What kind of hiking do you enjoy or anticipate? Consider how well your new addition will fit your plans. A dog's breed, size, age, physical condition, and even its coat are things to consider.

While there are exceptions to everything, small or toy breeds such as pugs, bichons, and Boston terriers are usually best at light hiking or suburban/urban walking. At the same time, I've seen some small doghikers fly up and down trails. Some avid hikers tuck their small dogs into the top of their packs for parts of longer outings, or tailor hikes for their dog's capacity and enjoyment.

Patch easing it—Balsam Mt Catskills.
—Emily Johnsen

Our vet feels any medium-sized dog can match 90 percent of human athleticism for hiking. Larger dogs—like huskies, pointers, labs, goldens, herders, and ridgebacks—can be tireless doghikers, as can mixes of these or similar breeds.

Extra-large or giant breed dogs such as rottweilers, Danes, Saint Bernards, and Newfoundlands are generally limited by their size. Getting them out of the woods in the event of an emergency can be difficult.

Dogs with long noses (hounds, retrievers, labs, spaniels, and pointers) have an aerobic advantage when hiking. Brachiocephalic breeds, such as pugs, shih tzu, Pekinese, Boston terriers, King Charles spaniels, and bulldogs of any variety, have more problems hiking. In addition to their reduced aerobic capacity, they overheat more quickly because they can't cool the air they breathe as effectively as dogs with snouts. Additionally, their eyes are much more commonly traumatized than the eyes of long-snouted dogs.

Pointers, vizslas, ridgebacks, labs, and similar breeds with short fur have easy-maintenance coats. Burrs don't easily adhere and, when they do attach, they are easy to remove. These dogs can more easily negotiate prickers, brush, beggar-ticks, burdock, or nettles, and provide less post-hike agita than dogs with long or curly fur. A few passes with a brush or comb on short-fur dogs and the hitchhiking attachments are quickly gone. Dogs with long or curly fur or possessing long tail feathers are burr magnets. When your dog inevitably

Shiloh drinking from Bill's hydration hose.
—Steve Shumway

rolls in something offensive—and it *is* inevitable—a short-fur dog is a quick hosing away from a return to polite company.

Dogs age and, like their human companions, they slow down when they get older. The spirit is there, but mileage, pace, and elevation usually need to be adjusted. If you adopt an older dog, or as your puppy matures through adulthood, their comfort and safety is paramount.

Most dogs are food beggars and it's hard to resist their imploring eyes as they ogle your snack or meal. For overweight dogs, build an exercise regimen to slowly develop endurance and conditioning. Overweight dogs need a gradual introduction to vigorous exercise. See the "Safeguarding Your Dog" chapter for more details.

Canines bred for cold or water environments have thick or double coats. They can handle all but the worst of winter conditions but labor in warm weather, especially when heat is combined with the exertion of hiking and climbing. It requires more vigilance to keep them cool, comfortable, and well hydrated in hot weather, a slightly lesser challenge with short-fur dogs.

As the weather warms in spring, look for shady trails and ones near streams or waterbodies, regardless of the dog's coat. I try to avoid brutally hot days and summer usually finds me carrying four to five liters of water to share with my dog. Look to their hydration before yours.

Vets and trainers strongly believe that separating puppies from their mother before eight weeks of age can harm the dog in a variety of ways. Leaving the comfort and security of its mother and littermates is stressful. Irresponsible breeders or rescue organizations will sometimes seek to move puppies at six weeks to save money or make space. This may lead to separation anxieties, fear, and destructive behavior.

Responsible shelters and breeders also strongly discourage taking home a "Christmas puppy." It's stressful enough for a puppy to be separated from her comfortable environment without adding the trauma of holiday food, distraction, noise, and being handed around to "strangers." Posing with your new puppy and its red ribbon may make a heartwarming social media moment, but it's not good for a puppy's well-being. Put a photo of the puppy in an envelope under the Christmas tree and pick her up the next day.

Homes with small kids should have a child-free zone for their puppy, a refuge where she can rest and recover, undisturbed by young children in her new surroundings.

There's a reason for the adage "a tired puppy is a good puppy." The time you spend keeping them busy chasing balls and playing with gnaw-worthy objects will pay off by saving your shoes, furniture legs, and other unsuitable objects. Mentally engaging and challenging puppies is equally important. A small dollop of peanut butter or a puppy biscuit inside of a hard rubber dog toy can keep the youngster occupied as they try to figure out how to get at the treat. In warm weather, scatter your dog's kibbles in a small area of your yard and watch the pup take the time to hunt down every morsel.

Friends.
—Joanne Hihn

Training

In order to really enjoy a dog, one doesn't merely try to train him to be semi-human. The point of it is to open oneself to the possibility of becoming partly a dog.

—Edward Hoagland

I've always felt that dogs first learn from you when they are puppies, then you learn from them for the rest of their lives. As they grow, so does your relationship, as the training and hiking come together.

There are too many dog training techniques and systems to cover them all in one chapter, but I've included some tips, techniques, ideas, and methods used by trainers and added a few of my own. Remember that every dog is different so be prepared to adapt and modify as needed.

Training begins the day your new dog comes home. Trainers agree that your new pup should spend nights in a crate to avoid problems while getting accustomed to a new environment. Although you might have a couple of nights of whining and crying, sticking with the crate will spare your furniture, rugs, and likely your sanity over time.

Get outside and play with your puppy, away from roads, dogs, and other distractions. She'll likely shadow you as if you're her mother. As the puppy slowly gains confidence, she'll extend her distance, providing the opportunity to begin those first steps toward the all-important "recall." As you walk, most puppies will look to see where you are. If she returns when you say her name, clap, or whistle, reward with treats, rubs, and praise. When an independent puppy ignores you, turn and slowly walk away. This will usually prompt a follow.

Loudly praise, stroke her ruff, make a fuss, and treat. Effusive praising and rewards are important in building a solid recall. Repeat, repeat, repeat at every opportunity, rewarding with extravagant praise and treats. This can be practiced in your yard, local woods, or indoors, and is the foundation for off-leash hiking. If your puppy has a mind of her own, you can use a long training lead that trails behind her as she walks. A soft pull as you call her name, followed by treats and praise, will have most young dogs catching on to the benefits of coming when called. Be certain to remain away from distractions, roads, or other hazards as puppies will be able to outrun you in just a few short weeks.

When teaching any new skill, use a small treat every time it's successfully completed. Once they "get it," treat at decreasing intervals to keep them from expecting a reward every time a task is completed. Real "yummies" are best for important behaviors. Use ones they'd climb a tree to get at. Some examples are microwaved hot dog slivers, jerky, or cheese. Never completely cut out rewards, as dogs quickly learn when rewards aren't coming.

Trainers and vets believe it's critical to start socializing and temperament-training puppies in their first weeks by introducing them to all types of sights, sounds, people, and experiences. The time invested will pay off with a more neutral reaction when your dog encounters people along a trail.

Dog trainers offer structured socialization sessions where puppies of a similar age play and interact, learning bite inhibition. Not having hands, dogs experience the tactile world with their mouths. All puppies chew and bite, so peer play allows them to learn what those pointy things in their mouths can do, testing bite pressure and the boundaries of play. Bite too hard and their playmate provides an immediate reaction, a yelp or return nip, teaching what's playful and what hurts. By biting other puppies in play, they learn bite inhibition, called "soft mouth," discovering that other dogs are fun. Trainers agree that this crucial skill needs to be learned well prior to eighteen weeks of age.

Fear is the most common cause of aggression and inadequate socialization is its most common cause. When puppies nip your fingers by accident or on purpose, many trainers suggest a loud "OUCH," startling them as you pull your hand away and reinforcing that they've done a no-no. This takes a little time for a puppy to grasp, but usually works. Dogs bite for any number of reasons, primarily fear, aggression, or protection. The most unpredictable is the fear biter. Even with proper socialization, some dogs will be fear biters and owners need to keep those dogs on leash, off trails, and away from people. Protective biting may occur as they guard their territory, food, owner, or self. Aggression can come from a variety of sources, including previous abuse or a strong alpha personality.

At four to five months, puppies can be enrolled in structured dog training classes. The stated purpose of classes is to "train the trainer," where you're taught techniques to train your dog. These sessions are often once a week for six to eight weeks, providing a week to work on what was learned in the previous class. You'll discover there's a sharp divide between dog training schools of thought.

Some trainers believe that coercion, including restraint, with choke or prong collars is the correct way to train. I strongly recommend a training philosophy that uses encouragement, reinforcement, and reward instead. One of the noncoercive training methods involves the use of a clicker. As soon as a dog responds positively to a desired behavior, you draw its attention with a loud click, reinforced with a reward. Our labs, Bookah and Toby, were trained by this method.

Good trainers demonstrate how to seamlessly incorporate training into daily life activities. "Sit," "wait," and "OK" are simple commands to work with your dog.

Trainers will provide tips on how to practice loose leash walking, so you're not towed every time you walk. Teaching a dog to "wait" before going out of doors or vehicles is not only an easily learned behavior but one that could someday save your dog's life. Having your dog "wait" before their dinner takes repetition and patience and is an easily transferable skill. We sometimes extend the meal waiting period to reinforce the command. Using small dog treats to reinforce a variety of daily behaviors sounds like a hassle, but it soon becomes second nature.

If you've read this far, it's likely that you're interested in having a well-behaved doghiker. Trainers offer advanced classes, including Canine Good Citizen and Therapy Dog. The elements of good dog behavior are transferable to trails. You may discover that working with your dog in class, in the woods, or at home is not only fun, but leads to a satisfying, mutually rewarding relationship that builds over the years.

It really isn't important if your dog doesn't shake paws, roll over, fetch, or beg, but she needs to have a solid, 100 percent recall for her to be off leash. This eliminates a lot of bad trail behavior and could someday save your dog's life. Your goal is to have your dog respond immediately to a voice or whistle, rewarding her with treats

Toby, wait.
—Barbara Via

and praise throughout her life. I prefer a one syllable, loud plosive that carries over distance. Mine is "HUP." I don't use it in the back yard, in the house, or at play. It's saved for occasions when I want my dog to immediately stop what she's doing and return to my side. Toby was once racing across a farm field, aching to dive into a pond located two hundred yards away. At "HUP," she skidded to a stop, did a U-turn, and raced back to the waiting treat, ear scratch, and "good girl."

I'm a proponent of having a young dog-in-training learn from an experienced doghiker on unoccupied trails or woods. The young 'un will typically follow the older dog, sniffing, exploring, and imitating. When the experienced doghiker responds to a recall, the young dog will usually follow.

When adopting a puppy or older dog, carefully evaluate temperament and personality if possible before making the lifelong commitment. Getting details on the dog's earlier life can often help you decide if you're right for each other. Keep in mind that once a dog has reached four months of age, its personality is mostly set and beyond an age where she would likely benefit from formal socialization sessions. Training presents a significant fork in the road. Will your new dog be trainable, stay close, and under control? If not, she'll need to be on leash or kept home.

Most trainers agree on the "Three Ds" of dog training: distance, duration, and distraction. Once you've trained your prospective doghiker to sit and wait, up the difficulty by practicing at farther distances. Your aim is to have her remain in place until your enthusiastic "OK" summons her to praise and a treat. This is the first "D," distance. Start moving farther away each session. If your dog breaks and runs for you, walk her back and begin again.

As distance increases, so does the waiting time, the second "D," duration. Lengthen the time she waits without breaking and reward, reward, reward on recall. As you continue to lock in distance and duration, introduce the most challenging "D," distraction. Begin at a short distance and have a friend come close or throw a ball. It requires a lot of practice and praise to have your dog remain in place while distracted and it can be a fun technique to train. Training in different places and environments adds another variable.

When you're satisfied with what your dog has accomplished, make things more challenging. With your dog on "wait," begin backing up, then turn and walk away. Breaking eye contact and moving away adds a challenging new dimension to training. Look for a different location and environment to practice. Try the three Ds in a wooded environment or trail when others aren't around. You may discover that the successful training done elsewhere needs more work when in a different or trail environment.

"Leave it" is a vital life skill, a behavior that can be introduced with the Three Ds. Broaden the training by rewarding your dog when she "leaves it" in a variety of situations. This can be avoidance of an unknown substance, not rolling in animal remains, or not picking up something she shouldn't. Treating is a strong reinforcement. "Leave it" is a key component of therapy dog training.

You may discover that adding hand signals to the voice commands is helpful. I snap my fingers to get my dog's attention. A palm up means "sit." Closed fingers, palm down means "down." And rolling my palm over in the "ta-da" motion with the verbal command "relax" is the signal for her to roll onto her side and back. This last is a handy skill. It allows for a child to pet her, or for me to check for ticks or examine for injury. Incorporating hand signals into training allows communication in loud environments or at a distance.

Dog training can be time consuming, challenging, or a chore if training maintenance is approached as such. You can make it fun and interesting, and incorporate it into daily interactions with your dog.

This section merely touches on a range of training options, summarizing the wisdom of excellent dog trainers, with input from our veterinarian, and some of my own experience.

To repeat, you are an ambassador for other dog owners. Good training allows outings where hiker and dog enjoy themselves, leaving no sign of their passing and impacting others in a positive way.

Toby receiving her Therapy Dog diploma.
—Barbara Via

Safeguarding Your Dog

If you get to thinking you are a person of some influence,
try ordering someone else's dog around.

—Will Rogers

PROPER NUTRITION AND HYDRATION—There's a large variety of dog food options and feeding philosophies: grain-free, organic, low protein, raw, and kibble from large and smaller companies. Kibble from high-quality, smaller companies seems to have less frequent recalls. Kibble remains palatable for longer periods and is easier to feed on hikes. Dry food has the additional benefit of helping to keep a dog's teeth clean.

Consider large-breed puppy food for dogs that will be large when grown. It contains less protein and avoids accelerated growth during a puppy's first six months. Consult your vet for a professional's opinion at your first visit.

Dogs deserve to have fresh, clean water available at all times.

See the information on "stomach torsion" in the "First Aid" chapter.

EXERCISE AND CONDITIONING—Dogs need to be conditioned to exercise much the same as human athletes. Owners should be aware of the potential stresses to young bones and joints. Frisbee-chasing leaps where dogs come down on rear legs lead to more serious injuries than those that are hiking-related. Dogs who splay their legs while running on ice or slippery floors can experience hip problems as they age.

When training your puppy, slowly build up distance, allowing time for sniffing, exploring, and peeing. Runners often want to have their dogs accompany them on their training runs. Be aware that most dogs are not built for long-distance running without breaks.

Conditioning, age, and whether the dog is obese are considerations when deciding on the appropriateness of a particular hike for a dog. Your dog's body may age, but rarely does her spirit. She may enthusiastically participate in a long, tough hike, with little concern for her well-being. Be observant of fatigue in your dog, especially the day after. If your dog is sore the following day, she may have gone too far for her level of conditioning. Overdoing requires recovery time, but dogs in their prime generally recover overnight.

Glucosamine/chondroitin supplements are thought to be an effective preventative for joint problems in dogs. The impact of aging on a dog's conditioning and stamina is an important topic to discuss with your vet during annual exams.

DEVELOPMENTAL STAGES OF DOGS COMPARED TO HUMANS—Jennifer Bull, DVM, of Delmar Animal Hospital in Delmar, New York, provides a great explanation of how to raise and condition a dog. Dr. Bull compares the stages of development dogs go through with the stages children experience, pointing out that dogs are still growing until eighteen to twenty-four months.

At under four months, your puppy is at the toddler stage, where wandering at a leisurely pace is the norm. Like a toddler, your pup will be ready to turn back or quit at any time.

From four to nine months, your pup is at elementary school age, with more energy than stamina. They should be learning the "rules of the road." Short hikes with play, or longer, leisurely hikes with play and behavioral expectations are the norm, but no heavy hiking or climbing at this stage.

Between ten to fourteen months, your dog is like a middle schooler, with a more adult body, but a brain that's easily distracted and impulsive. They are starting to get ready for real physical exertion, meaning short but tough hikes should be okay.

At sixteen to twenty-four months, they approximate high school and college age and are ready for real challenges, needing some mentoring, but with better general behavior. It's unfortunate that this is the stage at which most dogs reach what is termed "social puberty." Puppies that used to happily greet everyone and were submissive may start barking at people and getting into scuffles with other dogs. Some dogs just beyond puppyhood may still act like a puppy when interacting with an older dog. The grownup may have an expectation that the youngster has reached social puberty and should be greeting and interacting in a more mature manner. This can sometimes result in a fight.

Redheads make great hikers.
—Jason Cristman

DOG PARKS—I recognize these serve a purpose for the busy or others who perceive few alternatives, so my views may likely be unpopular with fans.

Most dog parks have "regulars," owners and dogs who know each other. Canines are pack animals and when a new dog or puppy comes through the double gate, they're usually greeted or surrounded. Depending on the personality of your pooch, her introduction to the pack will vary from eye avoidance and submissiveness, to a friendly, "Hi guys, glad to meet you, what's up?" Too often I've seen terrified newcomers cowering when the dog park alphas surround them. I liken this to prison movie perp walks where the seasoned prisoners comment on the "new fish" being paraded in.

In today's connected world, many owners are paying attention to their phones, missing the opportunity to observe and interact with their pets, or correct problem behavior. A more serious issue is dog owners who bring dogs that are unwelcome elsewhere, possibly exposing your dog to one who is dangerous or has serious behavior problems. Dogs can also be exposed to other animals who may not have been inoculated or are sick. If your dog doesn't show enthusiasm as you pull up to the park, she's telling you something.

Unless you're without options, consider other alternatives for your dog's daily exercise and play time.

PET SITTERS, DOG WALKERS, DOGGY DAY CARE—These can be great ways to take care of your dog while you're at work or away. Professional pet sitters or dog walkers can come to your home or bring them out for daily exercise. Ask friends for recommendations as the quality of care can vary greatly. Most cities have doggy day care businesses where your dog can be dropped off for the day. Check out the facility for cleanliness and observe how staff interacts with the dogs under their care. Do they screen dogs who don't interact well with others? Are there opportunities for outdoor play and activity?

DENTAL AND EAR CARE—From an early age, accustom your puppy to regular ear and mouth examinations. This makes it easier for you or your vet to examine and clean ears and brush teeth. Cotton balls with ear-cleaning medicine designed for canines should be a regular part of your routine. Doggy toothpaste with a dog toothbrush or finger brush will spare you extra visits to the vet.

LYME DISEASE—This is the most common tick-borne hazard for dogs, although there are three other diseases carried by ticks in New York State. Spring nymphs can transmit Lyme and are the size of the period at the end of a sentence. Annual Lyme vaccine inoculations provide an approximately 80 percent protection rate, or protection for an average of eight out of ten bites. A newer, dual-injection vaccine improves effectiveness to 93 percent. Check your dog after every outing, including use of a tick comb, Furminator deshedding tool, or lint roller.

Lyme symptoms can show up eight days to eight months after the infected tick bite, but symptoms can also appear so quickly that the test is not yet positive. There are different manifestations of Lyme, the most common being Lyme arthritis that generally shows up with a variety of symptoms ranging from "something's wrong," to fever, limping, lethargy, and poor appetite. The symptoms can show up so quickly as to give the impression of a broken bone. Antibiotics are the normal treatment for Lyme and very successful with the arthritis form.

Rarer forms of Lyme are neurological and cardiac forms, but vets worry most about the nephrotic or kidney variation where symptoms don't manifest until kidneys are failing, with limited treatment abilities.

Vaccines, when combined with tick-killing medication, can be quite protective. Those medications are available in both topical and ingestible forms. Most veterinarians recommend that medication not be suspended during winter as ticks can be active any time there is exposed ground. The topical forms of medication can be a little messy and leave a sticky residue on the dog's fur for a few days. Its effectiveness wears off more quickly with dogs that spend time in water. If your home contains children, you may not want them cuddling or petting your dog until the greasy medication disappears off your dog's back. The ingestible form of the tick medication circulates in your dog's bloodstream and kills a tick when it first attaches, before it can transmit Lyme.

GIARDIASIS AND LEPTOSPIROSIS—These are waterborne diseases.

Giardiasis, or giardia, presents symptoms including diarrhea with or without your dog feeling poorly. The diagnosis comes from a positive fecal sample or blood test. It is successfully treated by antibiotics. Giardia is colloquially called "beaver fever" when it occurs in humans. Dogs (and people) can contract it when they drink water that is contaminated with spores passed into the water through feces.

Leptospirosis is uncommon, but not rare. Dogs contract it from water contaminated with wildlife urine. It can be present in standing or moving water sources and is more common in periods of flooding in summer and autumn. Symptoms can include, but are not limited to, fever, lack of appetite, vomiting, lethargy, over or under drinking, changes in urinary habits, loss of weight, and dehydration.

Diagnosis is dependent on extensive blood work and a positive diagnosis might result in hospitalization. At that point, the dog is shedding spirochetes in its urine. If it reaches this stage, the urine is contagious to humans, dogs, and other mammals if it gets into a water source. If clearly ill or receiving late treatment, the dog can suffer temporary or permanent kidney and liver failure. Early intervention is often successful with full recovery after two cycles of antibiotics over a four- to six-week period.

HEARTWORM—This is a parasitic roundworm transmitted by mosquito bites from an infected host. Through various stages of growth, the parasite passes through the heart and lodges in the pulmonary artery. Heartworm can be prevented with a monthly chewable medication.

OTHER INTERNAL PARASITES—The medication used for heartworm prevention is also an effective monthly deworming for other internal parasites, with the exception of tapeworms. Tapeworms are generally visible as short segments at a dog's anus or tail, or on a dog bed. When visible, they are easy to treat with oral medication. With dogs being brought into the area from the south, vets often recommend dogs receive heartworm preventative medicine twelve months a year.

WILD ANIMAL AVOIDANCE—Seldom will healthy wild animals approach you and your dog. Any animal that appears to be stumbling, stupefied, and actively approaching likely has something wrong with it. Skunks, coyotes, raccoons, or foxes that don't run away may have rabies and you need to get away quickly.

Porcupines always waddle away, but their getaway "speed" is slightly faster than a tortoise. If your dog attempts to bite one, her face, chest, mouth, nose, and paws will collect quills. See "First Aid" for removal and treatment.

You and your dog share the same woods with bears. Though eyesight is a bear's weakest sense, they can hear and smell your approach, often from a long distance away. They usually do their best to avoid people, but cubs, especially small ones, increase the chance of contact. My dog wears a large bell during spring and early summer cub seasons, especially in the Catskills with its large bear population. When I am hiking or bushwhacking alone with my dog, I speak loudly to her, knowing that momma bear can hear our approach and can avoid us.

Spring fawns can't escape predators in their first days. They curl up motionless and hope to remain unnoticed. At this stage of development, they're completely defenseless. If your dog discovers a fawn, lead him away. The doe is nearby and will return to nurse it.

Rev with fawn.
—Mike Arthur

HUNTING SEASONS—These include archery, turkey, and a variety of firearms. Here are a few tips about how to comfortably coexist with hunters and enjoy the autumn woods. Camo-covered bowhunters shouldn't alarm you. Archers can hear you coming from a distance and you'll often walk by them completely unaware of their presence.

Turkey mating colors are bright red and blue, good colors to avoid during the spring turkey season. Unless you're trying to resemble a bear or deer, avoid black and white during bear and deer seasons. Black clothing looks like bear fur and white looks like the rear of a running deer.

Large dog bells are a wise precaution during firearms hunting seasons, another layer of protection to announce a dog is nearby. Avoid bushwhacks and remote trails where you're more likely to encounter and surprise hunters. Steep trails are good places to hike as hunting clothing and gear is heavy and you're less likely to encounter hunters on rugged terrain. Blaze orange vests for hikers and dogs allows hunters to see you coming.

DOGFIGHTS—The most likely negative encounter your dog will have with another animal is a dogfight. Most dog bites bleed, hurt, and can get infected, but are survivable. Serious damage can be done when one dog has the other by the throat or is biting the stomach or genital area.

Trying to break up a dog fight with your hands is a good way to get bitten. Rather than reaching in between the combatants, a safer way to break up a fight is by whipping them with the soft part of a leash or grabbing your dog's collar if they separate. If your leashed dog is confronted by an aggressive one, drop the leash, as it allows your dog to escape.

To protect yourself, a hiking stick, poles, or pepper spray are defensive tools. Try a trick I've used many times when chased by dogs while running on rural roads. Reach down as if picking up a rock. This can be surprisingly effective as aggressive dogs are usually accustomed to having things thrown at them. Whatever you do, don't run.

HOLIDAY TIMES AND HAZARDS—Meals and celebrations present food hazards other than the turkey carcass. Chocolate in even small amounts can be poisonous for small dogs. Holiday gatherings often bring dogs into contact with nondog people who've been drinking or want to treat your dog with what they are eating.

Tiring your dog out with a good workout before guests arrive is a good idea. Peanut butter-filled toys can keep your dog busy and not underfoot. When guests arrive, the open door can be a hazardous invitation for your dog to greet arriving guests. A Christmas puppy waiting under the tree with noise and confusion is not the way to introduce your new pet to the family.

POISONS—Ethylene glycol–based antifreeze is sweet tasting and poisonous. A dog licking radiator leaks at trailheads, streets, or on driveways is serious. It can lead to sudden kidney failure. Sugarless gums and diabetic candies containing xylitol are very liver toxic to dogs.

TRAVEL SAFETY—A crate in the cargo area of an SUV is the safest way for your dog to travel. Next safest is riding free in the cargo area. Consider using a special harness that attaches to the seatbelt in the rear passenger section of a vehicle. Dogs can generally ride in the cargo area of your vehicle around town, but should be crated for travel to and from trailheads. Traffic accidents are sometimes caused by dogs interfering with drivers. Puppies who haven't learned to stay in place should be attached to seatbelts with the harness or in crates 100 percent of the time.

Drivers coming and going around trailheads are not looking for a dog wandering in their paths. Beware of dogs who are itching to get hiking, running across trailhead parking areas or the nearby highway. Keep your doghiker leashed or in your vehicle before or after hikes.

POISONOUS SNAKE ENVENOMATION—If your dog is struck by a copperhead or timber rattlesnake, you need to evacuate her and seek immediate veterinary treatment.

FOOT PROTECTION—Many dogs don't like having their paws handled. Get them accustomed to it early in life. Dogs that are out on trails year-round usually don't require frequent nail trimming, but when it's required, your vet or groomer will thank you for having a paw-friendly dog.

MICROspikes® and snowshoe or boot crampons don't interact well with the tops of dog's paws. Take care where you step. Dog's pads, like new hiking boots, need to be gradually broken-in, a consideration when deciding on the appropriateness of hikes. Their pads will toughen, but unless sufficiently conditioned, they can bleed from a day of running up and down rocky trails.

LOCATING YOUR LOST DOG—Having your dog microchipped is essential. Shelters, animal control officers, and veterinarians will scan a dog and the chip will display your programmed contact information.

A local vet will be the first place an injured dog will be brought. Microchip companies offer a service where they'll send out electronic lost-dog flyers to animal control, shelters, and veterinarians within a twenty- to fifty-mile radius. Be certain to have an up-to-date digital image ready to provide. Having photos of your dog on your phone and posting lost dog notices at all nearby trailheads is often successful.

Keep calling local dog shelters, animal control officers, and other likely places where a lost dog might show up. This can sometimes take weeks. Found dog notices often show up on Craigslist and people sometimes hang onto a lost dog for a few days before deciding to look for the owner.

Keep returning to the area where your dog was lost as they'll often remain nearby. A friend's dog took off late in the afternoon on a snowy winter day. We left the owner's sweaty shirt on the ground before finally leaving. The dog was curled up on it the next morning.

One of the most successful ways of locating a lost dog is by leaving details on Facebook. Post a photo with your contact information and your dog's tendencies on Facebook and other social media sites. Ask that readers share to their pages. This has an amazing success rate with so many people looking and on alert.

Doghiker spa—Plattekills.
—Joanne Hihn

First Aid

FIRST AID KIT—Hikers carry first aid kits. Many items can do double duty for dogs. Here are some essentials for yours.

Multitool with needle-nose pliers

Sterile nonstick gauze pads and vet wrap

Antiseptic wipes and nitrile gloves

Duct tape for splints and bandages

Super glue for paw pad or other cuts

Betadine antibiotic ointment

Pawz booties

Bandana for adding pressure to active bleeding

Benadryl® for bee stings, itching, swelling, and bug bites (1mg/lb every eight hours)

Pain medication—Ask your veterinarian at exam time for a dose to be included in the kit

Rounded-tip first aid scissors

Stretchable waterproof tape

QuikClot® or similar product to stop blood loss

SAM® splint

Parachute cord

Hydrogen peroxide with irrigation syringe for disinfecting or inducing vomiting (see below)

Coated aspirin (it can interact with other pain meds or anti-inflammatories)

NO Motrin®, ibuprofen, or Tylenol®

FIRST AID FIELD SUBSTITUTES—

Sanitary napkins or pads and disposable diapers can be used to staunch bleeding.

Rolled magazines and newspapers can be used as emergency splints.

Expedient bandaging can include socks, bandanas, and tissues. Ziplock bags, socks, and plastic newspaper or grocery bags can serve as temporary foot bandages.

Tourniquets can be fashioned from hoodie strings, belts, or from any material that's somewhat giving, such as pantyhose legs, strips of Lycra®, yoga pants, or long johns. The best tourniquets are not too tight or too long.

FIELD TREATMENT—Backwoods emergencies require thought and calm judgment. Even though dogs are tough and usually heal well, when animals are injured and frightened they are most likely to bite, even people they love, without warning. If necessary, muzzles can be fashioned with duct tape or a roll of gauze. It does neither of you any good if you're both injured in the field or when returning to your vehicle.

If there is *penetration by a stick*, the stick should be cut or broken off close to the surface and left in place. Sticks should not be pulled out. Veterinarians worry that a penetration may have hit a deep artery and removing the stick can lead to internal bleeding and the inability to staunch blood flow. They also warn that pulling a stick from an eye should never be done, no matter how tempting.

Clean T-shirts and hand towels can be used for *washing your dog*, *wrapping large wounds*, and *applying pressure* for active bleeding. Keep a large, warm blanket in your car to treat for shock.

Heavy-duty contractor's bags, ponchos, soft shells, or other parkas can be used as *stretchers*.

Dog electrolytes can be made with diluted chicken or beef broth with restaurant sugar and salt packs.

Cuts to foot pads can happen with glass, sharp rocks, or other objects, and foot pads can bleed impressively. Super glue may be appropriate to close cuts until you return to the trailhead. *Deep lacerations* may require stitching and a long period of inactivity.

The *best method for taping wounds* or applying dressings is to cross your dog's coat at a ninety-degree angle. If you tape toward or parallel with the fur, you'll rip out much of the fur when removing the tape, hurting more than necessary.

Lucy gets a ride in the rain.
—Alan Via

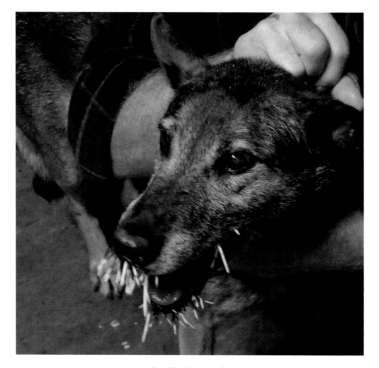

Quilled muzzle.
—Heather Rolland

Porcupines and dogs don't mix. The needle-nose pliers in your multitool is essential for removing quills. Not everyone will be comfortable de-quilling a dog and a vet can do it under sedation. I grasp the quills firmly with the needle-nose, as near to the skin as possible, and pull straight out.

Quills deep in the mouth are common among prey-driven dogs that aggressively bite porcupines and they may be difficult to remove without anesthesia. If away from medical care, dogs with mouth quills can have water but not food. If you can't remove the quills, cut them off, leaving enough so your vet has something to grab for removal under anesthesia.

A headlamp, even in daylight, provides excellent, up-close illumination.

Stomach torsion, or "bloat," is a life-threatening, though uncommon, emergency. It mostly occurs with deep-chested and extra-large breed dogs. It can happen any time, but it presents a higher risk when your dog eats or drinks (more than two cups) rapidly before or

Quilled paw.
—Heather Rolland

after heavy exercise. Providing modest amounts of water or food at reasonable intervals should be a preventative.

Symptoms of bloat include, but are not limited to, repeated retching or vomiting, distress, panting, poor color of the pink section of the mouth, sudden weakness or collapse, and varying degrees of a swollen, bloated abdomen. If your dog eats or drinks and vomits it right back up, STOP feeding and watering and slowly walk them out of the woods. Be prepared to rest often, or even carry the dog back to the trailhead and veterinarian.

Hydrogen peroxide can be used to induce vomiting if your dog ingests something it shouldn't. Although not necessary, an irrigation syringe is a handy way to administer the H2O2 while holding your dog's mouth open. There is no standard dose; it should be administered "to effect." It's safe to use but won't work on every dog in every case. Having them run around after ingestion will often result in an eruption of vomiting.

It's faster if you fly!
—Sandy Allen

Doghiker Gear

If your dog is fat, you aren't getting enough exercise.

—author unknown

LEAVE NO TRACE (LNT)—There are few things more important than keeping our dogs from having an impact on the environment. Always carry a few nonperforated plastic bags so you can double bag and carry out dog waste. Don't leave filled bags along the trail or at the trailhead as other hikers shouldn't have to pick up or carry out your dog's waste. In a pinch, dig a hole and bury waste 100 feet from trails, water, and campsites, if bagging and carrying out is impractical.

COLLARS—Flat collars are best. Avoid choke, prong, or other tightening-type collars such as martingales, all of which can be potential strangulation hazards on trails.

Use *electronic collars* with care and only when there are no alternatives. Electronic collars that deliver shocks can harm a dog's training. An out-of-sight dog may not have heard a recall or misunderstood a command. The unpleasantness and fear of receiving a shock at the wrong time can undo and, in some cases, permanently ruin a desirable behavior.

LEASHES—I carry what I refer to as a "sling leash," a four-foot lead, worn bandolier-style over, not under, pack straps, allowing quick access to snap onto a dog collar. At four feet, it's long enough to fit crosswise over your shoulder, but not long enough to snag on branches. If a hike involves a road walk, extended time on leash, or sharing a summit or viewpoint with others, pack a six-foot leash to attach your dog to your pack, tree, or other object.

Retractor leashes are popular and ubiquitous but have serious drawbacks. Inattentive use allows a dog to run into traffic, get into trouble, or bother others. Bystanders, as well as yourself, can be

Electrified dog.
—Eileen Catasus-Chapman

burned by the thin nylon as it quickly deploys across a limb. If a dog gets a running start, the retractor can be jerked out of your hand or knock you over when the dog reaches the end of the unwound leash.

COLD WEATHER—Insulated vests allow dogs not otherwise suited for cold weather to enjoy winter outings on days when the temperature is not dangerously cold. Dog booties and Musher's wax can help prevent snow buildup on the bottom of a dog's paws, but some dogs will try to pull off booties. Road salt can irritate paws.

COLLAR TAGS—Putting your name, address, and phone number on your dog's identification tags is the surest way to reunite with her if she is lost.

MICROCHIPS—Injected under the skin, these allow veterinarians, animal control personnel, and any dog facility to scan and locate owners.

VESTS AND BELLS—Dogs should wear blaze-colored vests during hunting seasons. Blaze orange or green are unnatural colors and

Bookah's bell.
—Eileen Catasus Chapman

contrast sharply with any forest background. Some dogs wear hiking vests that have side pockets for carrying food or other supplies.

The sound made by a large dog bell carries a long way in the forest, alerting mother bears and hunters that a dog is in the area.

TRAIL TREATS—A ziplock bag with dog treats is a handy way to get and hold your dog's attention and has the additional benefit of keeping biscuit crumbs from lining the bottoms of your pockets.

NUTRITION AND HYDRATION—Carry extra water and a collapsible water dish. Dogs can't remove their fur coats and their hydration should come before yours. They can be trained to drink water squirted into their mouths from hydration pack hoses. Read the "First Aid" section pertaining to eating and drinking during strenuous exercise. In warm weather, look for wooded trails that pass streams or other bodies of water.

RUFFWEAR—Makers of some of the best active dog gear. Their leashes, harnesses, portable water bowls, vests, and collars are the real deal. You won't find any rhinestones or similar stuff that self-destructs during hikes. Our home has an array of their gear. Ruffwear leash buckles snap on quickly and are difficult to unclip accidentally.

COAT CARE—A lint roller, loofah, or hooked sponge is a good way to remove ticks from dogs.
Furminator® makes an amazing tool for dogs with medium- to thick-density fur. During fall or spring shedding, a Furminator can harvest unbelievable quantities of fur. Nest-building birds will quickly recycle the fur, making it disappear from bushes, shrubs, and birdfeeders.

ILLUMINATION—Small blinking lights designed for attachment to dog collars, or collars and leashes with reflective material, are excellent for twilight or after-dark dog walking. If your hikes include predawn starts or after-dark exits, the light from headlamps can illuminate reflective dog collars.

MULTITOOL—You'll see this listed as a must-have in a dog first aid kit. Small versions (approximately three inches) can go on keychains or inside packs. Be certain you have a model that contains needle-nose pliers and scissors.

The Hikes

Soon the trout lilies will be blooming. Their pretty yellow flowers follow the sun during the day and close at night, only to turn into dreams. Then they follow other kinds of suns during the night and open at daylight, becoming once again pretty yellow flowers.

John P. O'Grady

Trout Lilies — Audrey Sallese

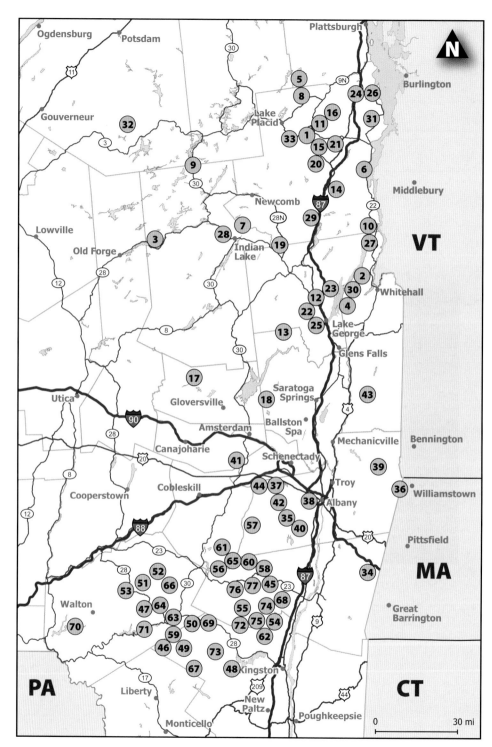

Peakfinder Map

36

Key to Hike Ratings

Difficulty: 1 = Easy   3 = Moderate   5 = Challenging
Views: 1 = Few Views   3 = Very Nice   5 = Drop Dead Gorgeous
Hydration: 0 = No Water   1-2 = Carry Extra Water   4-5 = Plenty of Water

Destination	County	Highest Point	Mileage (mi)	Elevation Gain (ft)	Difficulty	Views	Hydration/Swimming
North Region							
1. Baxter Mt	Essex	2440	2.7	750	2	4	0
2. Black Mt	Washington	2640	5.7	1200	3	5	4
3. Black Bear Mt	Hamilton	2440	4.9	700	3	3	3
4. Buck Mt - Hogtown Trail	Washington	2334	4.3	1125	3	5	3
5. Catamount Mt	Clinton	3169	4.0	1545	4	5	2
6. Cheney Mt	Essex	1350	2.5	575	2	3	4
7. Clear Pond - Chain Lakes	Essex	1735	7.0	525	3	2	4
8. Cobble Lookout	Essex	2375	2.5	270	2	3	3
9. Coney Mt	St. Lawrence	2250	2.0	515	2	3	2
10. Cook Mt	Essex	1225	3.4	960	3	3	1
11. Crows	Essex	2815	2.0	1000	2	5	1
12. Hackensack Mt	Warren	1357	2.6	750	4	3	1
13. Hadley Mt	Saratoga	2675	3.5	1500	4	5	2
14. Hammond Pond	Essex	965	2.0	150	1	2	5
15. Hopkins Mt	Essex	3155	6.0	2050	5	5	2
16. Jay Range	Essex	3580	7.5	2800	5	5	1
17. Kane Mt	Fulton	2180	2.4	650	2	3	1
18. LeVine Preserve	Saratoga	1283	3.0	400	1	2	5
19. Moxham Mt	Essex	2450	5.0	1400	3	4	2
20. Noonmark Mt	Essex	3556	6.3	2075	5	5	3
21. Owls Head Lookout	Essex	2530	5.0	1300	3	5	4
22. Pine Mt	Warren	1790	3.0	1200	3	3	0
23. The Pinnacle	Warren	1280	1.5	450	1	4	0

Destination	County	Highest Point	Mileage (mi)	Elevation Gain (ft)	Difficulty	Views	Hydration/Swimming
24. Poke-O-Moonshine Mt	Essex	2180	4.2	1275	3	4	3
25. Prospect Mt	Warren	2030	6.0	1350	3	3	2
26. Rattlesnake Mt	Essex	1310	3.0	950	2	5	0
27. Record Hill	Washington	1255	2.0	750	3	3	1
28. Sawyer Mt	Hamilton	2620	2.0	600	2	3	0
29. Severance Hill	Essex	1635	2.6	755	2	3	2
30. Sleeping Beauty Mt	Washington	2310	7.3	1400	3	4	5
31. South Boquet Mt	Essex	1170	2.0	550	1	3	2
32. Tooley Pond Mt	St. Lawrence	1750	2.3	250	1	1	4
33. Mt Van Hoevenberg	Essex	2866	4.4	900	3	5	2
Central Region							
34. Beebe Hill	Columbia	1760	2.0	360	1	3	5
35. Bennett Hill Preserve	Albany	1135	3.7	500	2	2	2
36. Berlin Mt	Rensselaer	2798	5.3	1280	3	3	1
37. Bozen Kill Preserve	Albany	500	2.9	160	1	1	4
38. Capital Hills	Albany	225	5.2	315	1	2	4
39. Dickinson Hill	Rensselaer	1760	2.9	325	1	3	4
40. Holt Preserve	Albany	1072	3.0	600	2	2	4
41. Schoharie Creek Preserve	Montgomery	640	1.4	180	1	2	5
42. Thacher Park	Albany	1370	3.0	350	2	1	4
43. Thunder Mt	Washington	840	2.3	450	1	2	3
44. Wolf Creek Falls Preserve	Albany	840	3.7	240	1	2	3
South Region							
45. Acra Point	Greene	3100	5.1	1200	3	4	3
46. Alder Lake	Ulster	2220	1.5	100	1	2	5
47. Andes Rail Trail	Delaware	1800	3.8	575	2	2	1
48. Ashokan High Point	Ulster	3080	7.0	2000	5	4	3
49. Balsam Lake Mt	Ulster	3720	6.0	1140	3	4	3
50. Belleayre Mt	Ulster	3420	3.5	900	2	4	0
51. Bramley Mt	Delaware	2817	3.9	875	3	3	2
52. Catskill Scenic Trail	Delaware	1650	8.9	-200	3	3	4

Destination	County	Highest Point	Mileage (mi)	Elevation Gain (ft)	Difficulty	Views	Hydration/Swimming
53. Delhi Trails	Delaware	2050	3.1	900	3	2	0
54. Huckleberry Point	Greene	2500	4.5	1165	3	4	2
55. Hunter Mt	Greene	4040	6.9	1940	5	5	3
56. Huntersfield Mt	Greene	3423	4.0	1000	3	2	2
57. Huyck Preserve	Albany	1885	5.7	750	3	2	3
58. Jennie Notch	Greene	2440	2.0	400	1	2	3
59. Kelly Hollow	Delaware	2245	4.0	500	2	2	4
60. Lake Heloise to Jenny Notch	Greene	2720	5.5	1250	3	2	2
61. Leonard Hill	Schoharie	2615	3.4	545	2	2	1
62. Overlook Mt	Ulster	3140	5.0	1400	3	5	1
63. Pakatakan Mt	Delaware	2510	3.5	1100	3	2	1
64. Palmer Hill	Delaware	2325	3.7	600	2	2	2
65. Mt Pisgah	Greene	2912	3.5	1100	3	2	1
66. Plattekills	Delaware	3340	3.7	1250	3	4	0
67. Red Hill	Ulster	2980	2.6	815	2	5	3
68. Rip's Ledge	Greene	1800	5.3	950	3	4	3
69. Rochester Hollow	Ulster	2285	6.5	1200	3	2	3
70. Rock Rift	Delaware	2382	5.5	1470	3	1	2
71. Shavertown Trail	Delaware	1800	2.0	500	2	3	3
72. Silver Hollow Mt	Greene	3000	4.5	1200	3	2	2
73. Slide Mt	Ulster	4180	7.5	1750	5	3	2
74. South Escarpment	Greene	2420	6.0	900	3	3	1
75. Twin Mt	Greene	3640	5.8	1800	5	5	2
76. West Cave - Cave Mts	Greene	3100	5.3	1700	4	4	1
77. Windham High Peak	Greene	3524	6.0	1550	4	3	3

Pat and Toby on Baxter bad weather bypass.
—Alan Via

Hike Map Legend

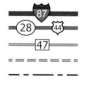

Interstate Highway	Parking Area
State/U.S. Highway	Campsite
County/Local Road	Cross-Country Skiing
Unpaved Road	Lean-to
County Line	Fire Tower
	Waterfall
Hike Route	Horse Trail
Other Trail	Building
	Scenic View
DEC/DEP Lands	

North Region

The life of a good dog is like the life of a good person,
only shorter and more compressed.

—Anna Quindlen

Baxter Mt.

HIGHLIGHTS AND SUMMARY: A great family and dog hike just outside of the High Peaks Wilderness Area but close enough to enjoy the spectacular views. Bring a map to pick out peaks and a wildflower guide to identify the large variety common to the hike. A nirvana for blueberry enthusiasts.

MILEAGE: *2.7 mi r/t.*

ELEVATION GAIN: *750 ft.*

DIFFICULTY: *2*

VIEW RATING: *4*

LEASH: *Not required, but appropriate on summit and near other hikers.*

DOG SAFETY AND HAZARDS: *Trailhead parking on shoulder of a busy highway.*

WATER: *No reliable water.*

HIKER TRAFFIC: *Busy, especially on weekends and holidays.*

TRAIL CONDITIONS: *Excellent.*

BEST TIME TO HIKE: *Spring through foliage season.*

GETTING THERE: *Turn onto NY 9N at the intersection (N44° 14.024', W73° 46.956') with NY 73, continuing 2 mi to a NYS Department of Environmental Conservation (DEC) sign at the 1675 ft trailhead (N44° 13.237', W73° 44.947'). Park on the wide shoulder.*

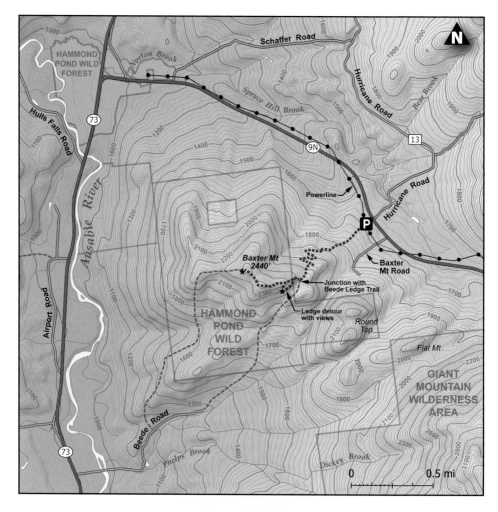

Baxter Mt. Map

The BLUE trail begins in a conifer forest scented with balsam, passing under a power line and gaining less than 200 ft in the first 0.3 mi. As you ascend, maple, birch, and beech predominate. Near 1950 ft, the trail steepens, but the effort is eased by the well-placed switchbacks. Near 2145 ft, bear RIGHT as the trail passes the Beede Ledge trail intersecting on the LEFT (N44° 12.959′, W73° 45.515′). The trail again steepens and leads to another switchback.

There's a tall rock ledge (N44° 12.940′, W73° 45.577′) near 2200 ft that may present an obstacle when wet or icy. Look for an unmarked bad weather bypass on the LEFT. It leads to a series of blueberry- and wildflower-bordered ledges that begin with a view of Tripod Mt. over the summit of Round Top and the rocky cone of Hurricane Mt. and its fire tower. A wildflower guide will be handy to spot bane- berry, trillium, Indian cucumber root, wild sarsaparilla, bearberries, pale corydalis, and many more.

This 0.2 mi unmarked path passes across one open ledge after an- other, providing almost continual views. Giant, Hurricane, the Dixes, Noonmark, Nippletop, Dial, Bear Den, Colvin, Blake, and the Great Range are on display. With an absence of trail markers, don't attempt this detour unless you are comfortable off trail, and you and your dog are comfortable scrambling up small ledges.

The path rejoins the marked trail (N44° 12.927', W73° 45.904') near 2320 ft. Continue to Baxter's wooded SE summit where a 30 ft path on the LEFT leads to another viewpoint. The trail descends less than 100 ft into a shady col and then climbs to Baxter's 2440 ft summit. This short piece of trail, laden with conifer needles, is bordered by blue- berries and bracken ferns. Near Baxter's summit there are faded trail signs pointing toward the Beede Farm trailhead. While Baxter's high point is deficient in views, the large rock a few yards away will be your lunch spot of choice, where views of the Dix Range, Noonmark, and a gaggle of other summits are your dessert.

As you return to the trailhead, look for a large rock on the SE summit for the beginning of a short path that parallels the trail and provides more views on your way down. Bring water for your dog as there is no reliable water. Given the amount of hiker traffic, the trail is in remarkably good shape. Though not required, there's enough hiker traffic that dogs should be leashed around people.

Black Mt.

HIGHLIGHTS AND SUMMARY: A deservedly popular hike to a rocky summit. The views of Lake George and its islands, surrounding peaks, and clear-day views of the High Peaks are impressive. It's unlikely you'll have the trails or summit to yourself, but a loop option has ponds and less traffic.

MILEAGE: *5.7 mi r/t. Pond loop adds 1.7 mi.*
ELEVATION GAIN: *1200 ft.*

DIFFICULTY: *3*

VIEW RATING: *5*

LEASH: *Not required but appropriate at trailhead and summit.*

DOG SAFETY AND HAZARDS: *Trailhead proximity to road.*

WATER: *Along trail and ponds.*

HIKER TRAFFIC: *Busy.*

TRAIL CONDITIONS: *Well-worn and eroded in places.*

BEST TIME TO HIKE: *Spring and autumn; more challenging in winter.*

GETTING THERE: *From Whitehall, continue on NY 22, crossing the South Bay of Lake George. Turn onto CR 6 (N43° 37.889′, W73° 26.756′) and then onto Pike Brook Rd. (N43° 37.376′, W73° 29.390′). Follow to the 1450 ft trailhead (N43° 36.707′, W73° 29.596′).*

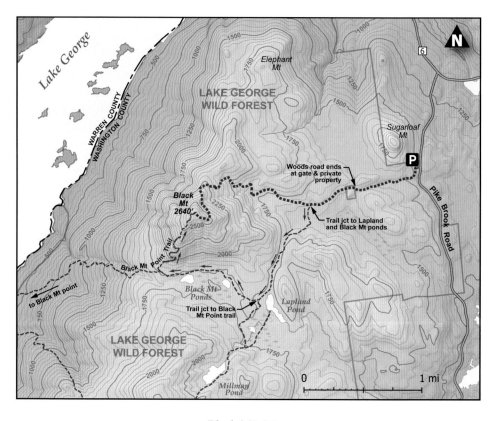

Black Mt. Map

Michele with Layla and Toby—Elephant Mt.
—Alan Via

Pass a small stream as you start uphill out of the trailhead on RED markers on a woods road that quickly flattens. Enjoy ferns, wildflowers, and a trailside marsh dogs will appreciate. The road reaches a gate and private property at 0.7 mi, where the road becomes a trail. The trail turns RIGHT at a sign pointing 1.8 mi to the summit. The trail also has DEC snowmobile markers.

A trail junction (N43° 36.454′, W73° 30.704′) at 1640 ft leads to Lapland and Black Mt. Ponds. This is an alternative and less busy trail to the summit, and optional return route. Continuing ahead on RED markers, the trail crosses a brook at 1810 ft, then another before the climbing gets steeper and the footing alternates between an eroded streambed and rock slabs.

Once the trail hits Black's N ridge, the grade eases, the eroded section is left behind, and the canopy transitions to areas of open sky. Watch for a small herd path just below the summit; it leads to a stone foundation and ledge with views of Lake George and surroundings.

A minute of climbing puts you at the summit with a classic view of Lake George at your feet, extensive mountain vistas in every direction, and clear-day views of the High Peaks. You'll usually find company at the top. The summit is the site of a decommissioned fire tower that's been converted to an emergency communication antenna, with solar panels, windmill, and protective fencing. Look for a trail junction (N43° 36.391', W73° 31.846') just below the summit. The trail leads toward Black's steep SSW ridge and the ponds previously mentioned. This trail adds an additional 1.7 mi to the day's outing but has nice views and more canine hydration opportunities.

Black Bear Mt.

HIGHLIGHTS AND SUMMARY: Great dog hike with gorgeous summit views. The N trail is less busy and drier. Trails are easy to follow, but markers are sparse and confusing in places. Hard to think of a better autumn foliage hike in the area.

MILEAGE: *Summit trail, 4 mi r/t. N trail, 5.6 mi r/t. Loop 4.9 mi.*

ELEVATION GAIN: *700 ft.*

DIFFICULTY: *3*

VIEW RATING: *3*

LEASH: *At the trailhead and at summit.*

DOG SAFETY AND HAZARDS: *Trailhead is near busy highway. Steep sections on summit trail and summit cliff.*

WATER: *Streams and wet sections.*

HIKER TRAFFIC: *Busy on weekends.*

TRAIL CONDITIONS: *Very wet, a quagmire section on the summit trail.*

BEST TIME TO HIKE: *Spring through autumn. Some trails are marked for cross-country skiing and mountain biking.*

GETTING THERE: *The sizable trailhead is located on NY 28, between Inlet and Eagle Bay.*

The nicely graded trail leaves the 1750 ft parking area (N43° 45.845', W74° 47.638') on rolling terrain through deciduous woods. At 0.3 mi, the trail begins ascending, reaching a poorly marked intersection (N43° 46.045', W74° 46.824') on the RIGHT in a small clearing at 0.75 mi. This is the shorter summit trail.

Bear LEFT on YELLOW markers for the slightly longer and more enjoyable N trail. It's marked for skiing and mountain biking

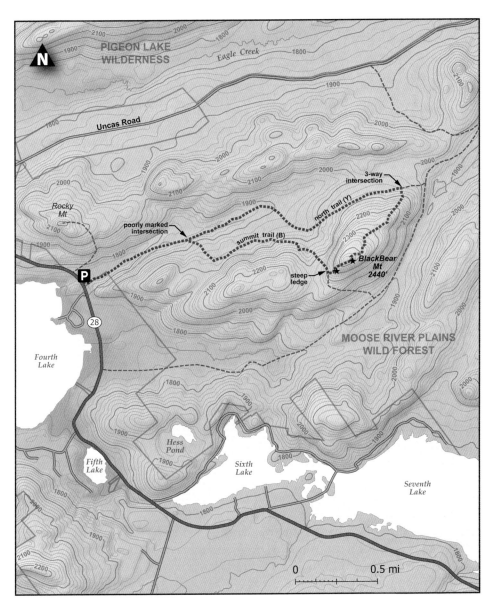

Black Bear Mt. Map

and crosses rolling terrain before starting uphill, passing five small streams along the way. The N trail descends for a short distance, then gains 350 ft in the next 0.25 mi to a three-way intersection (N43° 46.299', W74° 45.277'). It's 1.5 mi to Uncas Rd. and 2.2 mi back to the

Purple Finch.
—Barbara Via

trailhead, but turn RIGHT for a 400 ft ascent in 0.65 mi to Black Bear's summit along its NE ridge. As the trail ascends, the forest transitions from deciduous to dense conifers. The trail is drier and less eroded than the summit trail. You emerge from the dark forest onto rock ledges 0.1 mi from the summit.

Trail markers are sporadic here but keep heading up and you'll be on top in a few minutes. Sixth and Seventh Lakes preside over the foreground and Little Moose and Snowy Mts. are standouts. There's a panorama of smaller peaks and lakes visible in the West Canada Lake Wilderness Area. Wander NE a short distance for the best vista. Look down on a large bog and, in the distance, Blue Ridge, the Santanonis, Blue, Seward, Kempshall, and an array of other mountains populate the horizon.

The summit trail is a more direct route to Black Bear Mt.'s summit. Bear RIGHT at the poorly marked intersection noted earlier, gaining 100 ft in the first 0.25 mi. The trail is eroded, with wet, muddy sections. The trail levels off and turns NE, passing a small meadow. The wet and muddy conditions continue, causing hikers to rock hop, balance on branches, or create side trails to escape a mud paddy.

At 1.6 mi, the trail begins a steep 400 ft climb, meeting a 15 ft rock step near 2190 ft. It calls for caution when slippery and may provide difficulty for some hikers or dogs. Another steep section follows, this one having a bypass trail. The trail becomes rougher and rockier, alternating between smooth bedrock and soft hemlock needles, my favorite section. Approaching the summit, you reenter heavier canopy before emerging onto the open rock. Summit cliffs and other hikers suggest dogs should be leashed for their safety and the enjoyment of others.

Buck Mt.—Hogtown Trail

HIGHLIGHTS AND SUMMARY: Buck Mt. is the most prominent peak in the Lake George area. The spectacular views of the lake, surrounding mountains, and distant High Peaks make Buck a deservedly busy destination. The Hogtown Trail on the mountain's E side offers an uncrowded alternative trail to the summit.

MILEAGE: *4.3 mi r/t.*

ELEVATION GAIN: *1125 ft.*

DIFFICULTY: *3*

VIEW RATING: *5*

LEASH: *Leash your dog on the crowded summit.*

DOG SAFETY AND HAZARDS: *None.*

WATER: *Streams along the way.*

HIKER TRAFFIC: *Light until reaching the summit.*

TRAIL CONDITIONS: *Beautiful in the lower half, rocky and eroded in the upper section.*

BEST TIME TO HIKE: *Autumn. Midweek is best. Avoid winter due to seasonal road maintenance.*

GETTING THERE: *Turn N on Buttermilk Falls Rd. at the intersection (N43° 24.264', W73° 35.734') with NY 149. The road becomes Sly Pond Rd., then Shelving Rock Rd. The small trailhead (N43° 32.153', W73° 34.281') is 1.25 mi past Owens Rd. (Hogtown Rd.) and generally known as the Hogtown trailhead to differentiate it from the much busier trail from Pilot Knob Rd.*

Buck Mt. is visible from many locations on the S and W sides of Lake George and the trail from the lake side (Pilot Knob Rd.) is always busy. Following the Hogtown Trail, beginning at 1200 ft, BLUE markers lead into the forest. The lower portion of the trail gains a mere 200 ft in the first 1 mi. Along the way, cross a series of small streams and enjoy the beautiful hemlocks. The trail begins to gain elevation at

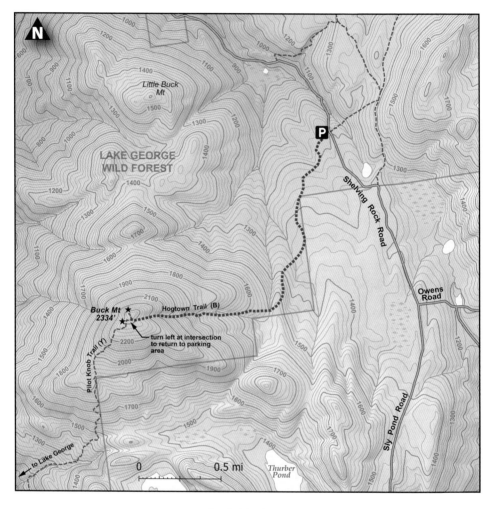

Buck Mt. Map

1400 ft, turning W. It becomes an eroded streambed where the footing is rocky and rough. In wet seasons dogs may find water, but it is often dry.

The Hogtown Trail intersects the Pilot Knob Trail 0.1 mi from the summit. Turn RIGHT and climb over a short section of bedrock, then stroll out onto Buck's 2334 ft rocky top. It's a good idea to leash dogs as you approach the summit as you'll seldom have it to yourself. The views are stunning, with Lake George below and too many mountains to enumerate. Pass through a small screen of trees to another rocky outcrop with N views that on clear days include the High Peaks. The peaks surrounding Lake George are very prominent from the summit. Leaving the summit, be certain to turn LEFT at the trail intersection so you don't inadvertently end up at the wrong trailhead.

Catamount Mt.

HIGHLIGHTS AND SUMMARY: The "WOW" you feel when seeing the mountain from the road is only surpassed by hiking this double-topped rocky peak. The shady forest at its feet abruptly changes as you emerge onto open rock. Pick a clear day and be certain you and your doghiker are comfortable on the summit rock slabs.

MILEAGE: *4 mi r/t.*

ELEVATION GAIN: *1545 ft.*

DIFFICULTY: *4*

VIEW RATING: *5*

LEASH: *Not required.*

DOG SAFETY AND HAZARDS: *Consider leashing on the open rock and around other hikers.*

WATER: *A few small streams. Dry and exposed beyond the first summit. Carry dog water.*

HIKER TRAFFIC: *Busy on weekends.*

TRAIL CONDITIONS: *Irregularly placed small cairns above first summit make route-finding difficult. Rocky sections slippery when wet or icy.*

BEST TIME TO HIKE: *Luminous in autumn.*

GETTING THERE: *Take NY 431 out of Wilmington, turning onto CR 18 before the entrance to Whiteface Memorial Highway. Turn RIGHT onto Roseman Lane (N44° 25.511', W73° 55.363') and RIGHT onto Forestdale Rd. (Plank Rd.) to the 1625 ft trailhead (N44° 26.575', W73° 52.767').*

Follow YELLOW markers from the gate onto a woods road through a dense, boreal bog. At 0.45 mi, pass a metal gate where the Wilmington Snowmobile Trail you've been sharing enters private land and the 8 ft wide road now turns into a trail. The first 0.6 mi from the parking area gains only 100 ft and the trail is bordered by areas of reindeer and club mosses, with blueberries in sunny spots.

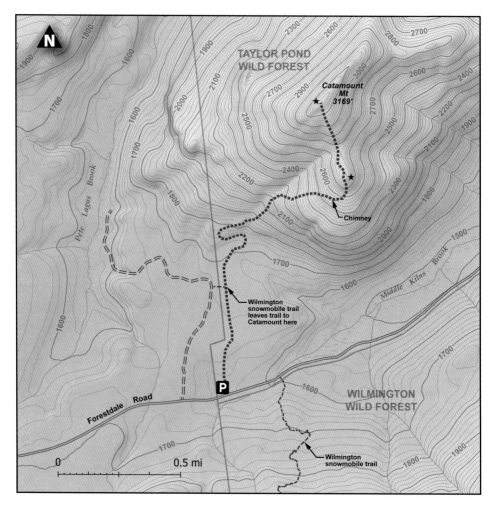

Catamount Mt. Map

The forest transitions as you ascend, beech now predominating with occasional large white birch. Near 1700 ft, cross a bridge over a small stream. This is the beginning of the first pair of trail reroutes. They bypass steep, eroded, unrecoverable sections, replacing them with switchbacks that take advantage of the natural terrain. Stonework has been placed to form steps where the trail parallels and crosses streams in a couple of other places. Where the second reroute joins the existing trail, there are filtered views of the Stephenson Range.

You can glimpse the rocky terrain above where the trail steepens near 0.85 mi. Ledges and boulders sit at the foot of a narrow rock chimney, one of Catamount's most photographed and talked about features. With hand and foot holds, it's not difficult or steep. Some dogs might need coaxing, though, and it helps to have them enter ahead of you. The remainder of the way to the 2770 ft first summit consists of short rock scrambles. You can take a break and enjoy the great views from here or turn around if you're uncomfortable on the terrain above. Otherwise, continue through a shallow, wooded col at 1.5 mi. Once on the rock slabs above, you're out in the open, exposed to the elements. Without trail markers, pay attention to your route on the remaining 400 ft of scrambling.

The ascent to the summit has little actual climbing exposure, but the open rock might intimidate some hikers or dogs who haven't had much experience above tree line. Save Catamount for a clear day, not only because of the views, but for ease in picking your way back down to avoid getting off-route. The 360-degree views from the 3169 ft summit are stupendous. Taylor and Union Falls Ponds, Silver Lake, and waves of summits populate the W and NW. There are up-close views of the Wilmington and Stephenson Ranges with Whiteface looming over Esther. The Green Mts. and many of the other Adirondack High Peaks are visible. Bring a container for the ample blueberries on this spectacular mountain.

Emma above it all.
—Kevin Talbot

Cheney Mt.

HIGHLIGHTS AND SUMMARY: Short hike with multiple view-points, wildflowers, blueberries, and perched wetlands. It's an ideal hike for families with dogs or someone looking for a half-day doghike courtesy of the Champlain Area Trails (CATS) organization.

MILEAGE: *2.5 mi r/t.*

ELEVATION GAIN: *575 ft.*

DIFFICULTY: *2*

VIEW RATING: *3*

LEASH: *Required.*

DOG SAFETY AND HAZARDS: *Heavy truck traffic at trailhead.*

WATER: *Perched wetlands.*

HIKER TRAFFIC: *Very light.*

TRAIL CONDITIONS: *Excellent, well-maintained.*

BEST TIME TO HIKE: *All three seasons.*

GETTING THERE: *The trailhead (N44° 04.807′, W73° 28.954′) is located on Pelfershire Rd. (CR 54), midway between NY 9N and CR 7, near Mineville or Port Henry.*

The roomy trailhead is marked by a large sign. Be careful with kids and dogs due to the large amount of weekday truck traffic. Begin following CATS trail markers through a grassy field from where Camels Hump and Mt. Mansfield in Vermont are visible. The trail register is in woods on the other side.

From the trailhead, start climbing through a mixed forest, turning uphill onto a woods road. The trail leaves the road at a LEFT turn (N44° 04.606′, W73° 28.887′), climbing towards Cheney's NNW ridge. Near 1100 ft, you'll pass a cliff and trailside wet areas where dogs can drink. There are a pair of trail signs at 1215 ft in a small col (N44° 04.540′, W73° 28.722′) on the ridge. One points LEFT to "North Lake Overlook," where there are views of the N part of Lake Champlain, Camels Hump, and Mt. Mansfield. The other sign points to "Seventh Mine–High Peaks Overlook" and "Champlain Bridge Overlook." They are farther along the ridge beyond Cheney's summit.

The remaining 0.25 mi to Cheney's summit is bordered by ferns, sedge, and wildflowers. Like the rest of the trail, it's easy walking on

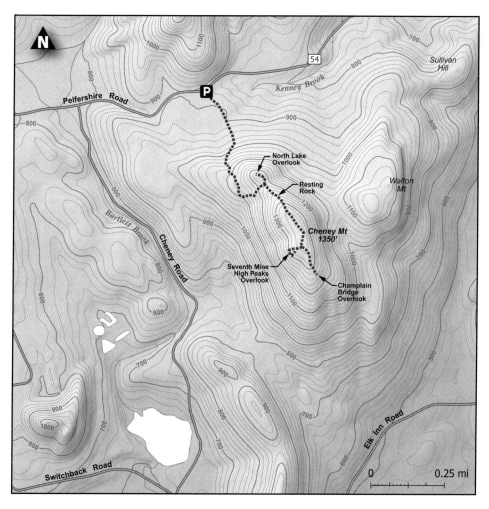

Cheney Mt. Map

the hard-packed surface, often cushioned by conifer needles. Resting Rock is at 1300 ft, a large flat boulder in the middle of a shady hemlock grove. It's located near a number of perched wetlands, making it a perfect location for a canine break. After snowmelt or periods of rain, it's a refreshing place for dogs, but midsummer mud may have you wishing you'd arrived in someone else's car.

Cheney's 1350 ft summit is surrounding by small oaks that provide peek-a-boo views of Lake Champlain. Compensation for the blocked perspective is the variety of spring wildflowers and ample blueberries. Descend past the summit for a short distance to a trail junction (N44° 04.361′, W73° 28.575′) and the nicest of the perched wetlands. It's large and deep enough for a dog to swim, drink, and cool off. One sign points to "Champlain Bridge Overlook" and the other, "Number Seven Mine–High Peaks Overlook." Descend 50 ft to the Champlain Bridge overlook (N44° 04.279′, W73° 28.515′) for a view of the bridge and lake through an opening between small oaks.

Descend slightly from the trail intersection to the Number Seven Mine and High Peaks Overlook (N44° 04.352′, W73° 28.618′) where a commemorative bench provides views of the iron ore mine, the Dixes, Great Range, and other High Peaks. There's a short trail on the LEFT leading to another viewpoint.

Clear Pond—Chain Lakes

HIGHLIGHTS AND SUMMARY: The Gooley and Polaris Clubs were stewards of this land before its sale to New York State in 2007. Though crossed by roads, the area is as close to walking through wilderness as most people will ever experience. Clear Pond is the table-setter for a day's explorations that include views of the Hudson, Cedar, and Indian Rivers. Mountain bikes, snowshoes, and cross-county skis are other ways to explore the area. It would be hard to imagine a place more suited for doghikers.

MILEAGE: *7 mi r/t.*

ELEVATION GAIN: *525 ft.*

DIFFICULTY: *3*

VIEW RATING: *2*

LEASH: *Not required.*

DOG SAFETY AND HAZARDS: *None.*

WATER: *Clear Pond and multiple ponds and streams.*

HIKER TRAFFIC: *Light.*

TRAIL CONDITIONS: *Excellent.*

BEST TIME TO HIKE: *Spring until road is closed for winter. Great snowshoeing and cross-country skiing.*

GETTING THERE: *Turn onto Chain Lakes Rd. from NY 28 (N43° 47.119′, W74° 14.439′) E of Indian Lake village. The curvy road becomes seasonally maintained at 1.8 mi and travel is sketchier and less suitable for low-clearance cars beyond the parking area at 3.1 mi (N43° 49.014′, W74° 12.400′).*

The trailhead (N43° 49.640', W74° 12.034') is situated at the former Outer Gooley Club clubhouse on a scenic bluff overlooking the Hudson River, 4 mi from NY 28.

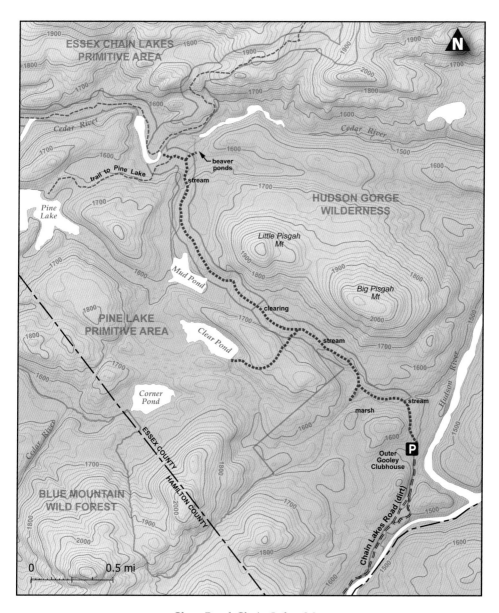

Clear Pond Chain Lakes Map

Following the road, the BLUE-marked trail begins on the other side of a gate, leading over the shoulder of a small hill. Turning W, the road crosses a stream at 0.3 mi and follows it for a short distance, upstream toward a marsh. The road is bordered by large birch and, in varying locations, areas of ferns, wildflowers, and in sunny areas raspberry bushes. Bypass an unmarked road leading to a sand pit on the LEFT (N43° 49.964', W74° 12.433').

The Clear Pond trail (N43° 50.277', W74° 12.888') intersects on the LEFT 1.4 mi from the trailhead. The YELLOW markers lead 0.5 mi to the pond, not 0.3 mi as the DEC sign describes. The trail follows the old Gooley trail, gaining 80 ft then losing 100 ft to Clear Pond's SE shore. Although the forest is deciduous, the pond is encircled by conifers. There's an ancient cedar adjacent to the old beaver dam that helps impound Clear Pond. Dun Brook Mt. and the Fishing Brook Range are profiled in the distance. Tall cliffs on the pond's E side, loon calls, and moose tracks bolster a wilderness atmosphere and will entice you to return.

Which way? Bones and Fletcher.
—Kim Waples

Back on the road, a series of small ups and downs lead to a gate and clearing (N43° 50.388′, W74° 13.160′) on the RIGHT. If you're a bushwhacker, follow an overgrown woods road out the back of the clearing that leads toward Little and Big Pisgah and their gorgeous views.

Beyond the clearing, enjoy areas of berry bushes in sunny sections as you continue, passing Mud Pond and surroundings, now mostly marsh and beaver ponds. Just under 3 mi from the trailhead the road crosses two streams. A short distance ahead is an unmarked woods road (N43° 51.150′, W74° 13.701′) on the RIGHT that leads to active beaver dams and an old road that parallels the Cedar River.

In another 0.25 mi (3 mi from trailhead), look for a short trail on the RIGHT that leads to a high bank overlooking the Cedar River, the site of a possible future bridge. There's a trail sign on the road pointing to beautiful Pine Lake, just under 1 mi beyond.

Cobble Lookout

> **HIGHLIGHTS AND SUMMARY:** This was a popular locals-only hike before DEC created a trail. Though short in length, it's an excellent forest hike with spectacular views from the ledge and superb autumn scenery.

MILEAGE: *2.5 mi r/t.*

ELEVATION GAIN: *270 ft.*

DIFFICULTY: *2*

VIEW RATING: *3*

LEASH: *Not required, but leash near hikers and at ledge.*

DOG SAFETY AND HAZARDS: *Busy road traffic and ledge at Cobble Lookout.*

WATER: *Two seasonal brooks.*

HIKER TRAFFIC: *Very busy.*

TRAIL CONDITIONS: *Eroded and rocky in places. A few muddy sections.*

BEST TIME TO HIKE: *Spring and autumn. Midweek is best.*

GETTING THERE: *Follow NY 431 out of Wilmington, bearing RIGHT onto CR 18 just before the entrance to Whiteface Memorial Highway. Look for the trailhead (N44° 24.231′, W73° 52.732′) 0.35 mi ahead at a DEC sign. There is pull-over roadside parking outside of the small trailhead lot.*

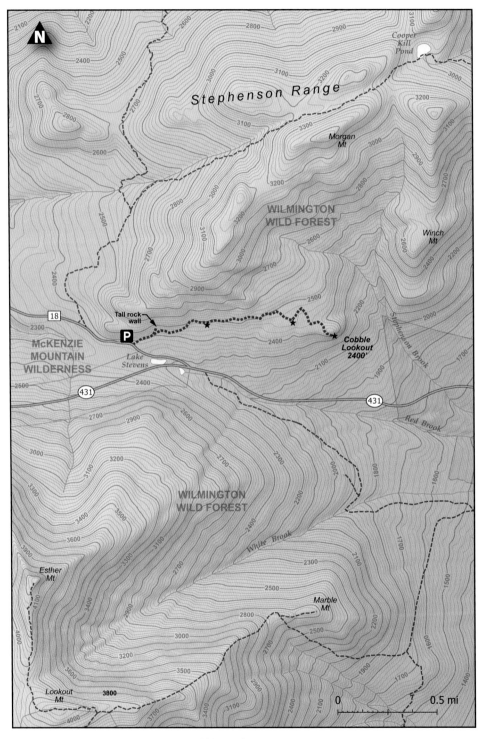

Cobble Lookout Map

Begin hiking on BLUE markers on a woods road that leads into a bo-real forest. Watch for an unmarked path on the LEFT at 0.15 mi. The 50 yd path leads to a tall rock wall that's ice-draped in winter, but watch for scattered broken glass. The conifers at the hike's beginning are soon replaced by a deciduous forest allowing screened views that include Esther and Marble Mts. as you hike. In the autumn, the foli-age is gorgeous. The trail has areas of exposed roots on the otherwise hard-packed dirt surface with a few muddy sections where you can rock-hop to keep your boots dry.

You'll discover that for most of its length, the trail is a series of short ups and downs, none of great consequence. Depending on the season, areas of ferns and wildflowers abut the trail. Near 0.4 mi, the small, skinny maples of a pole stand provide views when leafless. Ahead, the trail crosses a short bridge where there's seasonal water for dogs and more filtered mountain views.

At 0.25 mi from trail's end, conifers reappear as you hike next to and then cross the outflow of a small bog on a short bridge over another stream. Beyond, wooden planking crosses a muddy section. At 1.25 mi, the trail makes a negligible descent as you emerge from the forest to the bright Cobble Lookout. From the sandy and rocky lookout, you're greeted with views of Esther and Marble Mts., a line-up of small peaks, and valleys in two different directions. With the lookout's popularity, you're likely to have to wait your turn to take a photo of the "posing rock."

Coney Mt.

HIGHLIGHTS AND SUMMARY: A wonderful short hike to a rocky summit that provides views in every direction. A real favorite with families and doghikers. An especially nice outing during the autumn foliage season.

MILEAGE: *2 mi r/t.*

ELEVATION GAIN: *515 ft.*

DIFFICULTY: *2*

VIEW RATING: *3*

LEASH: *Not required.*

DOG SAFETY AND HAZARDS: *Keep dogs leashed near busy highway and at summit.*

WATER: *A stream near the beginning, otherwise dry. Carry dog water.*

HIKER TRAFFIC: *Busy, and more so on weekends and in the summer.*

TRAIL CONDITIONS: *Very good.*

BEST TIME TO HIKE: *Autumn foliage is spectacular.*

GETTING THERE: *The 1740 ft trailhead (N44° 06.036', W74° 31.784') is located on NY 30, a few minutes S of Tupper Lake's South Bay. Look for a DEC sign, "Horseshoe Lake Wild Forest—Coney Mt." The trailhead has room for only four to five vehicles. There's another parking area 100 yd away on the opposite side of NY 30.*

Follow BLUE markers through a beech forest, soon passing over wooden planking next to a glacial erratic with a cap of ferns resembling a toupee. Immediately beyond, the trail makes a 90-degree

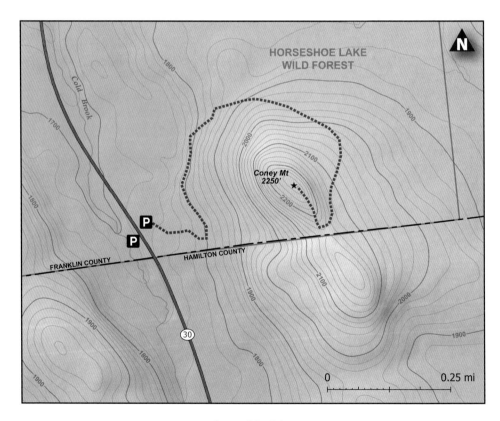

Coney Mt. Map

Gizmo and Marley—Mt Arab.
—Shane Holmes

LEFT turn at a stream deep enough for dogs to lay down, hydrate, and cool off. Continue N for 0.25 mi, gaining little elevation as the trail swings around the N side of Coney before corkscrewing its way uphill toward the summit.

The trail is a rocky, well-worn path, and though it sees a lot of use, it's well maintained and has water bars to divert runoff and keep erosion and mud to a minimum. One look at the map will show why the trail follows a spiral course. It avoids the steep terrain on the W, NW, and N sections of this little mountain. You'll enjoy the in-season wildflowers that are complemented with areas of summer ferns.

As the trail swings around to Coney's SE ridge, the grade steepens in the last 100 ft and bare rock offers a hint of the views waiting ahead. Paint blazes replace the trail markers immediately below the top, leading to the rock rib that forms the 2250 ft summit.

Blue Mt. dominates the stupendous 360-degree views in the S, with the Seward and Santanoni Ranges arrayed across the E skyline. Large and small peaks and ponds fill every point of the compass. The summit is large enough for multiple people to enjoy the views, but with its popularity, please keep dogs leashed so others can enjoy their summit experience.

Cook Mt.

HIGHLIGHTS AND SUMMARY: A Lake George Land Conservancy (LGLC) property that packs views, blueberries, birding, and a little history into its trails. Review the map at the trailhead kiosk as trail signs and markers may be confusing.

MILEAGE: *3.4 mi r/t.*

ELEVATION GAIN: *960 ft.*

DIFFICULTY: *3*

VIEW RATING: *3*

LEASH: *Required.*

DOG SAFETY AND HAZARDS: *Leashes near road.*

WATER: *Small stream and beaver marsh. Carry water for dogs.*

HIKER TRAFFIC: *Light, a little busier on weekends.*

TRAIL CONDITIONS: *Generally good, a little wet in places.*

BEST TIME TO HIKE: *Spring birding and autumn foliage.*

GETTING THERE: *The Cook Mountain Preserve (N43° 49.010′, W73° 26.306′) is located S of Ticonderoga on the W side of Baldwin Rd. and has roadside parking.*

Walk past the trail register and pass a small stream before arriving at the first intersection at 0.25 mi. This is the E end of the Beaver Marsh Trail Loop. Continue LEFT to another intersection (N43° 48.989′, W73° 26.577′), where a side trails leads in 0.3 mi to a civil war gravesite. Returning to the intersection, bear LEFT on YELLOW markers through large conifers, along the bottom of Cook Mt.'s steep E slope, to another intersection (N43° 49.153′, W73° 26.614′). Turning RIGHT takes you around the Beaver Marsh Loop back toward the trailhead.

Turn LEFT to climb Cook Mt. on the Ridges Trail following RED markers. The first 600 ft are continually steep with no reliable water for dogs in the deciduous forest. The steepest part of the ascent is over at 1020 ft as the trail levels for a short distance. It then turns LEFT for the remaining 0.4 mi and under 200 ft climb to the summit. The trail now passes through a mixed forest of conifers and small oaks with part of the path covered by conifer needles. In spring, this

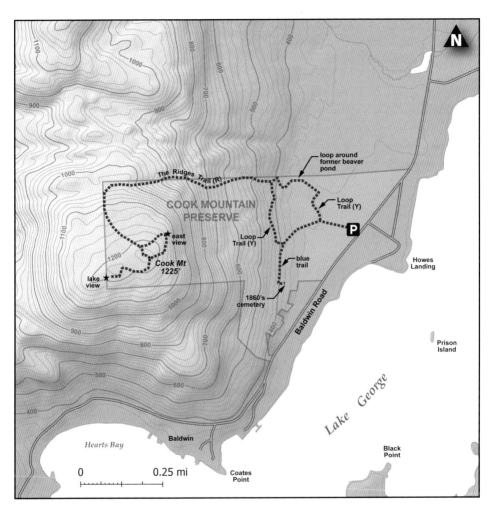

Cook Mt. Map

portion of the trail has wildflowers and, in summer, alternating sections of blueberries and ferns.

A trail junction just under the summit is marked by two red ar-
rows. "View Lake" points toward the summit; the other arrow reads,
"East View." Blueberries cover every inch of arable ground on Cook's
wooded and rocky top, and scattered small oaks grow out of rock
crevices on this interesting summit. With no views from the high
point, descend back down on the "Lake View" trail (N43° 48.960′,
W73° 27.069′) for a marvelous look at Lake George, Anthony's Nose,

Flat Rock, and other mountains. Roger's Rock is visible from a clearing, framed by a ring of small oaks and blueberry bushes. Enjoy the view from one of the large rocks or the small bench that command the clearing.

A short descent from the summit leads to the "East View" that overlooks the N end of Lake George and a portion of Lake Champlain, and provides views of the Green Mts. The trail continues, offering more views before turning uphill to rejoin the main trail just below the summit. You'll quickly shed the hard-earned elevation on the way to the trailhead. Be certain to turn LEFT onto the trail with YELLOW markers for the Beaver Pond Loop. There's a section of shady white pines, soft needles, and areas of boardwalk to keep your boots dry. This section of trail is a great location for spring birding.

The Crows

HIGHLIGHTS AND SUMMARY: A popular short hike over Big and Little Crow. The views from both of these puny, but rocky, summits are superlative. Though steep, the hike is short in duration, and provides a destination any doghiker can accomplish.

MILEAGE: *2 mi r/t.*

ELEVATION GAIN: *1000 ft.*

DIFFICULTY: *2*

VIEW RATING: *5*

LEASH: *Not required.*

DOG SAFETY AND HAZARDS: *Leash dogs at busy trailhead and around other hikers.*

WATER: *A small stream near the beginning, but otherwise dry. Carry water for doghikers.*

HIKER TRAFFIC: *Light during the week, busy on weekends.*

TRAIL CONDITIONS: *Very good.*

BEST TIME TO HIKE: *Spring through autumn.*

GETTING THERE: *Turn onto CR 13 (Hurricane Rd.) from NY 9N in Keene. Bear LEFT onto O'Toole Rd. (N44° 15.449', W73° 44.967'), which climbs 470 ft in 1.2 mi to the Crow Clearing trailhead (N44° 15.695', W73°*

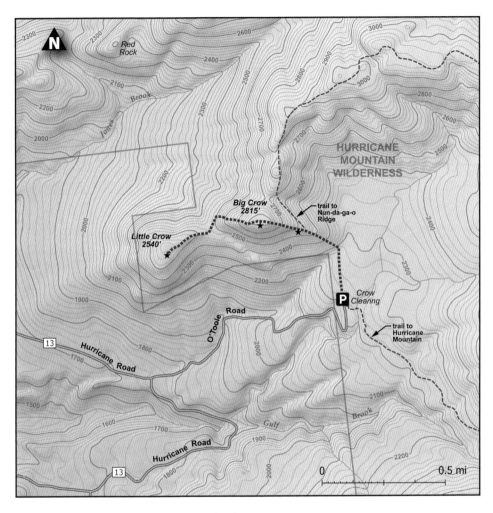

The Crows Map

44.005′). The busy parking area serves trails for Hurricane Mt. and Nun-da-ga-o Ridge as well.

The RED trail from 2215 ft Crow Clearing gains little elevation in the first 0.2 mi, where it crosses a small stream. This is the only reliable water on the hike. The trail then climbs steeply, switchbacking and alternating between forest and rocks. Your first great view is from a ledge at 0.4 mi. From this point upward, you're in and out of ledges

Frosty Emma.
—Kevin Talbot

until reaching continual open rock for the last 100 ft to the 2815 ft Big Crow summit.

The breathtaking views take in nearby Hurricane, Chase, Weston, Tripod, and Baxter Mts. Cascade, the Sentinel Range, Pitchoff, Giant, Dix, and other mountains claim the skyline. Walk 100 ft across the summit for views of Little Crow, Oak Ridge, Red Rock, Esther, Whiteface, and the Great Range. Continue W, descending 330 ft into the col with Little Crow.

With under 100 ft of climbing, you'll find yourself on the summit of Little Crow, where more great views await. The high point of Little Crow is in the dense woods, but the views are from the trail. Please don't take the more lightly used trail to Hurricane Rd. from Little Crow. It passes through private land and is inadvisable for doghikers. Reverse your route and enjoy a second helping of views from Big Crow.

Hackensack Mt.

HIGHLIGHTS AND SUMMARY: The kiosk at the entrance to this park gives the origin of the name "Hackensack" as Algonquin, meaning where two rivers meet. The Hudson and Schroon Rivers are visible from the summit, as are dozens of mountains in the area. This small peak is encircled by trails, with the steepest being the most direct route to the top. Trails on the N side have unmarked intersections. Great summit views.

MILEAGE: *2.6 mi r/t loop.*

ELEVATION GAIN: *750 ft.*

DIFFICULTY: *4*

VIEW RATING: *3*

LEASH: *Required.*

DOG SAFETY AND HAZARDS: *A steep section of the RED trail might challenge older dogs.*

WATER: *None.*

HIKER TRAFFIC: *Light.*

TRAIL CONDITIONS: *Some wet areas. Rocky and eroded in places.*

BEST TIME TO HIKE: *Spring and autumn.*

GETTING THERE: *Turn onto Emerson Ave. (N43° 29.707', W73° 46.377') from US 9 in Warrensburg, then RIGHT on Prospect St. to the trailhead driveway (N43° 29.797', W73° 46.171'). There's a second, lesser-used trailhead with residential street parking at the intersection (N43° 30.029', W73° 46.450') of Warren St. and Hackensack Ave.*

The RED trail starts beyond large boulders on the RIGHT of the kiosk. Ignore side trails, descending slightly before climbing to the intersection with the PURPLE trail. The RED trail leads directly to the summit and PURPLE continues around the E and N, climbing Hackensack's NW ridge.

The RED trail is short and steep, climbing 560 ft in 0.75 mi, with the first 0.15 mi a gradual ascent through mixed forest. A rocky, steep, and ledgy section follows through conifers, crossing an area of large boulders resulting from an old rockslide. As the grade eases

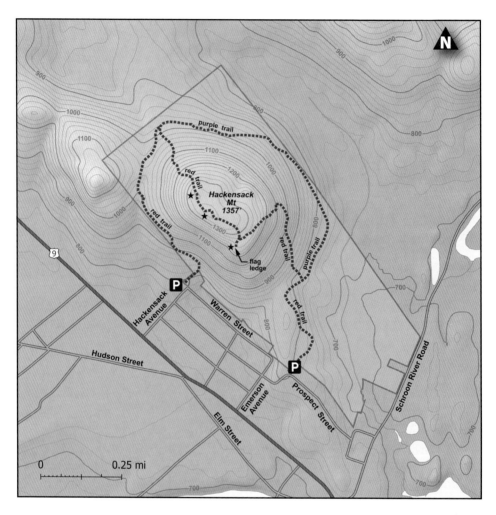

Hackensack Mt. Map

near 1160 ft, the forest transitions to short oaks. The trail passes over rock slabs that offer SE views.

Look for an unmarked path (N43° 30.153′, W73° 46.341′) on the LEFT that descends to a ledge with a makeshift flagpole. Nice views follow in the remaining 0.25 mi to the summit, with the best vantage point the open rock just beyond the top. You can see the rivers and an array of peaks, with the Three Sisters most prominent.

To hike a loop, instead of proceeding straight up the RED trail, turn onto the PURPLE trail at the intersection (N43° 30.050′, W73° 46.116′) previously mentioned. It's a woods road that descends slightly, then begins a slow climb along the N side of Hackensack. This less-used trail is mostly shady, and grassy and overgrown in sunny locations. Pay attention to your route and ignore multiple unmarked woods roads and snowmobile trails, as it's easy to get sidetracked.

The PURPLE trail ends at its intersection (N43° 30.440', W73° 46.631') with the RED trail on Hackensack's NW side. Follow RED markers SE as the trail climbs a steep 350 ft in 0.3 mi to the open rock NW of Hackensack's summit. From the top, follow the RED trail back to your vehicle. Bring lots of water for your dog as there aren't reliable water sources.

Hadley Mt.

HIGHLIGHTS AND SUMMARY: Enjoy great views, blueberries, and wildflowers. You don't have to climb the fire tower to enjoy the sights from Hadley's rocky summit. On clear days, views include the Adirondack High Peaks, the Green Mts., and the Catskills.

MILEAGE: *3.5 mi r/t.*

ELEVATION GAIN: *1500 ft.*

DIFFICULTY: *4*

VIEW RATING: *5*

LEASH: *Not required, but suggested at trailhead, summit, and near other hikers.*

DOG SAFETY AND HAZARDS: *None.*

WATER: *Seasonal brooks, but mostly dry.*

HIKER TRAFFIC: *Always busy.*

TRAIL CONDITIONS: *Eroded and rocky.*

BEST TIME TO HIKE: *Spring and autumn. Less hiker traffic during the week.*

GETTING THERE: *Drive N from Lake Luzerne on CR 1 (Stony Creek Rd.) to a LEFT onto Hadley Hill Rd. (N43° 21.259', W73° 52.675'). Turn onto Eddy Rd. (N43° 21.833', W73° 55.144'), then LEFT on Tower Rd. to the large trailhead (N43° 22.425', W73° 57.033').*

Begin on RED markers, starting out through a short section of hemlocks. The woods soon transition to a deciduous forest. There's little warmup as the trail starts immediately climbing on the well-trodden

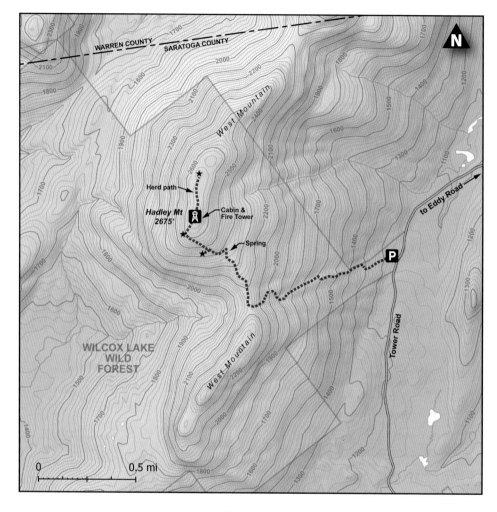

Hadley Mt. Map

and rocky trail over sections of worn bedrock, a gneiss (sorry!) beginning. Thanks to volunteers, the footing is kept it in good condition, no small challenge given the number of boots pounding it.

There are seasonal brooks, including a more reliable one near 0.5 mi, but plan to carry extra dog water unless it has recently rained. Pass an interesting trailside rock formation near 1850 ft. At 0.75 mi the grade eases, reaching a col at 2200 ft on the SSE ridge.

After an all-too-short respite, the trail resumes climbing. The forest canopy opens at 1 mi and small shrubs, ferns, and sedge line the

March sunrise.
—Deb Osterhoudt

trail. On sunny June days, linger and enjoy the fluttering scenery of tiger swallowtail butterflies attracted to white flowers on the blackberry canes. There's a small spring where the trail makes a sharp LEFT at 2350 ft, a perfect cooling-off place for dogs after the steady ascent. Not far ahead there's an unmarked path leading to a ledge and your first good view.

As the trail continues to climb, open rock slabs at 2650 ft provide views that are just an appetizer for those waiting on the summit, five minutes ahead. The observer's cabin and outbuilding are located just below the top and what at first appears to be a cave is in fact the fire lookout's cellar hole. The restored fire tower sits atop the rocky 2675 ft summit with views that include Great Sacandaga Lake, and Black, Gore, Snowy, Panther, and Buck Mts. More distantly, Killington and Camels Hump in the Greens, the Adirondack High Peaks, and Blackhead Range in the Catskills are visible on clear days.

Investigate an unmarked path N along the summit ridge. It's a peaceful 0.25 mi stroll through blueberry bushes, ferns, birch, and ash trees to the N ledge (N43° 22.792', W73° 58.237'). You may get a chance to see some of the creative cairns on the ledge and pink lady's slippers peeking from small alcoves along the path.

Hammond Pond

HIGHLIGHTS AND SUMMARY: Dogs and kids will enjoy this interesting and uncrowded short hike. There's a stream, pond, views, and an option to extend the hike.

MILEAGE: *2 mi r/t.*

ELEVATION GAIN: *150 ft.*

DIFFICULTY: *1*

VIEW RATING: *2*

LEASH: *Not required.*

DOG SAFETY AND HAZARDS: *Black Brook and Hammond Pond spillway during high water.*

WATER: *Black and Berrymill Brooks and Hammond Pond.*

HIKER TRAFFIC: *Very light.*

TRAIL CONDITIONS: *Excellent.*

BEST TIME TO HIKE: *Late spring through foliage season.*

GETTING THERE: *Turn onto US 9 from Northway exit 20 in North Hudson and continue N. In 2.5 mi, turn RIGHT onto CR 4C (N43° 59.147', W73° 43.018'), then onto Ensign Pond Rd. (CR 4) to the trailhead (N43° 59.517', W73° 39.688'), marked by a "Hammond Pond Wild Forest" sign, 2.5 mi ahead.*

The hike begins on a wide woods road/trail on RED markers, paralleling the S side of Black Brook. At 0.1 mi, cross a bridge over Berrymill Brook, which drains a series of ponds and small mountain slopes. There's a trail following it out of the trailhead. As you continue toward Hammond Pond, the trail takes you through a mixed forest paralleling Black Brook. At 0.65 mi the trail makes a sharp LEFT turn crossing the brook. Walk 0.2 mi slightly uphill to the outlet of Hammond Pond. There's a 50 ft wide wooden spillway that hikers and dogs can cross at low water. After periods of heavy rain or spring

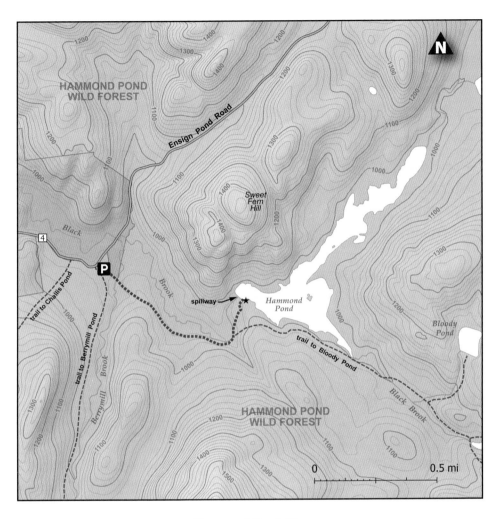

Hammond Pond Map

snowmelt, crossing the spillway, or dogs getting too close to Black Brook, is unsafe and inadvisable.

In times of "regular" water levels, dogs will love Hammond Pond and puddling around on Black Brook. When trees are bare you can see the cliffs on Sweet Fern Hill. Regardless of season, Bloody Mt. looks impressive across Hammond Pond. In addition to the usual wildflower cast of characters, be on the lookout for pink lady's slippers prevalent in the area. You can extend your hike by following the trail along the S shore of Hammond Pond or continue 1.2 mi to Bloody Pond.

Hopkins Mt.

HIGHLIGHTS AND SUMMARY: The Mossy Cascade Trail has just about everything—hemlock groves, giant white pines, waterfalls, cascades, blueberries, wildflowers, and spectacular views. It's one of the finest and most enjoyable hikes in the Adirondacks.

MILEAGE: *6 mi r/t.*

ELEVATION GAIN: *2050 ft.*

DIFFICULTY: *5*

VIEW RATING: *5*

LEASH: *Near trailhead and on summit.*

DOG SAFETY AND HAZARDS: *Busy highway trailhead.*

WATER: *First part of hike.*

HIKER TRAFFIC: *Very busy on weekends.*

TRAIL CONDITIONS: *Well-maintained, soft footing, with a few rocky sections.*

BEST TIME TO HIKE: *Spring flowers, summer blueberries, autumn foliage fireworks.*

GETTING THERE: *The trailhead (N44° 09.763', W73° 46.642') is a pull-off on the E side of NY 73, N of St. Huberts. Look for an easily missed "Hopkins and Giant via Mossy Cascade" trailhead sign.*

Beginning at 1100 ft, the RED trail starts at the road shoulder, crosses a small bridge, and passes a sign acknowledging the excellent Adirondack Trail Improvement Society (ATIS) trail work. It follows NY 73 for the first 100 yd on a woods road carpeted with conifer needles, then descends slightly toward the Ausable River at 0.1 mi. It continues on a woods road, passing behind a residence at 0.4 mi where dogs should be leashed.

Turn LEFT at an intersection followed by a RIGHT two minutes later. RED markers and an arrow keep you on track as you'll likely be gawking at the enormous white pines. Leaving the road at 0.5 mi, the trail now follows Mossy Cascade Brook and passes another white pine giant. The trail meanders near the brook, passing a path at 0.75 mi that leads to the cascades for which the trail is named. Once leaving the stream, the trail is mostly dry for dogs other than small, seasonal brooks, but it remains under a shady canopy almost all the way to the summit.

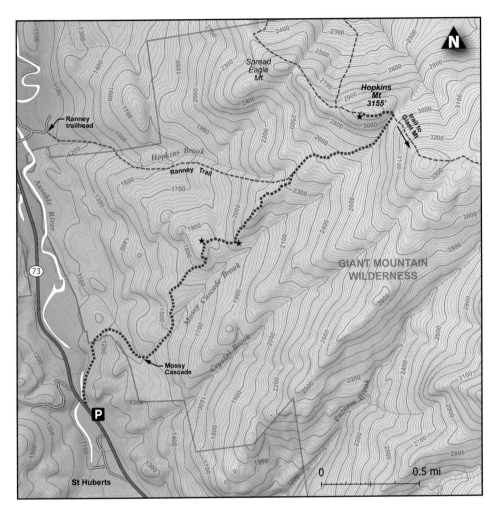

Hopkins Mt. Map

At 1.35 mi, the trail picks up a steep 200 ft of ascent followed by a level section with filtered sunlight, grasses, and sedge. There's a short descent to a small col, then another dip past a patch of Christmas ferns and wildflower showoffs. The steepest part of the hike up the SW ridge begins at 1900 ft, switchbacks easing the effort. Look for a viewpoint another 100 ft higher where you can see Bear Den, Noonmark, Nippletop, Dial, Colvin, and Sawteeth, and get a peek at Gothics.

The forest displays its diversity along the trail. Along with beech, ash, black cherry, birch, maple, and basswood, there's a small cluster of mountain ash in a sunny section, its favorite habitat. At 2.2 mi, the trail intersects the Ranney Trail (N44° 10.751′, W73° 45.360′), an alternative descent route to NY 73 (N44° 11.056′, W73° 47.128′). The Ranney Trail is slightly shorter than Mossy Cascade and has more water, but a portion passes through private property where dogs must be leashed.

Above the intersection, the trail climbs 550 ft to the col and intersection (N44° 11.000′, W73° 44.745′) with the Giant Mt. trail at 2.85 mi. This interesting portion of trail passes through a section of birch and ferns underneath cliffs on Hopkins Mt.'s SE side. Turn LEFT in the col on YELLOW markers for the remaining 0.2 mi to the summit, the trail a combination of eroded streambed, rock slabs, and loose rock. As you emerge from the dark hemlocks onto open rock, the views improve with every step. The spectacular summit has an abundance of alpine wildflowers, blueberry bushes, and unsurpassed High Peaks scenery.

Dogs should be leashed to protect the fragile terrain and because it's likely you'll be sharing the summit with others. Besides the views, Hopkins is known for the variety of flowers and abundant blueberries, and is a "must" destination in autumn. On your way back to the trailhead, follow the path mentioned earlier to get a closer look at the cascades and waterfalls. You can soak your dogs, all of them. They'll surely thank you.

Hey, take a look at this—Hopkins Mt.
—Rob Osterhoudt

Jay Range

HIGHLIGHTS AND SUMMARY: Considered one of the best hikes in the Adirondacks, the long sections of open ridge are the result of large fires in the early 1900s. The exposed ridge has almost continual views with the actual high point at its E end. This remarkable hike alternates sections of open rock with short, shady cols. Wildflowers, blueberries, birch glades, and spectacular views are all part of the day. Look for red garnet nodes embedded in the rocks. Carry lots of water for well-conditioned dogs.

MILEAGE: *7.5 mi r/t.*

ELEVATION GAIN: *2800 ft.*

DIFFICULTY: *5*

VIEW RATING: *5*

LEASH: *Not required, but leash around other hikers and near alpine vegetation.*

DOG SAFETY AND HAZARDS: *Dogs need to be in good shape.*

WATER: *There is no water. Carry lots of water for dogs as the ridge is hot and dry.*

HIKER TRAFFIC: *Busy, particularly on weekends.*

TRAIL CONDITIONS: *Very good, but slabs have slippery grit and sand.*

BEST TIME TO HIKE: *Springtime, and spectacular in autumn. Save for a stellar day.*

GETTING THERE: *Turn E on CR 12 (Glen Rd.) from NY 9N (N44° 20.094', W73° 46.479') in Upper Jay. Drive 3.5 mi, passing a number of side roads. The 1475 ft trailhead (N44° 18.953', W73° 43.242') is located at the intersection of Upland Meadows Rd. and Jay Mountain Rd. at "Jay Mountain Wilderness" sign. There's room for seven to eight vehicles and more at roadside.*

BLUE markers lead uphill from the trail register through a mixed forest to a view of Whiteface Mt.'s ski lifts and rock slides at 0.2 mi. The trail climbs at a steady and moderate rate under forest canopy, a contrast to the exposed ridges waiting above. At 1.2 mi the switchbacking trail curls around a 2323 ft knob and descends through a pair of shallow cols where dogs may find water at a small stream. The trail

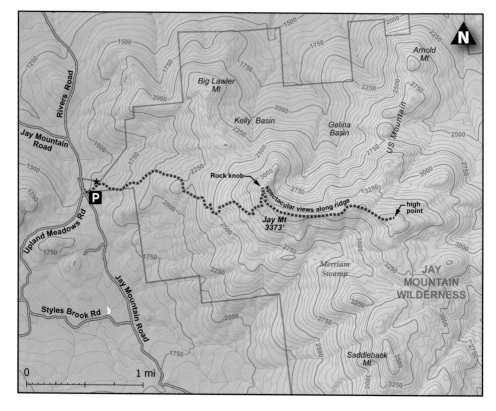

Jay Range Map

resumes its steady ascent through a deciduous forest, reaching a flat spot at 1.9 mi. The trail is now steeper, the effort lessened by numerous switchbacks.

There's an unmarked path on the LEFT at 2.25 mi. It leads to a rocky outcrop (N44° 18.948′, W73° 41.408′) with spectacular views of Hurricane, the Sentinels, Dixes, Great Range, and Lake Champlain, and a glimpse of the open ridge ahead. Some hikers consider the 1800 ft climb to his rocky perch a worthy-enough objective, but it's a mere 0.3 mi and less than 200 ft to Jay Mt.'s 3373 ft summit (N44° 18.748′, W73° 41.151′).

The 3580 ft high point of the Jay Range is another 1.15 mi of spectacular open ridge-walking beyond. The exposed rocky ridge is interrupted with cols filled with ferns, birch, mountain ash, and wildflowers. Midway along the ridge is Grassy Notch (N44° 18.751′, W73° 40.792′), well named and shady, providing views of Merriam Swamp and its devastation from Tropical Storm Irene. In the opposite direction is Gelina Basin and the ridgeline connecting the Jay Range to US and Arnold Mts.

There are three false summits beyond Grassy Notch before the tall cairn marking the high point of the range is reached, 3.75 mi from the trailhead. The ridge is a flower shop for flora enthusiasts. In addition to the usual suspects, summer brings a profusion of meadowsweet, fireweed, yarrow, pearly everlasting, harebells, and many others. The hike is a treat for well-prepared hikers but the dry, exposed ridge should not be attempted with doghikers who are not very well-conditioned. Be sure to carry an abundance of extra water for them.

Kane Mt.

HIGHLIGHTS AND SUMMARY: Located in the Shaker Mt. Wild Forest, this fire tower peak has multiple trails that can be hiked separately or combined. Wildflowers, fern glades, a swimming pond, and great views make this short hike a top destination for dogs and families.

MILEAGE: *N and E trails, 2.4 mi r/t.*

ELEVATION GAIN: *650 ft.*

DIFFICULTY: *2*

VIEW RATING: *3*

LEASH: *Trailhead sign states dogs must be leashed.*

DOG SAFETY AND HAZARDS: *None*

WATER: *No reliable water other than trailhead pond.*

HIKER TRAFFIC: *Busy, especially on weekends and holidays.*

TRAIL CONDITIONS: *Eroded and rocky in places.*

BEST TIME TO HIKE: *Summer and autumn.*

GETTING THERE: *Turn onto Green Lake Rd. (N43° 10.464', W74° 30.659') from NY 10 and 29A, N of Canada Lake. Pass shoreline camps to a LEFT into the narrow Kane Mt. driveway (N43° 10.752', W74° 30.293') at the top of a hill. "No Parking" signs on Green Lake Rd. indicate Kane's popularity.*

The E trail is shorter, but the longer N trail is less busy and a better ascent for doghikers. You can descend the E trail for a nice loop hike.

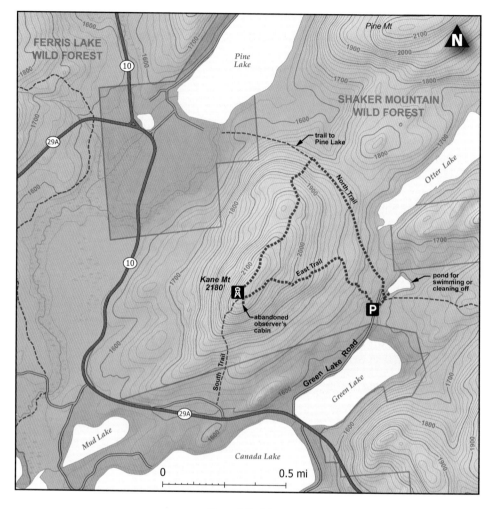

Kane Mt. Map

Follow the N trail 100 yd to a trail sign that points uphill on YELLOW markers. Before embarking, walk another minute to the small pond where dogs can drink and swim while you take in views toward Pine Mt.

The N trail starts uphill, making a sharp turn through a muddy, 50 yd section with exposed tree roots, eroded trail, and rocky footing. You may question why you didn't hike the shorter E trail. Have patience, your decision will be rewarded. Although YELLOW trail markers are sporadic, the trail is easy to follow, coinciding with the Pine Lake trail for its first 0.75 mi.

Rob and Toby—Kane Mt.
—Alan Via

At 1740 ft (N43° 11.328', W74° 30.571'), Kane's N trail leaves the Pine Lake trail. Turn LEFT, beginning a steep uphill climb, gaining 300 ft in 0.25 mi. This short section is a quad-burner, but the grade soon eases and the trail is in great shape. It's a pleasure to hike the rest of the way to the summit.

As the trail nears Kane's NE sub-summit, the forest canopy opens, and you're surrounded by ferns in every direction. The open forest and fern glades might tempt you to leave the trail to see if there's a view of the tower from the NW summit. Save the effort, there's nothing to see from its wooded high point. As you resume, the trail is mostly level before an almost imperceptible dip, then a leisurely climb toward the summit. A little under 0.2 mi from the summit, there is a series of erratics worth examining. Two of them are huge.

A sea of ferns engulfs the fire tower on Kane's 2180 ft summit. Pine Lake, Pine Mt., Canada Lake, Sheeley Mt., Little Roundtop, and a horizon filled with other small peaks and lakes are visible from the tower. Before departing, check out the now-abandoned observer's cabin. Three trails converge on the summit. Be certain you take the correct one back.

The E trail begins directly out of the parking lot. It's eight to ten feet wide in places, likely having been a woods road at one time. It's well-packed with some eroded places, but generally in good shape considering the number of boots that tromp this popular trail. The deciduous forest is mostly beech with some maple and ash and, like its N counterpart, there's no reliable water for dogs. The E trail climbs gradually for the first half, ascending more steeply the rest of its short way. Kane has a S trail that can be combined with either of the two trails described here. It's a long walk around, however, if you inadvertently descend it without a car spotted at that trailhead.

LeVine Nature Preserve

HIGHLIGHTS AND SUMMARY: This 177-acre Saratoga PLAN (Preserving Land and Nature) preserve is located in the foothills S of the Adirondack Blue Line. There are five trail loops and an abandoned road bisecting the preserve. The mixed forest has well-designed and maintained trails on rolling terrain. Long sections of trail follow Joby and Cadman Creeks, making this an ideal doghike.

MILEAGE: *3 mi all trails.*

ELEVATION GAIN: *400 ft.*

DIFFICULTY: *1*

VIEW RATING: *2*

LEASH: *Required.*

DOG SAFETY AND HAZARDS: *Proximity to Centerline Rd. and streams during high water.*

WATER: *Long sections follow streams.*

HIKER TRAFFIC: *Light.*

TRAIL CONDITIONS: *Excellent, well laid out.*

BEST TIME TO HIKE: *Three seasons and excellent cross-country skiing or snowshoeing.*

GETTING THERE: *Turn N off of NY 29 (N43° 03.710', W74° 01.131') onto Barkersville Rd. (CR 16), 12 mi W of Saratoga Springs. Turn LEFT onto Glenwild Rd. (N43° 05.690', W74° 02.313') and LEFT on Centerline Rd. (N43° 06.528 W74° 02.805). Continue 0.8 mi to the roadside parking area (N43° 06.212', W74° 03.626').*

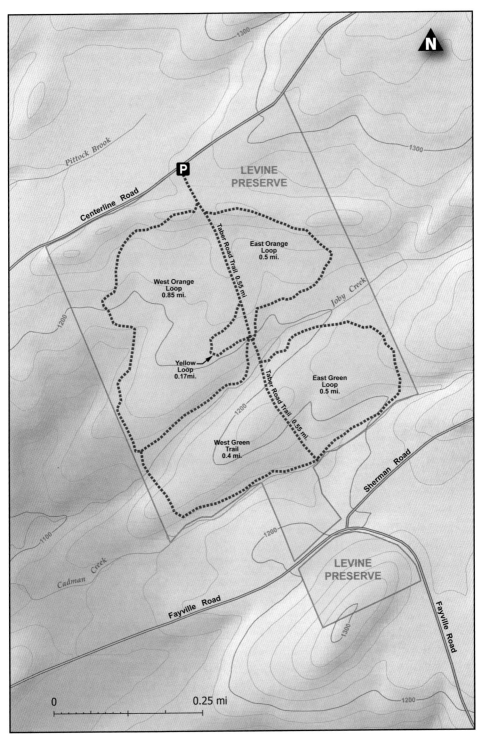

LeVine Preserve Map

LeVine Preserve.
—Alan Via

Pass a muddy bog right behind the kiosk area and begin hiking abandoned Taber Rd., which bisects the preserve. The Taber Road Trail is 0.5 mi long, crosses Joby Creek, and ends at a pair of benches overlooking Cadman Creek. Taber is a gradual downhill, bordered by stone walls, and the starting point for the preserve's four major and one minor loops. Its forest canopy provides dappled summer shade and is a splendor in autumn.

Within sight of the trailhead, the W and E ORANGE loops intersect Taber. Their trails swing away from the Taber Road Trail through mixed forest and generally head downhill toward Joby Creek. Even though the E ORANGE loop doesn't follow a stream, it passes a giant white pine log and its N end traverses an interesting narrow ridge.

Continuing S along Taber, you will come to the short, 0.2 mi YELLOW loop (N43° 06.149′, W74° 03.596′). The YELLOW loop takes you through a conifer forest and has a small but spectacular fern glade and a partial stone foundation, likely the remnant of an 1800s homestead. Continuing S again, Taber crosses photogenic Joby Creek, the first of two streams in the preserve. Both streams are excellent places for dogs to hydrate.

The W and E GREEN trails intersect Taber here. These trails have much in common. Beautiful stone fences crisscross trails that are as nicely designed as I've seen anywhere, taking maximum advantage of the streams and gently rolling terrain. The forest is mixed in places and, where conifers dominate, soft needles pave the trails. Long sections are next to or in sight of Joby and Cadman Creeks, offering doggy hydration and photo opportunities.

At the bottom of Taber Rd., the beautifully situated benches overlooking Cadman Creek are in a photogenic and contemplative location. You'll find LeVine a great destination to revisit once you've been there.

Moxham Mt.

HIGHLIGHTS AND SUMMARY: Moxham has it all—open ledges, small streams, spring wildflowers, summer ferns, blueberries, autumn foliage, and wonderful summit views. A great doghike.

MILEAGE: *5 mi r/t.*

ELEVATION GAIN: *1400 ft.*

DIFFICULTY: *3*

VIEW RATING: *4*

LEASH: *At the summit.*

DOG SAFETY AND HAZARDS: *Summit cliff and popular hunting area.*

WATER: *Two streams.*

HIKER TRAFFIC: *Can be busy on weekends.*

TRAIL CONDITIONS: *Excellent*

BEST TIME TO HIKE: *Spring through autumn. Popular snowshoe hike from where 14th Rd. is maintained in winter. Avoid during hunting season.*

GETTING THERE: *Turn onto 14th Rd. (CR 37) at the intersection (N43° 46.959', W73° 58.600') with NY 28N, SW of Minerva. Follow 14th Rd., bearing R at a fork. The macadam turns to dirt and starts downhill 0.2 mi before the 1530 ft trailhead (N43° 46.223', W74° 00.725').*

YELLOW markers lead uphill through a birch and beech forest to screened views along a fern-lined trail at 0.3 mi. The trail crosses a

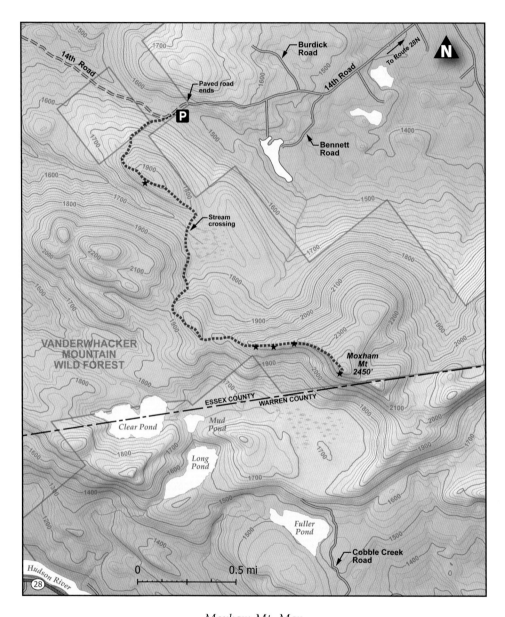

Moxham Mt. Map

ridge at 0.5 mi. Ledges with blueberry bushes and reindeer moss provide unobstructed views across a deep ravine through which Deer Creek flows. The views, berry bushes, and ledges continue for a distance. Don't be surprised to see bear scat in summer.

The trail descends 200 ft in the next 0.4 mi to a tributary of Deer

Bookah and Alan—Moxham Mt.
—Lin Smith

Creek, 1 mi from the trailhead. Unless it's been unusually dry, dogs can get a drink, splash, or take a break here. The stream drains a marshy meadow, likely a beaver pond at one time and a potential place to explore on snowshoes. The trail resumes climbing, passing glacial erratics and overlooking the marsh for 0.2 mi. There's another stream that feeds the marsh in this section of trail.

The grade gets steeper as it climbs onto Moxham's W ridge, passing gorgeous silver birch and blueberry-landscaped rock slabs with views of Peter Gay and Gore Mts. Other than the summit, this section of trail is my favorite, with wildflowers, ferns, summer berries, miniature oaks, and a section of trail where you balance along a rock rib. Visible are Moxham, Long, Mud, and Clear Ponds, a necklace of vleis and small ponds seemingly all connected.

At 2 mi there's a good look at the summit cliffs, 0.6 mi ahead. The trail descends into a shallow col, then ascends the last 400 ft up Moxham's W ridge.

The 2450 ft summit provides a ringside seat for superlative views of the Hudson River and Gore, Peter Gay, Bullhead, and Puffer Mts.

A gaggle of smaller peaks sprinkle the horizon. Looking down from the summit, you can see meandering tracks in the marsh SW of the summit. This is moose country and the tracks are likely where these large creatures emerge from the forest to forage the wetland vegetation. Rappel bolts driven into the summit rock should remind hikers to keep dogs away from the top of the cliff.

It's not all downhill back to the trailhead. Hikers often forget the almost 300 ft of ascent back to their vehicles.

Noonmark Mt.

HIGHLIGHTS AND SUMMARY: The summit is a rocky island surrounded by taller peaks, the stellar views a twelve on the scale of one to ten. This is the only trail to the summit of Noonmark on which dogs are allowed. The steep last mile and rocky terrain may have you feeling the hike is more challenging than either the mileage or elevation gain suggest. Keeping dogs leashed on the summit protects the fragile vegetation and allows other hikers to enjoy their day.

MILEAGE: *6.3 mi r/t.*

ELEVATION GAIN: *2075 ft.*

DIFFICULTY: *5*

VIEW RATING: *5*

LEASH: *Noonmark is in the new Outer High Peaks Zone of New York State's High Peaks Wilderness Complex; leashes are not mandatory in this zone. Leashes should be used at the trailhead for safety, around other hikers, and at the summit to protect alpine vegetation.*

DOG SAFETY AND HAZARDS: *Trailhead on busy NY 73.*

WATER: *Round Pond, small streams, and Boquet River crossing.*

HIKER TRAFFIC: *Sometimes busy to river intersection. Almost always busy on summit.*

TRAIL CONDITIONS: *Rocky in places, three steep rock sections on Noonmark's SE ridge.*

BEST TIME TO HIKE: *Summer through autumn. Midweek less busy.*

GETTING THERE: *The 1560 ft Round Pond trailhead (N44° 07.915′, W73° 43.911′) is located on NY 73, 0.8 mi SE of Chapel Pond, between US 9 and St. Huberts.*

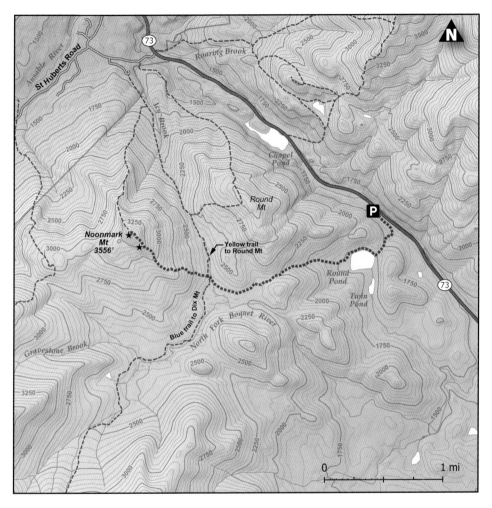

Noonmark Mt. Map

The small, roadside parking area is often fully occupied, requiring a leash walk along the shoulder of NY 73 to the trailhead. BLUE markers lead 50 ft uphill to the trail register, beyond which you pick up an additional 200 ft in the first 0.5 mi of rocky trail. At 0.7 mi, descend 75 ft to Round Pond, its surface reflecting the surrounding ridges. Hiking the 0.25 mi along its N side provides opportunities for photography or doggy fun.

    Leaving the pond's NW corner, the trail gains modest elevation in the next 0.35 mi, then begins to climb. The footing alternates between rocky and a little muddy and dogs will enjoy that the trail

A frosty Koda.
—Sathi Wagner

follows the pond's inlet for almost 0.5 mi. The trail is mostly level from 1.5 mi to a 2300 ft three-way intersection (N44° 07.370', W73° 45.510') at the Boquet River at 2.2 mi. BLUE markers lead SW towards the Dixes and the YELLOW trail leads toward Round Mt. This is the perfect location to grab a snack and allow dogs to cool and hydrate as the RED Felix Adler Trail to Noonmark's summit is steep and rocky, gaining 1215 ft in 1 mi.

Once across the N fork of the Boquet ("Bow-Khet," not the floral arrangement) River, there is no reliable dog water on Noonmark's SE ridge. The bottom half of the ridge is deciduous forest, the footing a mix of rock and dirt. The trail climbs a sometimes-slippery rock slab at 2550 ft. This is followed by another 100 ft higher. These aren't the only two places on the SE ridge that can be challenging when snowy or icy.

Peek-a-boo views and conifers appear midway up the ridge, beginning near 3250 ft. Open rock near 3440 ft provides a preview of what awaits 0.1 mi ahead. The trail ascends a tall, "be-careful" ledge just below the summit that will grab your attention, particularly when you're descending and especially if it's slippery. A little butt-sliding down the short middle section eases the descent.

As you step out of the forest onto Noonmark's rocky balcony, Giant, with its rockslides, the Dixes, and the Great Range are just a few of the dozens of peaks viewable from the 3556 ft summit. Many think Noonmark provides the best views-to-effort ratio in the High Peaks.

If you're comfortable hiking by headlamp, the summit is a fabulous place to watch a sunrise and July 4th fireworks.

Owls Head Lookout

HIGHLIGHTS AND SUMMARY: This rocky knob isn't a mountain but standing on the summit will have you feeling like you've climbed one. The summit provides close-up views of the High Peaks and a panorama of shorter peaks. The forest is an illuminated palette in autumn.

MILEAGE: *5 mi r/t.*

ELEVATION GAIN: *1300 ft.*

DIFFICULTY: *3*

VIEW RATING: *5*

LEASH: *Not required but recommended on the summit.*

DOG SAFETY AND HAZARDS: *Precipitous summit cliffs.*

WATER: *Stream crossings and small pond.*

HIKER TRAFFIC: *Moderately busy on weekends.*

TRAIL CONDITIONS: *Good, but the short summit spur trail is rocky and eroded.*

BEST TIME TO HIKE: *Autumn.*

GETTING THERE: *The trailhead driveway (N44° 12.780', W73° 40.751') is located on NY 9N between Elizabethtown and Keene. The large parking area is shared with trails to Giant, Hopkins, and Green Mts.*

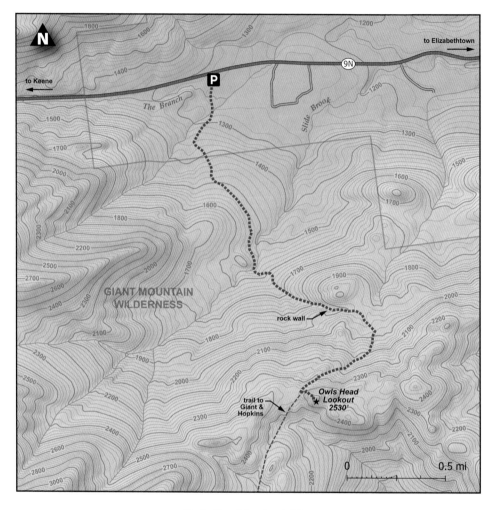

Owls Head Lookout Map

For the first 0.4 mi, the trail is on a dirt road through private proper-ty. Cross a bridge over a stream that drains the NE side of Knob Lock Mt. and make an immediate LEFT on RED markers. For much of the first 0.6 mi, the mixed forest trail is carpeted with conifer needles, adding to the pleasure of the 250 ft of easy ascent. There's little actual climbing until you cross the Slide Brook bridge at 1.1 mi. Dogs will be happy to discover a short herd path leading to the stream just before the bridge. After crossing Slide Brook, the trail is rockier as it steadily climbs through a forest that's now almost completely deciduous.

More canine refreshment is ahead where the trail crosses another stream at 1.4 mi. Just beyond there's a scenic rock wall at 1870 ft.

On bright days the sun casts beautiful shadows across its face and, in winter, large icicles adorn its facade. After a level section ahead, the trail resumes its ascent, the forest glorious when sun illuminates birch and beech leaves in autumn.

A trail junction (N44° 11.417', W73° 40.221') at 2.4 mi has a sign pointing toward Giant Mt. and Giant Mt. lean-to in one direction and toward Owls Head Lookout in the other. Look for a small pond 100 ft beyond the intersection on the trail to Giant Mt. In spring, its clear water is bordered by wildflowers, but it is muddy and covered with smelly algae by midsummer. The 0.2 mi YELLOW trail to Owls Head Lookout is a LEFT at the intersection. The first half of the trail is rocky and eroded, but switchbacks ease the steep 150 ft climb to the 2530 ft summit.

The contrast between the wooded forest through which you've been hiking and the exposed top is startling. Drop your pack and enjoy the stunning 270-degree view.

Whiteface, Pitchoff, Hurricane, Knob Lock, and the Sentinel Range take up one compass quadrant. In the E are Iron Mt., the Champlain Valley, and the Green Mts. Dominating the foreground are the summits of Green, Giant, Rocky Peak Ridge, and Bald Peak.

The summit is sizable, but significant cliffs or the presence of other hikers suggest dogs should be leashed. The lookout is a great spot to watch the upward progress of spring, or autumn march down the slopes of the surrounding mountains.

Pine Mt.

HIGHLIGHTS AND SUMMARY: Pine Mt. is one of a trio of peaks called the Three Sisters on USGS maps and is the ski mountain at Hickory Hill Ski Center. The hike ascends a service road curbed with ferns and wildflowers. Great over-the-shoulder views as you climb set the table for summit views. Hickory Hill has changed ownership; the new owners plan to reopen it in the future.

MILEAGE: *3 mi r/t.*

ELEVATION GAIN: *1200 ft.*

DIFFICULTY: *3*

VIEW RATING: *3*

LEASH: *Not required.*

DOG SAFETY AND HAZARDS: *None.*

WATER: *Bone dry, carry water.*

HIKER TRAFFIC: *Light to nonexistent.*

TRAIL CONDITIONS: *Dirt and grass service road.*

BEST TIME TO HIKE: *Spring and autumn; no hiking during ski season.*

GETTING THERE: *Turn onto NY 418 from US 9 in Warrensburg and cross the Schroon River bridge. Turn LEFT in 3 mi onto Hickory Hill Rd. (Katts Corners Rd. on some maps) immediately before NY 418 again crosses the river. The Ski Center access road (N43° 28.616', W73° 49.124') is 0.2 mi ahead. Park off the side of the access road before the gate and don't block the driveway.*

Walk 150 yd up the driveway to the bottom of the main lift and ask for permission if staff is around. The summit access road, known as "Ridge Run," is on the LEFT. It's a rough dirt road for the first 0.2 mi, after which the footing improves as you climb. It crosses ski runs and goes through wooded sections separating them. You can hike the ski trails for a more direct route, but Ridge Run is a more gradual and enjoyable hike.

On sunny days you're out in the open, particularly on the upper half. Carry extra water for dogs as the hike is completely dry other than a small stream near where you parked. Midway, the hiking is a steady climb, more like a trail than an access road. You'll likely marvel at the lush areas of ferns and cornucopia of showy wildflowers on both sides of the trail. In some places the roadbed is rock slab.

Doghikers always find the soft touch.
—Alan Via

The road is level near 1300 ft, then after the short breather it makes a sharp SW turn and the ascent is steeper for the next 0.2 mi. Be sure to turn around from time to time for the excellent views. Warrensburg and the Hudson River are prominent, as are Sugarloaf, Cat, and Thomas Mts. Once on Pine's NE ridge, additional peaks come into view, notably Buck Mt. and Pilot Knob. You'll pick up 450 ft of elevation

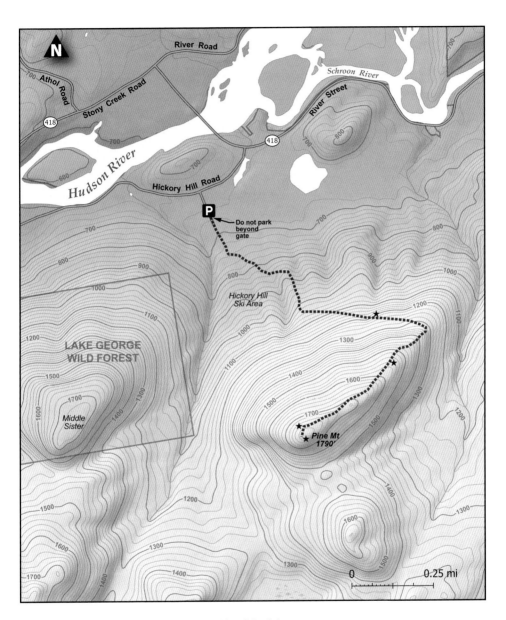

Pine Mt. Map

in the last 0.3 mi, the climb easing the closer you get to the 1790 ft summit. The top is thinly wooded and trees have been cleared in places. Walk through grass, ferns, and wildflowers for close-up views of Middle Sister and Bald Mt. The Hudson River and taller Adirondack summits are visible in the N.

The Pinnacle

HIGHLIGHTS AND SUMMARY: The Lake George Land Conservancy (LGLC) rescued this property from home development in 2015. This short dog- and family-friendly hike ends at an overlook that commands a spectacular view of Lake George and surroundings peaks. Renowned for its gorgeous sunrises, many also enjoy the spectacle of July 4th fireworks or winter snowshoeing here.

MILEAGE: *1.5 mi r/t.*

ELEVATION GAIN: *450 ft.*

DIFFICULTY: *1*

VIEW RATING: *4*

LEASH: *Required.*

DOG SAFETY AND HAZARDS: *None, except during the hunting season.*

WATER: *None.*

HIKER TRAFFIC: *Light during the week.*

TRAIL CONDITIONS: *Excellent.*

BEST TIME TO HIKE: *Spring and summer. Less traffic midweek.*

GETTING THERE: *The trailhead (N43° 33.505', W73° 40.947') is located on Edgecomb Pond Rd. W of Bolton Landing. A LGLC sign marks the drive-way. The Conservancy asks hikers to park at the Bolton Conservation Park 0.4 mi S of the trailhead if the parking lot is filled.*

Follow the RED markers on an easy incline past a metal gate. The trail steepens, nears a residence, and intersects a woods road at 0.2 mi. Follow trail markers off the woods road onto a section of foot trail that avoids private property. The grade gets steeper as the trail climbs the W side of the Pinnacle through a mostly deciduous forest. Climb a set of stone steps and turn RIGHT, back on the woods road, a steady up-hill with switchbacks to ease the short, but steep, section of trail.

The grade eases at 0.5 mi, the trail mostly level for the remaining 0.2 mi to the viewpoint. Along the way, pass a YELLOW-marked trail (N43° 33.748', W73° 40.808') on the LEFT (see more about the YELLOW trail at the end of this trip description). Continuing on RED markers, the trail is now more of a footpath and less like a woods road. The trail ends with a RED marker and arrow that points to the Pinnacle viewpoint (N43° 33.627', W74° 40.631') and bench.

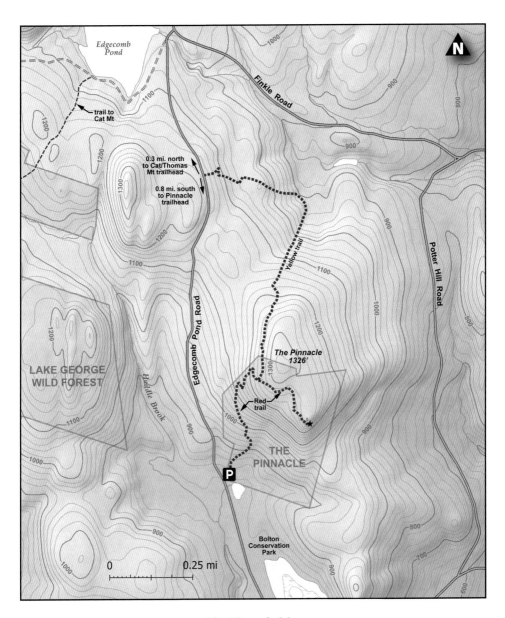

The Pinnacle Map

The spectacular ledge is encircled by blueberry bushes and wild-flowers. The LGLC has selectively removed trees to enhance the 270-degree view. Lake George dominates the foreground and the nearby Bolton Conservation Park is identifiable by its pond. There's a lineup of peaks across Lake George that include Tongue, Buck, Little

Buck, Erebus, Black, Shelving Rock, and Pilot Knob. The horizon is studded with others. The Pinnacle is known for its stunning sunrises and as a locale from which to watch fireworks. The LGLC did not route the trail over the wooded and viewless summit.

The YELLOW trail you earlier passed leads to Edgecomb Pond Rd. 0.8 mi N of the Pinnacle trailhead. The YELLOW trail loses much of the elevation you gained, reclimbs a ridge, and then drops to the road, where a 0.3 mi walk gets you to the Cat Mt. trailhead.

Poke-O-Moonshine Mt.

> **HIGHLIGHTS AND SUMMARY:** Not only is the mountain's quirky name interesting, its pair of trails are equally so. The Ranger Trail is shorter and steeper, with small streams and cliff-top views. The Observer's Trail is longer, has slightly more elevation gain, streams, two beaver ponds, and no cliffs until the summit. Both lead to a fire tower on the summit. Combine them for the full experience.

MILEAGE: *Ranger Trail, 3.3 mi r/t. Observer's Trail, 4.8 mi r/t. Through trip, 4.2 mi r/t.*

ELEVATION GAIN: *Ranger Trail, 1275 ft. Observer's Trail, 1410 ft.*

DIFFICULTY: *3*

VIEW RATING: *4*

LEASH: *Recommended at trailheads, summit, and cliffs.*

DOG SAFETY AND HAZARDS: *Both trailheads are adjacent to US 9. Cliffs at summit and viewpoints.*

WATER: *Small brooks and seeps on Ranger Trail. Streams and two beaver ponds on Observer's Trail.*

HIKER TRAFFIC: *Busy, especially on weekends.*

TRAIL CONDITIONS: *Ranger Trail is excellent. The Observer's Trail is very wet in places.*

BEST TIME TO HIKE: *Autumn.*

GETTING THERE: *The 1000 ft Ranger trailhead (N44° 24.129', W73° 30.169') and 840 ft Observer's trailhead (N44° 23.352', W73° 30.435') are located on US 9 between Northway exits 32 and 33.*

The Ranger Trail begins on RED markers from the S end of the closed

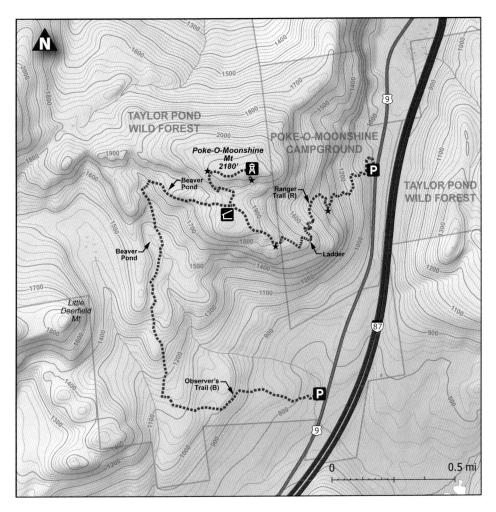

Poke-O-Moonshine Mt. Map

DEC campground. Cross a small bridge beyond the kiosk to a large boulder and the first of a number of interpretative stations. Ahead are 112 rock steps, installed as part of a phenomenal 0.5 mi rerouting of eroded trail sections by the Adirondack Mountain Club (ADK) professional trail crew. Dogs can get a drink at seasonal seeps located near 1340 ft. Ahead, the trail passes a ledge, the first of a few where dogs should be kept close.

Over much of the trail's length the deciduous forest is lit up and luminous in October. At 1550 ft, the trail leaves the ledges, heading

Joy.
—Kevin Talbot

into the forest and crossing a stream. Stone steps and switchbacks ease the climbing to a short, two-section trail ladder near 1700 ft. Dogs may need a little "encouragement," particularly on the first seven steps.

The forest transitions to conifers and the needle-strewn trail offers a view across Lake Champlain toward Burlington. Mt. Mansfield and Camels Hump are prominent. Oaks begin to infiltrate, with blueberries in sunny areas, making this a gorgeous section to hike. The trail passes a pair of rock slabs covered by reindeer moss. They offer views, but dogs should be kept close to protect the vegetation and to keep them away from the drop-offs. Ahead, when trees are bare there's a view of the tower.

At 1940 ft, the Ranger Trail intersects (N44° 24.006′, W73° 30.882′) the BLUE Observer's Trail at a lean-to. There's a chimney 50 yd beyond, what remains of the former observer's cabin. A sign points to the summit 0.3 mi ahead and the trail climbs past a view of the High Peaks at 2050 ft. The remaining 0.2 mi across the summit ridge sees a remarkable change. Short trees, scrubs, and black raspberries replace the large-tree forest you've been hiking through.

The fire tower is situated on a rocky knob with striking views of the Green Mts., Jay and Great Ranges, Lyon, Whiteface, and Giant. Views are abundant whether you climb the 35 ft tower or stay grounded. On clear days, you can see buildings in Montreal and peaks everywhere. Leashing dogs on the summit is not only a courtesy to other hikers, it protects the alpine vegetation and keeps dogs from the cliff tops.

Descending, bear RIGHT on BLUE markers at the lean-to for the Observer's Trail. What this trail lacks in views is made up for by the abundance of dog water and the absence of cliffs. At 1800 ft, pass a beaver pond at the base of a tall cliff. It's a scenic spot to linger while dogs swim and cool off. The trail below is wet and rocky in a few places where it follows a stream and passes a second beaver pond near 1460 ft. In spring or rainy periods, it's sometimes difficult to get through this area with dry boots. DEC will be rerouting the trail around it.

Below the pond the trail widens and is drier, following a woods road. To avoid private property the trail turns LEFT off the road at 1180 ft. It crosses a small stream, then rejoins the road. The trail again leaves the road, crosses a stream, and emerges from the forest at the Observer's trailhead next to busy US 9. You can walk 1 mi N to the Ranger trailhead if you haven't left a second vehicle here. There are plans for a connecting trail.

Prospect Mt.

HIGHLIGHTS AND SUMMARY: Most people think of Prospect Mt. as a rocky slog up the overused trail from Lake George Village, or a drive up the toll road. This hike follows a woods road above beautiful Big Hollow Branch through hardwoods and hemlocks to great summit views. It's a unique variation to one of the Lake George area's icons. There are no trail markers guiding you as you follow the woods road to the top.

MILEAGE: *6 mi r/t.*

ELEVATION GAIN: *1350 ft.*

DIFFICULTY: *3*

VIEW RATING: *3*

LEASH: *Not required. Dogs not allowed beyond the summit parking lot when the toll road is open.*

DOG SAFETY AND HAZARDS: *Near summit parking lot.*

WATER: *Big Hollow Branch. Carry extra water.*

HIKER TRAFFIC: *Very light.*

TRAIL CONDITIONS: *Woods road.*

BEST TIME TO HIKE: *Hike when Prospect Mt. Veteran's Memorial Highway is closed, from mid-November to early April, when dogs can go beyond the parking lot.*

GETTING THERE: *Turn onto Big Hollow Rd. at the intersection (N43° 26.408', W73° 43.337') with US 9, N of Lake George village. Drive to the 660 ft trailhead (N43° 26.341', W73° 43.619'), passing through tunnels under the Northway. Seasonal parking area is 0.15 mi before the tunnels.*

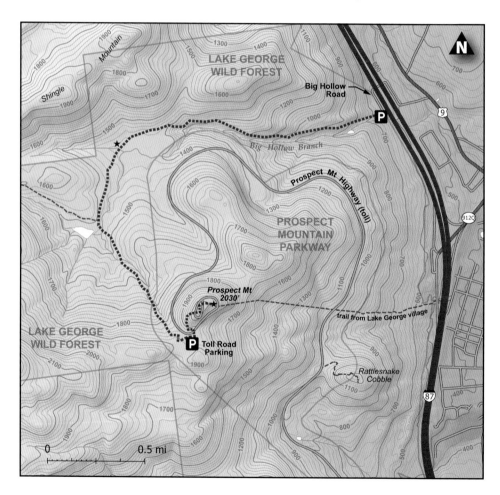

Prospect Mt. Map

From the trailhead, follow a woods road through a mixed hardwoods and hemlock forest that's gorgeous in autumn or spring. The first half of the hike parallels Big Hollow Branch. It's worth the short, steep, downhill detour to get a closer look at the stream's waterfalls and pools. At 1150 ft, the trail passes through an exceptionally attractive section of hemlocks. As the trail continues to climb, bear RIGHT at a fork in the road, taking the branch that goes uphill. There are no trail markers on the road, so hikers need to pay attention to where they are in a few places.

Pass under a power line at 1350 ft and again at 1430 ft. Look up through the trees here for a brief glimpse of the summit. The road enters a small clearing (N43° 25.890', W73° 45.340') at 1500 ft. There's an arrow pointing LEFT to avoid a side trail toward Big Hollow Reservoir. Keep LEFT just ahead at another junction, recrossing under the power line.

Walk out of the woods to the 1870 ft paved summit parking lot. When the toll road is open you can take a shuttle to the summit, or you can climb 200 ft on a paved trail. Although the Big Hollow Trail is an ideal dog hike, canines aren't allowed beyond the parking lot. Plan to leave your pooch with a group member here while you continue to the summit, or hike when the toll road is closed.

The rocky summit is always busy with people who have driven the toll road. Lake George, Buck Mt., Pilot Knob, and surrounding peaks are prominent. On a clear day, you can see buildings in Albany, the Blackhead Range in the Catskills, the Adirondack High Peaks, and Mt. Equinox and other Green Mt. summits. Be sure to check out the restored flywheel from the 7392 ft cable railway that took passengers from Lake George to the summit in the 1870s.

Carry extra water for the hike. Unless you detour down to Big Hollow Branch, the only water on the hike is seasonally dependent.

Rattlesnake Mt.

HIGHLIGHTS AND SUMMARY: This superb dog- and family-friendly hike has ledge views of the Adirondacks, Green Mts., and Lake Champlain. If the hike were more widely known, the trailhead would need a larger parking area. Thanks to Highland Forests LLC, which allows the nonmotorized public to enjoy this scenic hike.

MILEAGE: *3 mi r/t.*

ELEVATION GAIN: *950 ft.*

DIFFICULTY: *2*

VIEW RATING: *5*

LEASH: *Required.*

DOG SAFETY AND HAZARDS: *Parking area along busy NY 22.*

WATER: *None.*

HIKER TRAFFIC: *Can be busy on weekends and holidays.*

TRAIL CONDITIONS: *Excellent.*

BEST TIME TO HIKE: *Summer and autumn. Parking difficult in winter.*

GETTING THERE: *The trailhead is W of Lake Champlain's Willsboro Bay and E of Long Pond. Look for an unmarked parking area (N44° 23.429', W73° 26.833') on the W side of NY 22 across from Long Pond Cabins and a huge glacial erratic.*

Even without trail markers, it's easy to follow the woods road that starts the hike. The surface is sandy and dry except after rainy periods. The first 0.3 mi is mostly level, before the trail gains a little elevation and turns RIGHT off the woods road at 0.5 mi. The hike gains only 200 ft in the first 0.75 mi, picking up an additional 750 ft in the remaining 0.75 mi.

Toby running up the steeps on Rattlesnake Mtn.
—Cindy Kuhn Yourdon

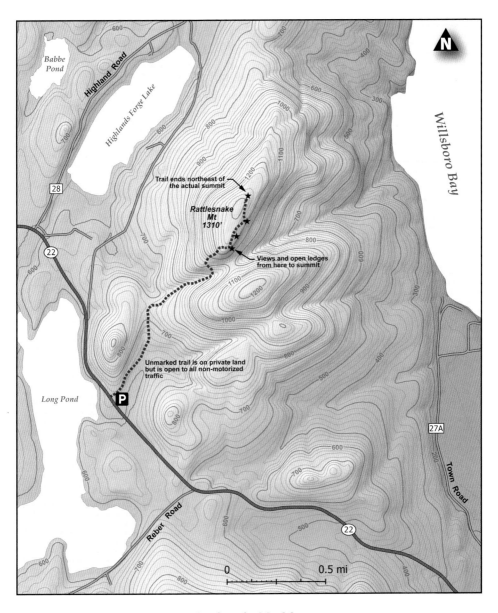

Babbe
Pond

Highland Road

Highlands Forge Lake

Willsboro Bay

28

22

Trail ends northeast of
the actual summit

Rattlesnake
Mt
1310'

Views and open ledges
from here to summit

Unmarked trail is on private land
but is open to all non-motorized
traffic

Long Pond

P

27A

Town Road

Reber Road

22

0   0.5 mi

Rattlesnake Mt. Map

The trail reaches the base of a steep ledge at 1100 ft. It's an
easy scramble when dry and ice-free, otherwise take the bypass on
the LEFT. The first views appear above the ledge on the RIGHT.
There's an unmarked path at 1215 ft leading to another ledge (N44°
24.000', W73° 26.146') with views that can modestly be described as

spectacular. Long Pond, the peaks of the Jay and Giant Wilderness Areas, and the High Peaks populate the horizon.

You can return to the trail or continue following ledges past blueberry bushes, wildflowers, stunted oaks, and junipers, treating yourself to almost continual views. Poke-O-Moonshine, Camels Hump, and the Ellen-Abraham ridgeline of the Green Mts. are strewn along the horizon above Lake Champlain's Willsboro Bay. The ledges merge with the trail 100 yd ahead. In the remaining short distance to the top, the trail meanders towards another ledge at 1300 ft where a large erratic is landscaped by blueberry bushes. The view overlooks much of Lake Champlain where, on summer days, sailboats feather their way across the lake, a foreground for Mt. Mansfield.

The trail ends N of the summit, but in the upper part of Rattlesnake, it really doesn't matter if you stay with the trail as paths parallel it on more open rock. The trail's high point is wooded on three sides, but offers more views of the lake and Green Mts. If you have to see the summit, the 1310 ft high point is 100 yd off the trail in a shady forest with a large erratic surrounded by small oaks, ferns, and wildflowers. With all the areas open to the sun, carry extra dog water as the hike is completely dry.

Record Hill

HIGHLIGHTS AND SUMMARY: Record Hill is part of the Lake George Land Conservancy's (LGLC) Anthony's Nose Preserve. After a brief section with little ascent, the trail is a steady climb up Record's SE ridge. There are gorgeous ledge views of Lake George and the surrounding mountains.

MILEAGE: *2 mi r/t.*

ELEVATION GAIN: *750 ft.*

DIFFICULTY: *3*

VIEW RATING: *3*

LEASH: *Required.*

DOG SAFETY AND HAZARDS: *None.*

WATER: *Small streams near beginning, otherwise dry.*

HIKER TRAFFIC: *Generally light, more on weekends.*

TRAIL CONDITIONS: *A wet area. Very steep trail.*

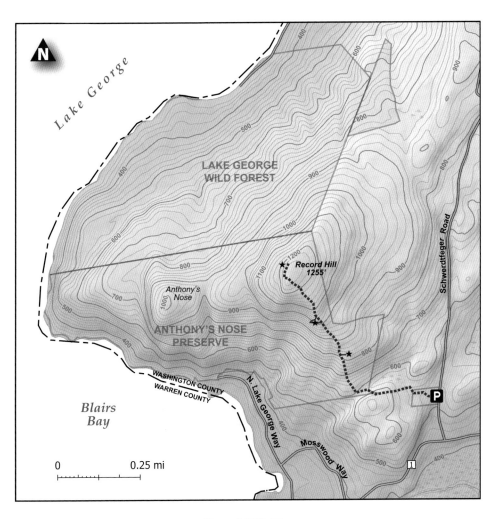

Record Hill Map

BEST TIME TO HIKE: *Spring and autumn.*

GETTING THERE: *Turn W off of NY 22 (N43° 46.238', W73° 24.796') onto Glen Burnie Rd. (CR 1). Turn onto Schwerdtfeger Rd. (N43° 45.997', W73° 26.849') in 1.8 mi and continue 0.1 mi uphill to the trailhead (N43° 46.106', W73° 26.860').*

BLUE markers lead through a mostly deciduous forest. The trail turns LEFT, crosses a brook, then turns RIGHT, passing a snow fence marking private property. Threading a narrow right-of-way through private land beyond the fence, the trail reenters LGLC property at a stream where dogs can drink. The trail turns LEFT after crossing the brook, climbs over a small rise, then descends through a wet area. Passing a 50 ft cliff, the trail again turns to stay on LGLC land.

At 0.4 mi, the trail gathers a head of steam as it meets the nose of Record Hill's SE ridge. It's the beginning of a steep 0.5 mi uphill with just a couple of short breathers. The forest is deciduous with grasses and sedge and areas of flowers—delightful but steep. At 800 ft there's a screened look at the Green Mts. on the RIGHT. Walk 100 ft W off the trail through small hickories and oaks to a ledge (N43° 46.229′, W73° 27.217′) with better views. There's a break in the trees at 1000 ft where a blueberry-bordered ledge (N43° 46.406′, W73° 27.323′) provides stellar views of Lake George.

The trail gradient eases in the final 200 ft to Record Hill's 1255 ft summit. It's wooded and viewless with small oaks, hickories, and scattered conifers. A 50 ft unmarked path weaves its way through small conifers and blueberry bushes to a rocky perch (N43° 46.440′, W73° 27.424′). The photography-perfect ledge commands views of much of the length of Lake George, Anthony's Nose, distant Pharoah Mt., and peaks on the W side of the lake.

A short distance ahead there's another viewpoint looking toward the N end of the lake with views of the imposing rock slabs of Roger's Rock and, in the distance, Cook Mt., another LGLC hike property. Don't be misled by herd paths leading off the ledges on the W side of the summit. They give the appearance of being trails but peter out, and by following them, you risk disturbing peregrine falcons during breeding season. Although the preserve is named Anthony's Nose, the trail ends on Record Hill. Avoid any paths leading to Anthony's Nose for the same reason you avoid the herd paths.

Sawyer Mt.

HIGHLIGHTS AND SUMMARY: A short and interesting hike suitable for two- and four-legged members of the family. There's an option for a short bushwhack from the end of the trail to the slightly higher S summit.

MILEAGE: *2 mi.*

ELEVATION GAIN: *600 ft.*

DIFFICULTY: *2*

VIEW RATING: *3*

LEASH: *Not required, but leash near other hikers.*

DOG SAFETY AND HAZARDS: *Parking on shoulder of busy NY 28.*

WATER: *Dry hike, carry water for dogs.*

HIKER TRAFFIC: *Busy on weekends.*

TRAIL CONDITIONS: *Good, but it's eroded in places.*

BEST TIME TO HIKE: *Spring and autumn.*

GETTING THERE: *The 1960 ft parking area (N43° 48.661', W74° 19.278') is along the shoulder of NY 28 between the villages of Indian Lake and Blue Mountain Lake.*

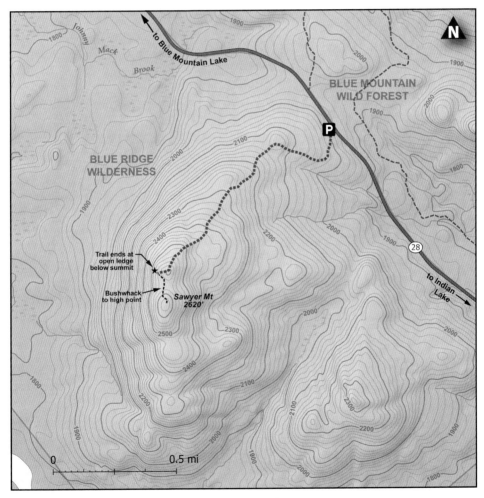

Sawyer Mt. Map

Ahhh Winter.
—Deb Osterhoudt

YELLOW markers lead into a shady beech forest beyond the trail register. Though heavily used, the trail is mostly easy walking but well worn. It climbs at an easy grade, ascending 250 ft in the first 0.5 mi. The trail continues climbing at a moderate angle, passing a series of rock slabs 0.2 mi from the summit at 2490 ft. Peek-a-boo views of Dun Brook, Fishing Brook Range, and Vanderwhacker appear as the trail gets a little steeper over the remaining distance. Look for a 20 ft unmarked path (N43° 48.234', W74° 20.012') on the LEFT at 2530 ft. It leads to an open ledge with views that make the hike worthy all by itself.

The trail passes under the first of Sawyer's completely wooded summits at 2600 ft. Descend slightly to a ledge (N43° 48.160', W74° 20.132') that faces W with views of Metcalf Mt., Blue Ridge, and Blue Mt., the end of the marked trail. If you're comfortable with off-trail hiking and want to step on Sawyer's highest point, here's an option. Leave the ledge on a SW heading, descending slightly into the adjoining col. Turn S on an indistinct herd path to Sawyer's slightly taller 2620 ft S summit. It's an easy 0.5 mi round trip with a miniscule 50 ft of ascent for experienced bushwhackers. I followed my dog, Toby, as she nosed our scents back to the trailed summit.

Severance Hill

HIGHLIGHTS AND SUMMARY: This is a popular "tourist" hike outside of Schroon Lake. Expect lots of hikers, dogs, and great views for a small effort. It's an excellent destination for families looking for a summer vacation option. Small children are able to do the hike, sharing the trail with their favorite doghiker. Look for the photogenic erratic midway along the trail.

MILEAGE: *2.6 mi r/t.*

ELEVATION GAIN: *755 ft.*

DIFFICULTY: 2

VIEW RATING: 3

LEASH: *Not required, but strongly advised given the number of hikers and dogs on most days.*

DOG SAFETY AND HAZARDS: *None.*

WATER: *A couple of small streams on the way up. Carry dog water, especially on warm days.*

HIKER TRAFFIC: *Very busy on weekends and summer vacation time.*

TRAIL CONDITIONS: *Worn down but in good condition with trenches directing water off the trail.*

BEST TIME TO HIKE: *Spring and autumn.*

GETTING THERE: *Look for a DEC sign marking the trailhead driveway (N43° 51.748', W73° 45.313') on the W side of NY 9, 1.25 mi N of Schroon Lake village.*

YELLOW markers lead out of the back of the 880 ft trailhead area, but the well-worn path makes them unnecessary. Protective fencing protects dogs from the roadway as you walk through a pair of tunnels under the Northway. Kids will really like this!

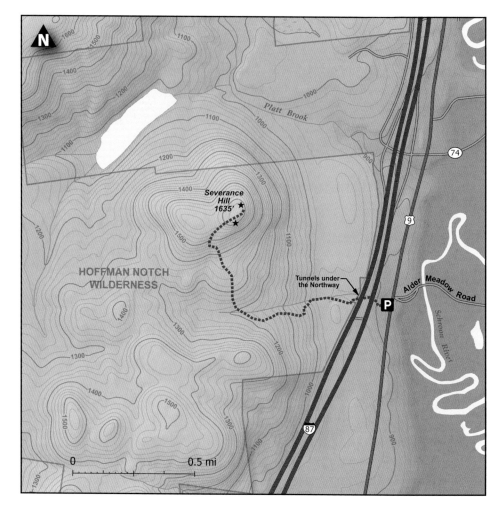

Severance Hill Map

The trail crosses a stream on the other side of the Northway and begins climbing at 0.3 mi, staying near the stream for a short distance. The grade steepens, with the trail climbing steadily to 0.6 mi. It passes over a stone staircase enclosed by logs with a rough-hewn handrail. After a section that could be described as strolling, the trail begins a continual climb to the summit. As light appears through the trees, you walk out to views of Schroon Lake and large Clarks Island. Pharoah Mt. is impressive, standing above the smaller mountains

Autumn.
—Barbara Via

surrounding it. Don't neglect a short, unmarked path leading NE from the view to another ledge where Paradox Lake and its smaller brethren are in view.

The forest throughout the hike is mixed conifers and deciduous trees. The rocky trail has areas of exposed roots, but it is in remarkably good condition and well cared for, as evidenced by the frequent water bars and erosion trenches.

Sleeping Beauty Mt.

HIGHLIGHTS AND SUMMARY: Two trailheads provide a second, shorter option during nonwinter months. This popular hike has great views, lots of water, and a large pond for dogs, and it offers trail options for hikers and their doghiker companions. The fairy tale name attracts costumed hikers on Halloween.

MILEAGE: *6.5 mi r/t from Hogtown trailhead. 3.5 mi r/t from Dacy Clearing trailhead.*

7.3 mi r/t for entire loop.

ELEVATION GAIN: *900 ft. 1400 ft for loop.*

DIFFICULTY: *3*

VIEW RATING: *4*

LEASH: *Not required.*

DOG SAFETY AND HAZARDS: *Busy trailheads and tall cliffs.*

WATER: *Streams and Bumps Pond.*

HIKER TRAFFIC: *Very busy on weekends.*

TRAIL CONDITIONS: *Rocky and wet in places.*

BEST TIME TO HIKE: *Spring and autumn. Don't miss the Halloween hikers.*

GETTING THERE: *Drive 6 mi E on NY 149 from the S end of Lake George. Turn N on Buttermilk Falls Rd. (N43° 24.261', W73° 35.734'), which becomes Sly Pond Rd. in 3 mi. Bear LEFT onto Shelving Rock Rd. and continue to the 1240 ft Hogtown trailhead (N43° 31.889', W73° 33.944'). Hike or drive 1.5 mi to the Dacy Clearing trailhead on a seasonal road.*

Hikers from the Hogtown trailhead share the bumpy dirt road to Dacy with slow-moving vehicles. It's an enjoyable hike through mixed forest with streams and short ups and downs and with a brief view of Sleeping Beauty where the road crosses a large stream before Dacy Clearing. YELLOW markers lead out of 1360 ft Dacy Clearing (N43° 32.972', W73° 33.350') on a usually busy trail shared with other hikers and dogs.

The trail climbs on an eroded woods road/trail through a mixed forest. It narrows at 1640 ft, turning sharply under Sleeping Beauty's S ridge. Dogs will appreciate the small streams and wet areas nearby. There's a large erratic at 1680 ft, marking where the Sleeping Beauty trail intersects the Bumps Pond trail (N43° 33.124', W73° 33.106').

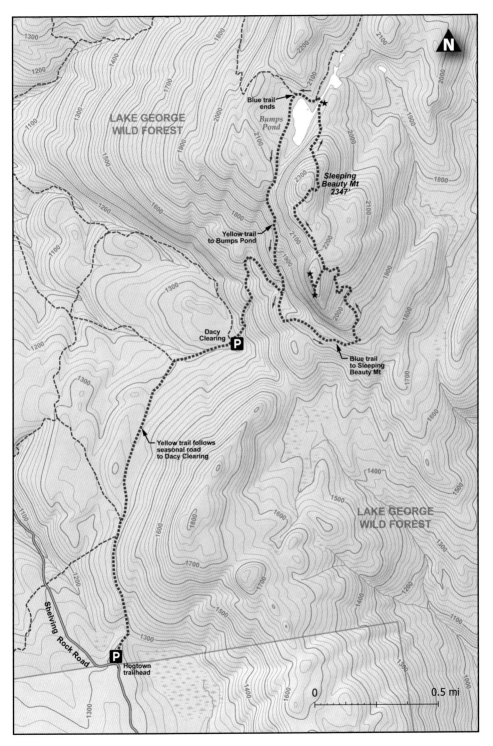

Sleeping Beauty Mt. Map

Rev on Sleeping Beauty.
—Mike Arthur

Keep RIGHT on BLUE markers to continue another 1.2 mi toward Sleeping Beauty. The trail narrows, passes through a short, wet section, crosses a small stream, then resumes climbing. There's a great piece of trail maintenance at 1750 ft, a series of short switchbacks and rock work that bypass steep cliffs on the mountain's SW side.

The trail enters a sunny section ahead where large white pines line both sides of the trail. A stream parallels the trail for 100 ft. This precedes a series of rock slabs through shady hemlocks. Reach a trail intersection at 2160 ft, where a sign points to Sleeping Beauty 0.1 mi ahead. The pair of rocky knobs are the destination for most hikers. Their 2175 ft and 2230 ft viewpoints offer grand views, but they are not Sleeping Beauty's summit.

The High Peaks line the hem of the N horizon. Tongue, Cat, Thomas, Little Buck, Buck, Pilot Knob, Crane, and others populate the front row. Keep dogs leashed as you'll seldom have the views to yourself and the cliffs are precipitous. Back at the intersection, you can return back to the trailhead or continue N on the loop that bypasses Sleeping Beauty's wooded summit and circles Bumps Pond. Less frequently traveled, the trail toward Bumps is in great condition and offers screened views that are better when trees are leafless. Ferns and wildflowers abound in areas of sun and shade.

The trail passes 40 ft under Sleeping Beauty's thickly wooded 2347 ft summit then descends 300 ft through birch and hemlock to a footbridge over an inlet of Bumps Pond. Dogs will enjoy the deep, clear stream. As the trail circles around the pond's N side, views include Sleeping Beauty's summit and you're back on YELLOW markers. The trail leaves the pond's SW side on an eroded woods road, shedding 440 ft to the trail junction with the large erratic described earlier. Stay with the YELLOW markers back to Dacy Clearing.

South Boquet Mt.

HIGHLIGHTS AND SUMMARY: A short hike courtesy of Champlain Area Trails (CATS). The trail is located on private property. Hikers must remain on the trail and dogs must remain on leash. There are terrific views along the summit ridge and it's a particularly nice spring wildflowers destination that includes white trillium.

MILEAGE: *2 mi r/t.*

ELEVATION GAIN: *550 ft.*

DIFFICULTY: *1*

VIEW RATING: *3*

LEASH: *Required.*

DOG SAFETY AND HAZARDS: *Road right next to parking area.*

WATER: *A stream and some wet areas.*

HIKER TRAFFIC: *Very light.*

TRAIL CONDITIONS: *Good, but damp in places after periods of rain.*

BEST TIME TO HIKE: *Spring and autumn.*

GETTING THERE: *The 605 ft parking area (N44° 17.505', W73° 26.608') is located on Brookfield Rd., W of NY 22 and Essex Station. Look for a sign, cable, and roadside parking.*

The grassy Wildway Overlook Trail begins on the other side of a trail register and vehicle-blocking cable. It passes through a mixed forest dominated by short deciduous trees following diamond-shaped GREEN and WHITE CATS markers that have a distinctive catamount

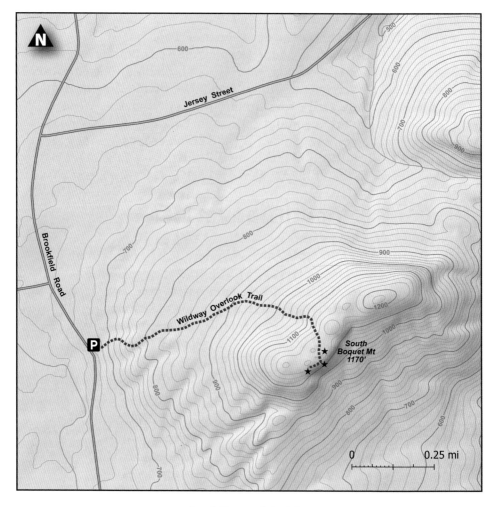

South Boquet Mt. Map

paw print. The stumps and tree heights indicate the area has likely been logged. At 0.5 mi, dogs can get into a stream at the side of the trail, while hikers savor ferns and a variety of spring and summer wildflowers.

The trail gets steeper in the last 0.3 mi to the ridgeline. Volunteers have installed water runoff trenches to keep the trail dry. You'll be greeted by screened views of Lake Champlain and the Green Mts. at 1170 ft when reaching the South Boquet ridge (N44° 17.475', W73° 25.761'). Turn RIGHT. A few yards ahead there's a blueberry-bordered ledge below the trail that commands a 180-degree unobstructed view that includes Coon and Split Rock Mts. and the Green Mts. across Lake Champlain. Continue SW along the ridge, being on the lookout for two more view-worthy ledges.

The trail along the ridge has areas of sedge and wildflowers amidst short hardwoods. In springtime, trout lilies, spring beauties, and foam flowers mix with ferns. Hike in early May looking for one of my favorites, white trillium. A "Trails End" sign marks the end of the CATS trail. In summer, don't hike without a container for blueberries.

Tooley Pond Mt.

HIGHLIGHTS AND SUMMARY: Tooley Pond Mt. is tucked away in the NW Adirondacks near Cranberry Lake. Its fire tower was removed years ago, and a pair of trails leads to the lightly hiked summit. After the trip, stop at nearby Tooley Pond for a post-hike swim and dog frolic.

MILEAGE: *2 mi r/t on E trail. 1.5 mi r/t on W trail. 2.3 mi loop with a short road walk.*

ELEVATION GAIN: *250 ft.*

DIFFICULTY: *1*

VIEW RATING: *1*

LEASH: *Not required.*

DOG SAFETY AND HAZARDS: *Light traffic, but ATVs use the road.*

WATER: *Small streams.*

HIKER TRAFFIC: *Very light.*

TRAIL CONDITIONS: *Good.*

BEST TIME TO HIKE: *Summer and autumn.*

GETTING THERE: *Turn onto Tooley Rd. (N44° 13.176', W74° 51.193') from NY 3 in Cranberry Lake, driving 6 mi to the E trailhead (N44° 16.502', W74° 55.228'). The W trailhead (N44° 16.754', W74° 55.738') is 0.5 mi beyond. It's an easy 0.5 mi walk between them. The parking areas for both trailheads have ample room for the light hiker traffic.*

The E trailhead is a pull-off on the N side of the road, marked by a DEC sign. The RED-marked trail begins on the other side of the road, 75 yd farther W. Walking into the woods, your first impression might

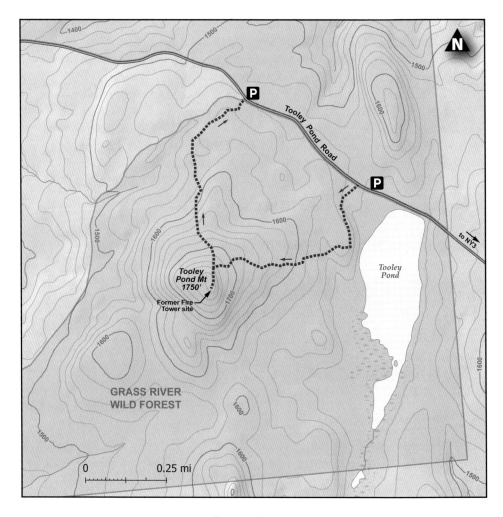

Tooley Pond Mt. Map

be that you've entered a fern nursery. Dense, summertime ferns drape over the footpath that leads into a deciduous forest of beech and maple. In two minutes, the trail takes a sharp LEFT and passes a small brook. There's little foot traffic or trail erosion on the easily followed and soft-footed path.

On the map, it appears as if the trail comes close to Tooley Pond, but it's a steep, downhill trek to reach its shore. You can see the pond through the trees, but there's a better look at it when trees are bare. At 0.4 mi, the trail dips through a shallow col to a stream, then resumes climbing. It follows, then quickly leaves, a woods road. Be certain you don't miss the quick RIGHT turn when leaving the road.

At 1725 ft, the E trail intersects the W trail at 0.75 mi. The remaining 0.25 mi passes through a fern glade immediately before the summit, goes under large conifers, and emerges on top. There's a 1942 benchmark set in a rock and remnants of the fire tower footings. The views are scant, a narrow window through a row of deciduous trees that will soon overtake it.

Descending, bear LEFT at the trail intersection onto the W trail. Pass a stream at 1670 ft and another at 1580 ft, both of which dogs will appreciate. The 1570 ft W trailhead is a short distance ahead. It's an easy 0.5 mi walk between trailheads.

Don't miss the opportunity to stop at Tooley Pond on your drive out to launch a kayak, swim, and let your dog cool off.

Mt. Van Hoevenberg

HIGHLIGHTS AND SUMMARY: The summit ledges have glorious views and stupendous close-ups of some of the Adirondack's highest summits. Mt. Van has about as much bang for the hiking buck as you'll receive anywhere. Observe care with children and dogs along the summit precipices. As this peak is located in the Central High Peaks Zone of New York State's High Peaks Wilderness Complex, leashes are required. There is another trail originating from the Mt. Van Hoevenberg Olympic Sports Complex.

MILEAGE: *4.4 mi r/t.*

ELEVATION GAIN: *900 ft.*

DIFFICULTY: *3*

VIEW RATING: *5*

LEASH: *Required.*

DOG SAFETY AND HAZARDS: *Caution at summit cliff tops.*

WATER: *At beaver dam and stream.*

HIKER TRAFFIC: *Busy on weekends.*

TRAIL CONDITIONS: *Wet near the beaver pond.*

BEST TIME TO HIKE: *Autumn.*

GETTING THERE: *Turn onto Adirondak Loj Rd. (N44° 14.613', W73°*

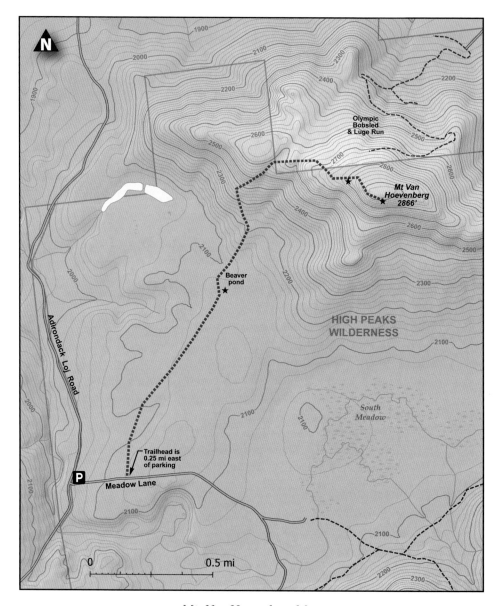

Mt. Van Hoevenberg Map

57.291') from NY 73, 4 mi E of Lake Placid. Drive 3.75 mi to Meadow Lane (N44° 11.613', W73° 57.328'), also known as South Meadow Rd. Park and walk 0.25 mi on Meadow Lane to the trailhead.

Begin hiking on Meadows Lane onto a woods road through a red pine plantation that transitions to mixed forest. The Mt Van trail

Gryffin and Tim—summit smooch.
—Tim Lucia

begins on the LEFT on BLUE markers, 0.25 mi from your vehicle. The trail descends slightly to a large, flooded beaver pond at just under 1 mi where the trail turns LEFT to skirt it. Linger for a moment to enjoy views of Van Hoevenberg's cliffs looming in the distance while your dog has a chance to hydrate. The trail has recently been rerouted to avoid the wet footing. In winter, deep snow and freezing temperatures allow you to venture off the trail for a little exploring through the wetlands on skis or snowshoes.

The trail is wet here but dries as it starts climbing at an easy grade, passing a stream through a mostly hardwood forest. It begins to steepen near 2260 ft and turns, passing under Van Hoevenberg's 2644 ft NW sub-summit through a drainage where dogs may find water. You get a breather as the trail reaches a col between Van Hoevenberg's main and minor summit at 2600 ft, a little over 1.5 mi from the trailhead. The trail turns E, dipping 25 ft, before climbing 325 ft in 0.4 mi along the NW ridge to the first ledge.

Mt. Van Hoevenberg summit view, pages 126–127.
—Joanne Hihn

There are a series of ledges, all sitting atop tall cliffs. The first provides breathtaking views of Big Slide, Saddleback, Basin, Phelps, Marcy, Colden, and the MacIntyre Range. The other viewpoints offer views as impressive as those from the 2866 ft summit. Keep your dog leashed around other hikers and safely away from cliff tops.

Doreen Alessi-Holmes with Gizmo and Marley on Mt. Van Hoevenberg.
—Shane Holmes

Central Region

Beebe Hill

HIGHLIGHTS AND SUMMARY: Tucked away in the northern part of Columbia County, this diminutive fire tower peak has a lot to offer. Enjoy a loop with an abundance of wild-flowers, excellent trails, plenty of dog water, and a lightly hiked woods road with two ponds. Beebe is a hike for all ages and doghikers.

MILEAGE: *2 mi r/t.*

ELEVATION GAIN: *360 ft.*

DIFFICULTY: *1*

VIEW RATING: *3*

LEASH: *Not required.*

DOG SAFETY AND HAZARDS: *None.*

WATER: *Streams, Barrett Pond adjacent to trailhead, and Opal Pond near summit.*

HIKER TRAFFIC: *Never heavy, but busier on weekends.*

TRAIL CONDITIONS: *Excellent.*

BEST TIME TO HIKE: *Spring and autumn.*

GETTING THERE: *The trailhead driveway (N42° 20.337′, W73° 28.429′) is located on CR 5 (Osmer Rd.), reachable from exit B-3 off I-90 or the Taconic Parkway SE of Chatham.*

The best way to enjoy a hike to Beebe is a loop. Ascend the main trail and descend the observer's road.

The main trail crosses the Barrett Pond outlet at 0.1 mi, immediately before reaching the trail register. Cross a second stream a few minutes later, then begin ascending. Scattered patches of ferns in the first part of the hike turn into a veritable pinnae parade nearer the

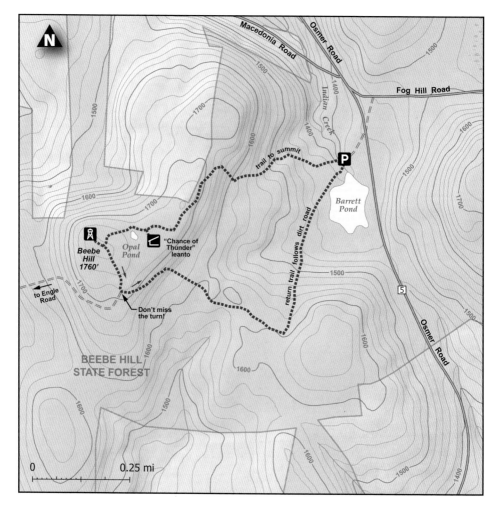

Beebe Hill Map

summit. The trail grade gets a little steeper in its middle section as it passes an impressive stone wall near 0.45 mi. There are exposed tree roots on the trail's lower half, but it's otherwise dry and in good condition. The forest is almost completely deciduous from trailhead to summit, mostly oak, maple, basswood, and black cherry.

At 0.55 mi, the grade eases. An unmarked path on the LEFT leads 75 ft to the Chance of Thunder Lean-to. I'm certain its name has an interesting origin. Once back on the trail, Opal Pond (N42° 20.190', W73° 29.054') is ahead, a small, well-named vernal pond dogs will

Rob signs us in — Beebe Hill.
— Alan Via

savor. From this point, it's an almost level hike to the summit, the trail entering into a grassy meadow with the observer's cabin on one end and the fire tower on the other.

You'll have to climb at least most of the way up the tower to enjoy views over the surrounding treetops on the 1760 ft summit. In addition to the rolling hills of Columbia and Berkshire Counties, the Catskills summits are prominent on the horizon, most notably Hunter, Windham, Overlook, and the Blackhead Range.

Returning to the trailhead by the tower observer's road makes a slightly longer, but nicer, hike loop. Grassy at its beginning, the way soon turns into a hiker-friendly dirt road, an interesting walk with good, dry footing and new terrain to explore. Don't miss the unmarked turn for the road (N42° 20.052', W73° 29.095') on the LEFT, 0.1 mi below the tower. Missing it lands you on Engel Rd., on the other side of Beebe Hill from the trailhead. Stone fences, a handsome deciduous forest, another stream, a small pond, and an ever-changing woodscape make this an attractive exit. The road passes next to Barrett Pond, a photographic and doggy treat just before the parking area.

Bennett Hill Preserve

HIGHLIGHTS AND SUMMARY: The 155-acre Mohawk Hudson Land Conservancy preserve features trails that are a mix of uphill and rolling terrain, a perfect destination for doghikers, snowshoers, or trail runners. Birders will appreciate an entry trail bordering a field favored by owls and red tails. Cows may sometimes be in the pasture just over the fence at the beginning of the hike.

MILEAGE: *3.7 mi r/t for all trails.*

ELEVATION GAIN: *500 ft. 800 ft for all trails.*

DIFFICULTY: *2*

VIEW RATING: *2*

LEASH: *Required.*

DOG SAFETY AND HAZARDS: *None.*

WATER: *Seasonal water and Bathtub Spring.*

HIKER TRAFFIC: *Light.*

TRAIL CONDITIONS: *Good, but trails can be wet in places during spring.*

BEST TIME TO HIKE: *Autumn.*

GETTING THERE: *Turn onto CR 312 (N42° 34.522', W73° 58.329') from NY 443, S of Clarksville. Make an immediate LEFT onto Bennett Hill Rd. Drive 0.3 mi to the trailhead (N42° 34.308', W73° 57.947'). It sometimes takes a couple of days for the trailhead to be plowed after a storm.*

Heading uphill into the woods from the kiosk, the trail is mostly level for the first 0.4 mi, with views of the Helderberg Escarpment across a pasture. Please keep dogs on the trail to avoid having them contact the electric fence wire or disturb cows in the adjacent pasture. The preserve has three trails. The GREEN entry trail ascends to an intersection (N42° 33.957', W73° 57.939') with the RED trail and it also continues ascending, meeting the YELLOW trail (N42° 33.810', W73° 57.773') that circles the summit rim. You can mix and match or repeat a section to cover the entire preserve in one hike.

The RED trail has an interesting variety of terrain and flora. It passes the edge of a grown-over meadow and skirts the bottom of a hemlock forest that populates the steepest terrain on the W and N sides of the preserve. You'll enjoy the well-designed switchbacks

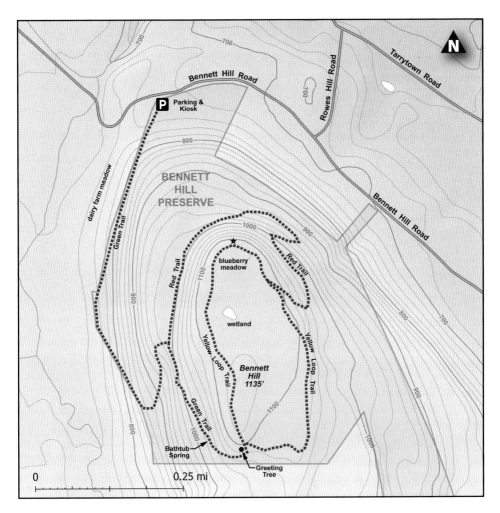

Bennett Hill Map

that lead to the intersection (N42° 34.030', W73° 57.701') with the
YELLOW trail that circles the summit rim.

The YELLOW trail has some of the most interesting features in
the preserve. There are alternating sections of oak, red pine, and other
conifers, and small clearings with Helderberg views. Look for a blueberry meadow 50 yd from the trail on the other side of screening conifers. The meadow provides a refuge from the cold, upslope winds
on blustery winter days. Bring snowshoes in winter, as winds deposit
deep snowdrifts along the N side of the trail. The best view from
Bennett is near a section of stunted oaks where a cleared viewpoint

Bennett Hill buddies.
—Alan Via

(N42° 34.103′, W73° 57.797′) overlooks Clarksville, the Helderbergs, and beyond.

Hikers may want to continue the Bennett tradition of adding a rock to the large, creative, and ever-changing cairn a little farther along the trail. The YELLOW trail skirts the 1135 ft summit of Bennett Hill on its SW side. The summit is easy to locate but is wooded and viewless. Look for the multi-trunk oak where the YELLOW and GREEN trails intersect. The "Greeting Tree" is where many group photos are taken.

The GREEN trail descends gradually through beech and oak woods, passing Bathtub Spring, where fresh water flows from an underground pipe into an old bathtub. Dogs always enjoy this iconic Bennett Hill landmark, a holdover from the days when the preserve was a pasture.

The preserve is a special place in winter. Depending on how soon you are there after a snowfall, you may find a broken trail or have the fun of being first. The woods are so open and inviting, they'll almost beg you to strap on your snowshoes and go exploring.

Treat yourself to breakfast or lunch at Clarksville's Jake Moon Restaurant Cafe. This small restaurant has an award-winning menu, plus a view of Bennett Hill out the windows.

Berlin Mt.

HIGHLIGHTS AND SUMMARY: Rensselaer County and the Taconic Crest Trail's high point, Berlin is the tallest mountain in this part of New York. The trail has an abundance of wildlife, butterflies, and wildflowers, and the open, grassy summit is a blueberry Eden.

MILEAGE: *5.3 mi r/t. 5.6 mi r/t with Mt. Raimer.*

ELEVATION GAIN: *1280 ft. 1580 ft with Mt. Raimer.*

DIFFICULTY: *3*

VIEW RATING: *3*

LEASH: *Not required.*

DOG SAFETY AND HAZARDS: *Trailhead on a busy NY 2. Avoid during deer-hunting season.*

WATER: *Seasonal springs and puddles. Carry extra water.*

HIKER TRAFFIC: *Light.*

TRAIL CONDITIONS: *Eroded near the beginning with muddy areas due to illegal ATV use.*

BEST TIME TO HIKE: *Late summer to early autumn.*

GETTING THERE: *The trailhead (N42° 43.405′, W73° 16.675′) is on NY 2 in Petersburg Pass, a high col on the Taconic Crest Trail. Located midway between Petersburg and Williamstown, Massachusetts, the trailhead is on the site of the former Mt. Raimer Ski Area.*

Begin hiking on diamond-shaped Taconic Crest Trail (TCT) markers from the RIGHT rear of the 2080 ft parking area. The trail gains 100 ft in the first 0.4 mi along the NW side of Mt. Raimer and another 250 ft to its SSW ridge. The latter section received a thorough scouring from Tropical Storm Irene, leaving a rocky, eroded chute that can be treacherous when coated in ice.

Ignore an unmarked woods road that intersects the TCT on Raimer's NW ridge. Look for an unmarked path (N42° 42.971′, W73° 17.123′) descending from Mt. Raimer's summit. It marks an alternative route that passes over Raimer. More details on this alternative can be found at the end of this trip description.

The TCT begins a 250 ft descent to the 2200 ft Berlin Pass (N42° 42.399′, W73° 17.425′). Side trails enter here from both sides, routes from more remote trailheads and entry points for ATVs. The trail is

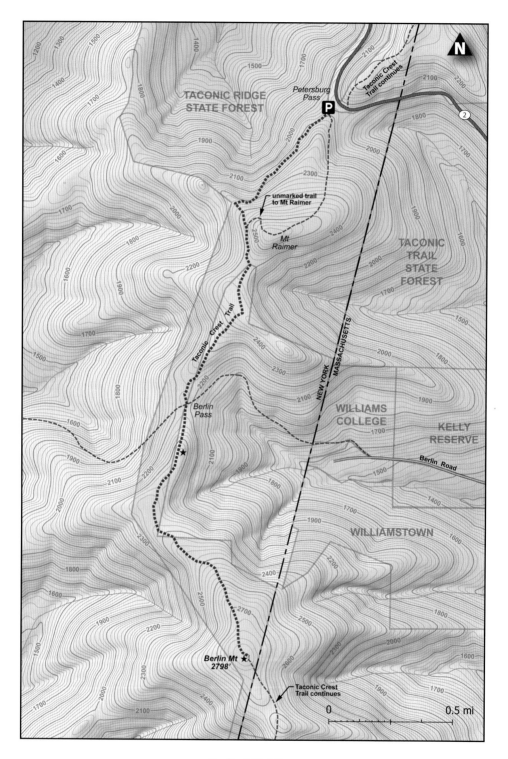

Berlin Mt. Map

a jeep road from Berlin Pass, ascending Berlin Mt.'s N and NW ridges. Trail erosion has exposed the bedrock in places and, though not steep, the footing can be slippery.

You're able to see the summit of Berlin Mt. from the trail, but this scenic section has sunny areas with no water for dogs. In the 600 ft climb to Berlin, there are extensive areas of wildflowers, ferns, berry bushes, and an interesting surrounding forest, a favorite section for spotting birds or butterflies. Berlin's grassy, bald top has views in numerous directions, though over the years, trees and bushes have encroached on the views. While slightly impeded, you can still see a long way from the open top. The most prominent peak is Mt. Greylock.

In summer, the summit is loaded with blueberries and, on warm mid-September days, buzzing with grasshoppers. The deep ferns near the summit crown are a cool, soothing place dogs will enjoy. Berlin's summit is seldom without a breeze, so packing a windbreaker is a good idea even on summer days.

A second route to Berlin begins LEFT of the trail register, midway across the rear of the parking area. An unmarked path beyond large rocks climbs the grown-over Mt. Raimer ski trails. Depending on the season, they can be easy or tricky to follow on the 300 ft climb to Raimer's 2572 ft wooded summit (N42° 43.405', W73° 16.675'). There are a few narrow views of White Rocks and Smith Hill across Petersburg Pass. From Raimer's summit, a path leads NW off the top, losing 250 ft and joining the TCT trail at the unmarked intersection mentioned earlier.

For winter hikers, the drive to Petersburg Pass is steep and can be treacherous in stormy weather. You and your dog will often be breaking trail to the summit.

Bozen Kill Preserve

HIGHLIGHTS AND SUMMARY: This Mohawk Hudson Land Conservancy (MHLC) preserve offers 214 acres of dog-friendly hiking. The terrain is interesting, and trails follow sections of stream where dogs can swim and hydrate. MHLC explains that "kill" is a Dutch word for stream and "bozen" means angry or raging, appropriate after heavy rain or spring runoff.

MILEAGE: *2.9 mi r/t.*

ELEVATION GAIN: *160 ft.*

DIFFICULTY: *1*

VIEW RATING: *1*

LEASH: *Required.*

DOG SAFETY AND HAZARDS: *Trailhead and first section of trail is adjacent to Westfall Rd. Caution near streams after heavy rainfall or snowmelt.*

WATER: *Part of hike follows the creek or crosses small tributaries.*

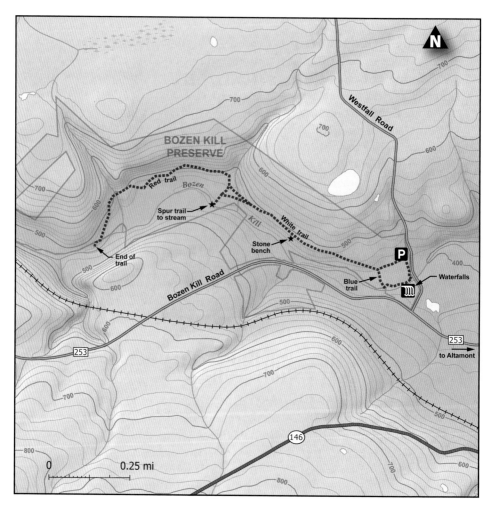

Bozen Kill Preserve Map

HIKER TRAFFIC: *Light.*

TRAIL CONDITIONS: *Very muddy in places during wet periods.*

BEST TIME TO HIKE: *Summer or autumn; waterfalls are impressive after rain.*

GETTING THERE: *Drive N out of Altamont on NY 146, continuing onto CR 253 (N42° 42.355', W74° 02.100'). Bear LEFT around a curve on CR 253 (Bozen Kill Rd.). Turn RIGHT onto Westfall Rd. and cross a bridge to the trailhead (N42° 42.895', W74° 02.794') immediately ahead.*

There are two options from the trailhead kiosk. Turn LEFT on the BLUE trail that parallels Westfall Rd. until reaching the stream. Take care with dogs, as this section of trail is close to Westfall Rd. The portion of the BLUE trail along the Bozen Kill has waterfalls and large pools and the 0.1 mi along the stream is heaven for water dogs and photographers. The trail turns RIGHT on a connector across a field to join the main WHITE trail.

You can also hike to this intersection straight across a meadow path from the trailhead and bypass the BLUE trail and stream. From the intersection, the WHITE trail begins ascending 65 ft to the trail's high point near 0.65 mi. It can be very muddy after snow thaw or heavy rain. The trail remains on the ridge above the Bozen Kill, coming to

Layla—Bozen Kill Preserve.
—Alan Via

a stone bench in a small trail alcove that has views of the stream. The trail descends slowly to an intersection (N42° 43.039′, W74° 03.376′) and a sign, "White Trail to Stream." This 0.1 mi spur passes through hemlocks and ends where dogs can get into the Bozen Kill.

From this point on the Bozen Kill, you can hike back to the intersection or take a shortcut to the main trail, now following RED trail markers on a section of trail more recently added to the preserve. Like the first part of the hike, this last 0.5 mi of trail passes through typical lowland forest, with open woods and an extensive area of hemlocks. The trail crosses tributary streams (with the most photogenic at N42° 43.091′, W74° 03.417′) before ending at the Bozen Kill and a "Trails End" sign. Near the end of the trail are a pair of deep pools and riffles doghikers will relish. The RED markers end at a long, deep pool bordered by a cliff. It's a perfect ending to a great trail. The MHLC preserve extends well beyond and is an interesting area to explore in winter.

Capital Hills at Albany

HIGHLIGHTS AND SUMMARY: A wonderful, dog-friendly golf course that welcomes four-legged hikers from mid-November until mid-April. It has perfect terrain for hiking, snowshoeing, skiing, or trail running with dogs across its rolling hills. Trails crisscross the forest in addition to five miles of paved cart paths. People come from all over with their canine companions to this remarkable place.

MILEAGE: *5.2 mi.*

ELEVATION GAIN: *315 ft.*

DIFFICULTY: *1*

VIEW RATING: *2*

LEASH: *Dogs are required to be under control of owners.*

DOG SAFETY AND HAZARDS: *Proximity to Normans Kill Creek during high water. Tall fencing separates the course from the Thruway.*

WATER: *A pond, numerous small streams, Normans Kill Creek.*

HIKER TRAFFIC: *Very busy on weekends, less during the week.*

TRAIL CONDITIONS: *Excellent.*

BEST TIME TO HIKE: *Late autumn through early spring. Doghikers can use the Power Line Trail year-round.*

GETTING THERE: *Turn onto O'Neil Rd. (N42° 39.215', W73° 49.269') from New Scotland Rd. and continue to the parking area.*

Capital Hills may seem like an unusual location for a dog hike, but it's a remarkably welcoming setting, a "must" for people already familiar with it. From when golf ends in November to the course reopening in April, it's one of the most enjoyable, dog-friendly locations anywhere. The course is divided into "Front" and "Back" Nines, their cart paths plowed in winter.

Leapin' Layla at Capital Hills. —Alan Via

A winter day at Capital Hills. —Barbara Via

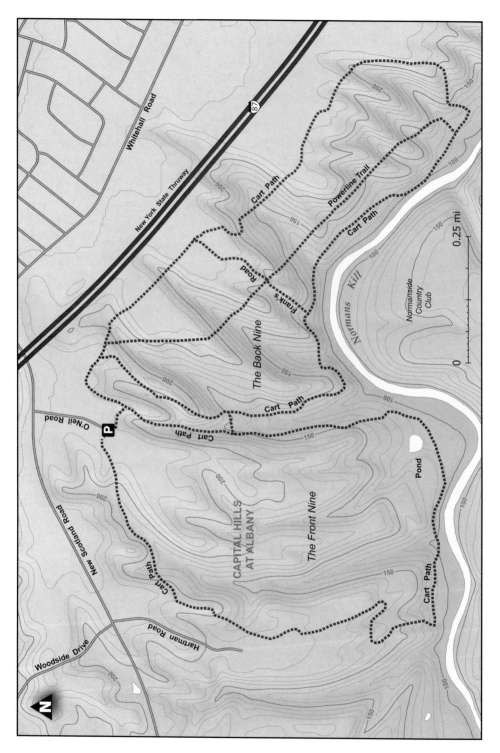

Capital Hills at Albany Map

Ganging up at Capital Hills.
—Mike Kalin

There are numerous marked and unmarked trails weaving their way through the hilly woods and meadows. For a workout, hike the Power Line Trail, an 8 ft mowed path with nary a flat section any-where along its entire length. A sign marks it as "Dog Trail." Frank's Road is a mowed path crossing the Power Line Trail, intersecting the Back Nine in two places.

Though located on the fringe of Albany, the rolling hills, wide fairways, and surrounding forest make you feel as if you're in a more isolated area. It's common to see deer running through the woods and red tails and merlins flying or perched in trees looking for prey. Whether you're hiking the cart paths or following a trail through the woods, you can always create your own route.

Long sections of both cart paths follow Normans Kill Creek. It's usually calm and slow moving, but dogs should be kept away after periods of heavy rain or when its surface has breakable ice. In addi-tion to the large pond, there are streams throughout Capital Hills. Hikers are strongly encouraged to pick up their dog's waste and make deposits in the many receptacles placed throughout the course. Regardless of where you wander, it's impossible to get lost. Just fol-low a cart path back to the parking lot. Winter snow is one of the best times to visit.

Dickinson Hill

HIGHLIGHTS AND SUMMARY: The summit is crowned by a sixty-foot fire tower constructed in 1924. The Friends of Grafton Lakes State Park group restored and reopened the tower after it fell into disrepair. Hike past ten interpretive panels to the tower that provides a different perspective on a multitude of mountain ranges. Long Pond is great for a post-hike swim and fun with dogs.

MILEAGE: *2.9 mi r/t. 0.75 mi for Chet Bell Trail.*

ELEVATION GAIN: *325 ft.*

DIFFICULTY: *1*

VIEW RATING: *3*

LEASH: *Leashes required while on the Grafton Lake Park portion of trails.*

DOG SAFETY AND HAZARDS: *Hunting season and Long Pond Rd. traffic.*

WATER: *Puddles, small brook, seasonal water, and Long Pond.*

HIKER TRAFFIC: *Light.*

TRAIL CONDITIONS: *Eroded woods road. Very muddy section from illegal ATV abuse.*

BEST TIME TO HIKE: *Late spring through early autumn. Avoid hunting season.*

GETTING THERE: *Turn off of NY 2 onto Long Pond Rd. (N42° 46.165', W73° 27.057') opposite a church in Grafton village. Follow Long Pond Rd. past Mill and Second Ponds to the 1600 ft Fire Tower Road trailhead (N42° 47.437', W73° 26.017').*

Begin hiking on the Fire Tower Road Trail, which is bordered by rock walls, fern patches, and wildflowers where sunlight illuminates it. The trail gains and loses 100 ft in its initial 0.4 mi, passing the intersection (N42° 47.495', W73° 25.615') with the Chet Bell snowmobile trail on the LEFT. It's an option to extend the hike on your way back to the trailhead.

Begin ascending, past the Spruce Bog Trail on the RIGHT, which leads to White Lily Pond. The Fire Tower Road Trail continues its easy uphill to 0.75 mi, where it becomes rockier, more eroded, and narrower. Most of the trail to this point is dry or you can rock hop to keep your boots dry. Illegal ATV use has turned a 100 yd section into a mud wallow where hikers have created a bypass trail. At 1.1 mi, the

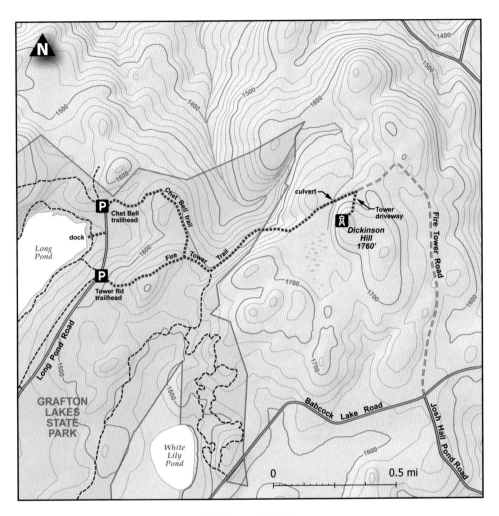

Dickinson Hill Map

trail passes a residence and immediately beyond is the first reliable dog water, where the trail passes over a large culvert, the outflow of the nearby marsh and pond.

Dogs will love the deep, clear water. The fire tower driveway (N42° 47.710′, W73° 24.786′) is 0.1 mi ahead, where a gate blocks vehicular traffic on the gravel access road. Dickinson Hill's tower offers unique views. Berlin Mt. and Mount Greylock are nearby standouts. The Green Mts. are visible, as are the Adirondacks. In the opposite direction, the Helderbergs and Catskills form a line along the SW horizon.

Dickinson Hill thistles.
—Alan Via

On your return, the Chet Bell Trail provides a couple of nice options. The hard-packed, dry snowmobile trail leads through a shady and relaxing deciduous forest. Its ORANGE markers are superfluous, as it would be difficult to lose your way. It ends at a parking area on Long Pond Rd. at N42° 47.675′, W73° 26.014′ where you can leave a second car or turn LEFT for the 0.45 mi hike back to the Fire Tower Road trailhead. Walking or driving, turn down the short access road to the beach, boat launch, and dock off Long Pond Rd. It's a superb place for you and your doghiker to enjoy a post-hike swim, fetch, or paddle.

Holt Preserve

HIGHLIGHTS AND SUMMARY: A Mohawk Hudson Land Conservancy preserve, Holt has two trailheads, an interesting variety of trails, and a spring-fed pond where dogs can wade or swim. The light foot traffic provides hikers the opportunity to observe nature while out hiking with their dogs. Holt is a favorite with snowshoers.

MILEAGE: *3 mi all trails.*

ELEVATION GAIN: *600 ft all trails.*

DIFFICULTY: *2*

VIEW RATING: *2*

LEASH: *Required.*

DOG SAFETY AND HAZARDS: *None.*

WATER: *Streams and pond.*

HIKER TRAFFIC: *Light, a little busier on weekends.*

TRAIL CONDITIONS: *Very good with a few muddy sections during wet weather times..*

BEST TIME TO HIKE: *Autumn and winter.*

GETTING THERE: *Turn onto Lower Copeland Hill Rd. (N42° 33.012', W73° 56.192') from NY 32, continuing 0.6 mi to the year-round (lower) trailhead (N42° 32.625', W73° 55.919'). The upper trailhead is reached by turning onto Appleby Rd. (N42° 32.003', W73° 55.423') from CR 108 (Copeland Hill Rd.), continuing past the old barn and snowplow turnaround (N42° 32.484', W73° 55.645') to the upper trailhead (N42° 32.640', W73° 55.645'). The road beyond the turnaround is unmaintained in winter.*

A rocky and undrivable woods road connects the lower and upper trailheads. Beginning at the lower trailhead, you can hike the road or start on the WHITE trail that begins 25 ft before the parking area. The WHITE trail crosses two skinny streams to an intersection. Turn LEFT on RED markers onto the Dr. Holt loop. A RIGHT turn leads toward the upper trails. The Dr. Holt is less traveled, formerly with wet and overgrown areas. This made the trail more suitable for a dry or cold weather hike. The trail has undergone a relocation, moving a portion of it to a drier area.

The YELLOW Ravine Trail climbs a hardwoods ridge that parallels the woods road that connects the trailheads. It follows above a stream where dogs can drink. The pond (N42° 32.675', W73° 55.566') is one of the highlights of the preserve, just minutes from the upper trailhead. Clean, deep, and spring fed, dogs can wade, swim, or retrieve. Be watchful for poison ivy around the pond and in other places in the preserve. Three trails are accessible from the upper trailhead and vicinity of the pond. Boundary, Plantation, and Helderberg Overlook each are excellent trails.

The Helderberg Overlook Trail follows the top edge of a steep W overlook that provides views of the Helderberg Escarpment in spring, winter, and late autumn. The Plantation Trail begins W of the pond, bisecting the upper preserve and climbing through sections of mixed forest. It's named for the red pine plantation through which the trail passes. The widely spaced conifers are an excellent place to look for animal tracks in winter. If you're quiet, in early evening you might hear barred owls in its lower section. The Boundary Trail originates

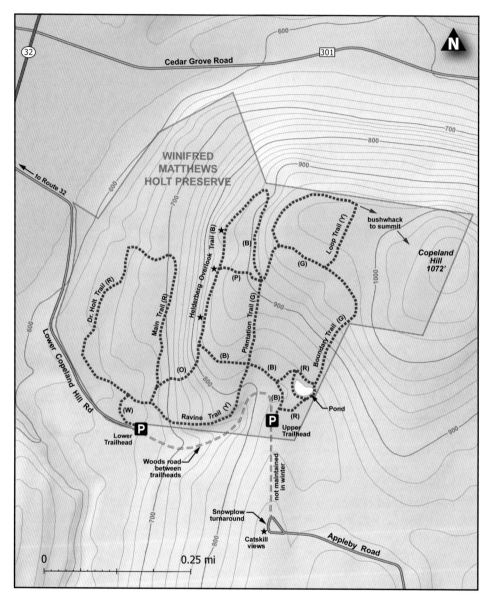

Holt Preserve Map

next to the pond and is aptly named, ascending on the E side of the preserve. Its top section passes through neat rows of red pines.

The short but beautiful YELLOW loop intersects the Boundary Trail in two places. Doghikers fully comfortable with off-trail travel can bushwhack to Copeland Hill (N42° 32.883′, W73° 55.281′), the highest point in the preserve. Head E from the YELLOW loop trail along the preserve border through deciduous forest before turning SE to Copeland's 1072 ft wooded summit. Best done on snowshoes in winter when trees are bare, you can follow your tracks back to the trail. Don't head home without checking the view of the Helderbergs and Catskills from near the snowplow turnaround.

Schoharie Creek Preserve

HIGHLIGHTS AND SUMMARY: The trail through this compact Mohawk Hudson Land Conservancy preserve follows sections of scenic Wilsey and Schoharie Creeks. Wilsey has picturesque waterfalls and the rocky Schoharie is the width of a river where dogs can splash or swim. Hikes kick off with dog fun at the trailhead pond.

MILEAGE: *1.4 mi loop.*

ELEVATION GAIN: *180 ft.*

DIFFICULTY: *1*

VIEW RATING: *2*

LEASH: *Required.*

DOG SAFETY AND HAZARDS: *Butler Rd. traffic and Schoharie Creek at high water.*

WATER: *Wilsey and Schoharie Creeks and trailhead pond.*

HIKER TRAFFIC: *Very light.*

TRAIL CONDITIONS: *Good.*

BEST TIME TO HIKE: *Spring and autumn.*

GETTING THERE: *Cross Schoharie Creek on CR 102 and turn RIGHT onto Burtonsville Rd. (CR 127). Turn RIGHT onto Butler Rd. in 0.85 mi and follow to the preserve driveway (N42° 49.027', W74° 15.892').*

Though the trail can be hiked from either direction, I prefer clockwise, hiking along a mowed path from the rear of the trailhead. It enters the woods at 0.2 mi, crosses a stone fence, and begins a gradual descent. You'll hear Wilsey Creek before you see it, as you follow above it on the trail. As you near the stream, you'll see the beginning of a succession of waterfalls. Wilsey is so photogenic it's hard to pick which cataract is a favorite. One of the nicest (N42° 49.246', W74° 16.009') has a 10 ft drop into a large pool. It's right below the trail and

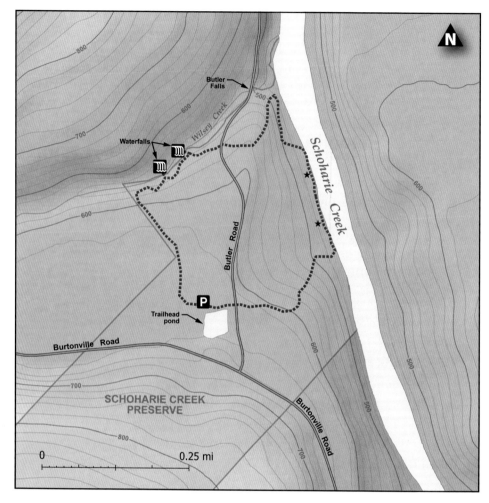

Schoharie Creek Preserve Map

easy to get streamside. Dogs will enjoy it and you'll likely be tempted to photograph them while they swim or chase sticks.

The trail leaves Wilsey Creek and crosses Butler Rd. Though it's not busy, be careful of vehicles when crossing. The trail resumes and descends, the forest open enough that you can see Wilsey's highest waterfall through the trees. Don't miss the sharp RIGHT turn (N42° 49.334′, W74° 15.822′). Missing the turn leads you down an unmarked path across a narrow, crumbling rock rib with steep and dangerous drop-offs to the Wilsey and Schoharie Creek drainages.

The trail continues to descend toward Schoharie Creek, climbing down wooden steps in a steep section. For much of the 0.2 mi it is

Toby in her office.
—Mike Kalin

creek-side, the trail is sandy and unshaded. The Schoharie is close enough that you can walk out on the rocks. Unless the water level is high, it's a wonderful place for dogs to wade and hikers to cool their feet. In summer, this section of trail has a showy stream-side display of flowers and bushes framing views of the surrounding hills. The trail switchbacks uphill into the forest away from the Schoharie, climbing 175 ft through a section of conifers whose needles cushion the trail. At the top of the brief ascent, recross Butler Rd. opposite the trailhead driveway.

Thacher State Park

HIGHLIGHTS AND SUMMARY: Located on the Helderberg Escarpment, Thacher has twenty-five miles of forested hiking trails—too many trails to cover in one book. This trip description introduces hikers to the trails that originate at the Paint Mine and Hop Field trailheads. Enjoy the hemlocks and hardwoods, ravines and ledges, and trails laced with streams and a variety of spring and summer wildflowers. Trailheads are open 9 a.m.–9 p.m. There is a $6 parking fee from May 1 through October 31, or an annual pass is available.

MILEAGE: *3 mi. Hikes vary from 2 mi to 5 mi.*

ELEVATION GAIN: *250 ft to 800 ft.*

DIFFICULTY: *2*

VIEW RATING: *1*

LEASH: *Required.*

DOG SAFETY AND HAZARDS: *The trailheads are busy and the Paint Mine Trail passes near a section of hazardous ravine. The BLUE trail parallels Beaver Dam Rd.*

WATER: *Streams and wet areas throughout the park. Many dry up in summer.*

HIKER TRAFFIC: *Busy on weekends.*

TRAIL CONDITIONS: *Generally good, with wet and muddy sections.*

BEST TIME TO HIKE: *Spring and autumn.*

GETTING THERE: *Turn onto NY 157 from NY 85 (N42° 36.945′, W73° 58.523′) near New Salem and continue into the park. A 30-mph speed limit is enforced on park roads. Stop at the Overlook (N42° 38.931′, W74° 00.375′) and Visitor's Center (N42° 39.268′, W74° 01.062′) for spectacular views.*

The Paint Mine trailhead (N42° 39.100′, W74° 00.869′) is large, set back from the road, and has rest rooms. The 1 mi Paint Mine Trail follows Mine Lot Creek uphill and features a variety of side trails. At 0.1 mi, look for an abandoned road on the RIGHT that sees little activity. It's an excellent place to listen for birds and the forest invites off-trail snowshoeing through open, hilly woods.

At 0.2 mi, the Paint Mine Trail passes a bridge that spans Mine Lot Creek, a section of stream with a series of small cascades, a downstream waterfall, and a large pool where dogs can drink or cool off. One end of the 1.2 mi Nature Trail loop intersects here on the LEFT. It crosses the bridge on RED markers, beginning with a short climb up a shale and dirt road into a magnificent hemlock forest. The loop takes you through mixed hardwoods and hemlocks before it rejoins the Paint Mine Trail above.

As you continue uphill on the Paint Mine Trail, it climbs above the stream, passing an area of cliffs with eroded edges that overlook the creek below. There's an unmarked road (N42° 38.649′, W74° 00.889′) on the RIGHT at 0.5 mi. This 0.35 mi grassy access road has a small sag where spring snowmelt sometimes accumulates, attracting ducks, and is a good place for a spring peeper symphony. Chewed trees give

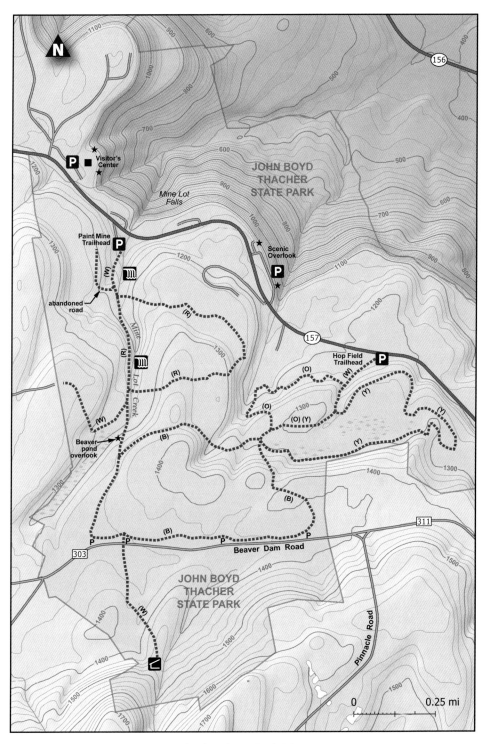

Thacher State Park Map

Wren.
—Barbara Via

evidence of nocturnal beaver activity and it's common to see deer or turkey crossing beyond where the road climbs through a cleft in a ledge. The road reaches private property at the park's boundary, at a small building where hikers must turn around.

Back on the Paint Mine Trail, there's a rocky ledge ahead on the RIGHT that overlooks a beaver pond. It's a rare spring day when songbirds, ducks, or geese aren't on or near the water. At dawn, beavers and muskrats are active here. The BLUE trail intersects the Paint Mine Trail nearby on the LEFT. The 1.8 mi BLUE loop parallels Beaver Dam Rd., passes through a mixed forest with small streams, then reunites with the Paint Mine Trail. Cross Beaver Dam Rd. to hike a trail on the opposite side. The 0.35 mi trail climbs through meadows to a lean-to just inside a woods line. Autumn through early spring is the best time to hike, before the meadow grows over in summer and ticks become a problem.

The spacious Hop Field trailhead (N42° 38.795′, W73° 59.948′) also has restrooms and its trails connect to those from the Paint Mine trailhead. Walk to the back of a grassy area and begin hiking uphill on a crushed shale road to the RIGHT of a waterfall, passing the E end of the ORANGE trail loop. The road reaches the intersection (N42° 38.650′, W74° 00.138′) with the 2 mi YELLOW trail loop in a couple of minutes, where you can turn LEFT or RIGHT.

For almost half of its length, the YELLOW trail is near the edge of a wetland. It's an excellent trail for spring birding or winter snowshoeing but has unavoidable wet and muddy sections. It crosses numerous streams, most with small bridges, and a 100 ft section has a boardwalk. Beyond, the gently undulating trail passes photogenic, moss-draped ledges and one of the most scenic hemlock forests in the park. You can connect with trails originating from the Paint Mine Trail on the W sides of the ORANGE or YELLOW trails. Though shorter than the YELLOW trail, the ORANGE loop is drier and hillier. Some of the wet and grassy sections of the Hop Field trails make great snowshoe hikes.

Thunder Mt.

HIGHLIGHTS AND SUMMARY: Though diminutive in size, the trail system in this park offers some interesting views. The pond near the trailhead is the former town reservoir. Dogs can swim or cool off here at the beginning or end of hikes. Wildflower enthusiasts will enjoy some of the trails around the pond.

MILEAGE: *2.3 mi all trails.*

ELEVATION GAIN: *450 ft.*

DIFFICULTY: *1*

VIEW RATING: *2*

LEASH: *Not required.*

DOG SAFETY AND HAZARDS: *The concrete pond spillway.*

WATER: *Trailhead pond and seasonal water along trails.*

HIKER TRAFFIC: *Light.*

TRAIL CONDITIONS: *Good, but a little overgrown around pond.*

BEST TIME TO HIKE: *Summer and autumn.*

GETTING THERE: *Turn onto Prospect St. (N43° 05.490', W73° 29.520') in Greenwich. Continue as Prospect becomes North Rd. to the metal gate (N43° 06.618', W73° 28.855') with large boulders and 0.25 mi driveway to the Village of Greenwich Recreation Department park.*

There are three trails in the park. The first is the loop around the pond, a second climbs Thunder Mt., and the third passes a historic site on the way to a bench with views.

The 0.3 mi loop that circles the pond has a grassy area and offers lots of doggy access to the water. It's a little overgrown in a few places, damp in others, and passes through a mixed forest, partially comprised of red pines. Be careful with dogs near the concrete spillway.

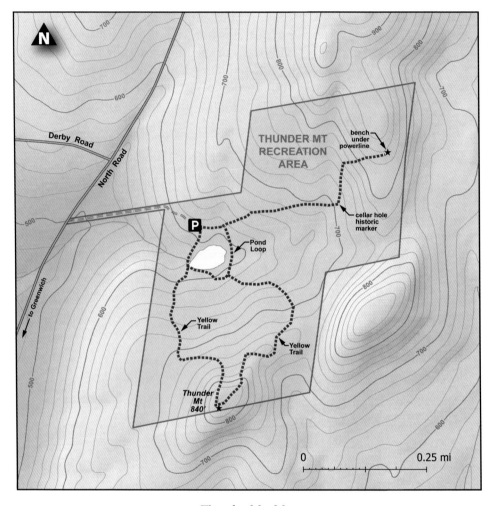

Thunder Mt. Map

A trail with RED markers intersects the pond loop at its NE corner. At 0.1 mi, the RED trail passes a woods road/snowmobile trail on the LEFT, one of a series in the N side of the park. Continue past it another 0.2 mi to a large old tree marking a historic cellar hole and sign explaining that the land was sold to the Village Waterworks in 1887. RED markers lead uphill to a bench (N43° 06.720′, W73° 28.109′) under a power line. The views of surrounding hills partially make up for the setting.

Returning to the pond, the YELLOW Thunder Mt. trail intersects the pond loop in two places. Starting from the pond's SE corner, the trail climbs steadily, never steeply, through a mixed forest, part of which is a red pine plantation. Ferns, seasonal wildflowers, and, in sunny places, berry bushes border the trail. As the trail continues to gain elevation, conifers disappear, and the forest becomes deciduous as you reach the 840 ft summit of Thunder Mt. There's a nice view from a clearing on the S side of the trail with views of Schuyler, Willard, and Whelden Mts. As you descend the NW ridge of Thunder, the trail at the top of the NW ridge is steeper than the trail you climbed, the gradient easing the closer you get to the pond.

Wolf Creek Falls Preserve

HIGHLIGHTS AND SUMMARY: This Mohawk Hudson Land Conservancy preserve has trails that border streams with picturesque waterfalls. Kids will love the Musical Bridge. The preserve is a great snowshoe hike and its waterfalls are best seen after rainfall or snowmelt.

MILEAGE: *3.7 mi to 1.4 mi.*

ELEVATION GAIN: *240 ft.*

DIFFICULTY: *1*

VIEW RATING: *2*

LEASH: *Required.*

DOG SAFETY AND HAZARDS: *Road crossing and streams after heavy rain.*

WATER: *Trails parallel or cross streams.*

HIKER TRAFFIC: *Light.*

TRAIL CONDITIONS: *Generally good with some very wet sections.*

BEST TIME TO HIKE: *Spring and autumn.*

GETTING THERE: *Follow CR 253 (Bozen Kill Rd.) 3 mi out of Altamont to the trailhead (N42° 43.299', W74° 05.125'). Parking is prohibited where the trail crosses Bozen Kill Rd.*

The preserve straddles both sides of Bozen Kill Rd. Begin hiking on the GOLD trail from the rear of the parking area into shady forest. The trail soon intersects a WHITE-marked loop trail that circles the S side of the preserve. Turn LEFT, passing a stream, the only reliable dog water on this side of the preserve.

The WHITE trail passes through a forest of hardwoods, white

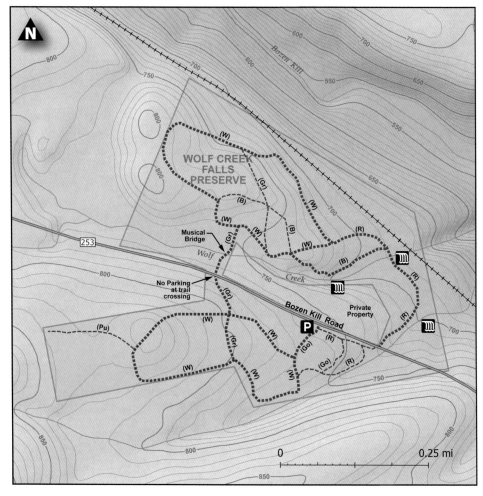

Wolf Creek Falls Preserve Map

pines, and hemlocks with little elevation change. The trails are soft, with muddy sections during rainy periods. Fans of stone fences will be in for a treat. Cross the GREEN trail that intersects with the WHITE trail in two places. Continuing, the WHITE trail slowly climbs over the preserve's 840 ft high point, then descends, again meeting the GREEN trail. Turn LEFT on GREEN markers, crossing Bozen Kill Rd. to the N side of the preserve 70 yd ahead. Take care crossing the highway as drivers won't anticipate people crossing here.

The GREEN trail enters the N side of the preserve, crossing Wolf Creek on the Musical Bridge. Eight of its boards were tuned to imitate

Gryffin and Amanda.
—Tim Lucia

the tones of a scale when tapped by walking sticks. Kids of all ages will be delighted, while dogs get a splash and drink. The trail climbs slightly and intersects (N42° 43.435′, W74° 05.283′) the WHITE trail that loops its way around much of the N preserve through a mostly hardwoods forest. Turning LEFT, the WHITE trail climbs over the 790 ft high point of the N side, then begins a gradual descent past a wetland to an intersection.

WHITE markers lead back uphill to Bozen Kill Rd. Turn LEFT on RED markers, passing close enough to rail tracks that dogs should be kept close for a short section. The trail nears Wolf Creek (N42° 43.407′, W74° 05.986′), presenting a couple of options. You can pick up the BLUE trail that parallels Wolf Creek past a large waterfall visible from the trail (N42° 43.385′, W74° 05.154′). It's spectacular during spring or after periods of rain. The BLUE trail intersects the WHITE loop, which you can also follow back to Bozen Kill Rd. The RED trail crosses Wolf Creek, turns uphill, following a scenic section of the stream with waterfall views. It meets Bozen Kill Rd. (N42° 43.271′, W74° 05.007′) SE of the trailhead. Cross the road and follow RED markers back to the trailhead or to another section of trail along the stream.

View of the Blackheads from Lunch Rock on Acra Point.
—Tony Versandi

South Region

Acra Point

HIGHLIGHTS AND SUMMARY: Acra Point has a little bit of everything. The hike begins with the photogenic Batavia Kill's waterfalls, sluices, and pools. The ridge walk is a wildflower delight, and a perfectly situated rock ledge has terrific views in exactly the right place for lunch. Hike up to the Burnt Knob viewpoint on your way back to the trailhead.

MILEAGE: *5.1 mi r/t. 5.7 mi r/t with Burnt Knob.*

ELEVATION GAIN: *1200 ft for loop. 1500 ft with Burnt Knob.*

DIFFICULTY: *3*

VIEW RATING: *4*

LEASH: *None.*

DOG SAFETY AND HAZARDS: *Caution at ledges.*

WATER: *Small streams and Batavia Kill.*

HIKER TRAFFIC: *Light on weekdays, busier on weekends.*

TRAIL CONDITIONS: *Good*

BEST TIME TO HIKE: *Spring or autumn.*

GETTING THERE: *Take CR 40 out of Hensonville. Bear LEFT onto CR 56 (Big Hollow Rd.) in Maplecrest (N42° 16.514', W74° 11.238') and continue to the trailhead (N42° 15.332', W74° 06.902') at the end of the road.*

Hike E from the trailhead on RED markers, starting out on the trail that leads toward the Blackhead Range. You'll enjoy the pools and small waterfalls on the beautiful Batavia Kill as much as your dog will. Cross two bridges and pass a trail intersection (N42° 16.999', W74° 0.473') at 0.5 mi on the RIGHT. The RED markers now turn toward Lockwood Gap, the Blackhead–Black Dome col. Continue ahead

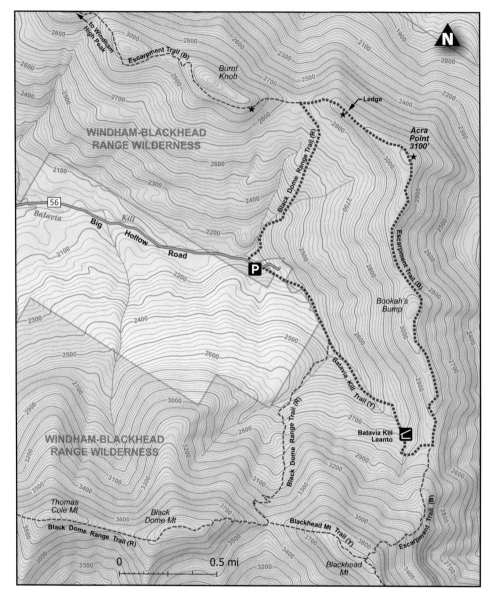

Acra Point Map

on YELLOW markers, climbing at an easy grade past the former site of the Batavia Kill lean-to, now relocated on a 100 yd side path.

The trail makes a sharp LEFT, steepens, then follows the topographic contour through large birches and hemlocks. At 1.5 mi, it reaches the Escarpment Trail in a shallow col (N42° 16.539′, W74°

05.886') at 2860 ft. Turn LEFT in the col on BLUE markers along Acra Point's S ridge. Begin through a section of white birch and conifers. The trail is in good condition but turns rocky where it briefly drops off the ridge before regaining it.

As you continue, the hike across the ridge is easy walking on a soft tread through deciduous forest. The trail gains about 300 ft of ascent from the col to Acra Point. Midway, the trail passes E and just below a 3060 ft high point, called Bookah's Bump, named after one of my Labs, the first dog to complete the Catskill 100 Highest summits. Depending on the season, wildflowers and ferns mix with birch and cherry trees on the negligible climb to a lichen-covered sandstone block marking the bump's high point. There are filtered views of the Blackheads from here when trees are bare.

The remaining distance to Acra Point is a favorite in early spring. Before leaves appear, there are views on both sides of the ridge and the trail has bouquets of spring ephemerals on the last section to Acra Point's 3100 ft wooded summit. The 0.7 mi and 330 ft descent to the 2770 ft Acra Point–Burnt Knob col is easy, but be certain to plan for a break at the rocky ledge midway to the col. It's a grand place for lunch and enjoying views of the Blackhead Range, Burnt Knob, Windham High Peak, and a horizon full of high and low summits and ridges. It's a 1 mi descent from the col to Big Hollow Rd. You can add a little extra to your day: 300 ft of climbing takes you to another beautiful ledge just below the summit of the trailless Burnt Knob.

Alder Lake

HIGHLIGHTS AND SUMMARY: A fun, short hike for families and dogs on a trail that circles a small lake. Explore what's left of the former late 1800s Coykendall mansion and enjoy views of surrounding peaks from the large meadow that used to be the mansion's lawn. You can hike, camp, fish for trout, or be lucky enough to see one of the shy otters inhabiting the lake.

MILEAGE: *1.5 mi r/t.*

ELEVATION GAIN: *100 ft.*

DIFFICULTY: *1*

VIEW RATING: *2*

LEASH: *Not required, but advisable near others or campsites.*

DOG SAFETY AND HAZARDS: *None.*

WATER: *Alder Lake and 5 stream crossings.*

HIKER TRAFFIC: *Can be busy on weekends.*

TRAIL CONDITIONS: *Muddy in places, depending on seasonal precipitation.*

BEST TIME TO HIKE: *Foliage makes autumn a favorite, but spring wild-flowers and summer temperatures and breezes make those seasons strong competitors.*

GETTING THERE: *Turn N onto CR 54 from CR 102 in Turnwood (N42° 01.458', W74° 42.557'), continuing 2.3 mi to the Alder Lake spur road (N42° 03.100', W74° 41.329'). If you're coming from the N, turn onto seasonally maintained Cross Mt. Rd. (N42° 05.813', W74° 42.986') from Millbrook Rd. The long, uphill drive is steep and rocky as it gets closer to Alder Lake.*

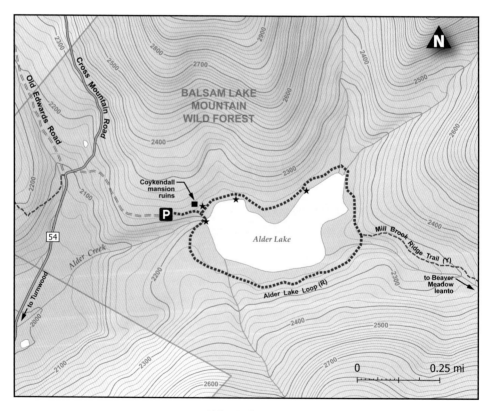

Alder Lake Map

Moonray smoothing it after Catskill 'whack.
—Alan Via

Hike from the rear of the spacious 2250 ft trailhead (N42° 02.992′, W74° 40.993′) past what remains of the mansion. The mansion was built by a canal and railroad magnate and subsequently owned by a sportsman's club and a Scout council. It was bought by New York State in 1980 and razed thirty years later. Visualize its glory days as you look at the stone steps and fireplace. Walk across a meadow that was formerly its lawn, overlooking Alder Lake and a trio of Catskill 100 Highest summits, Cradle Rock, Mill Brook, and Woodpecker Ridges.

Although you can walk in either direction, begin LEFT, clockwise around the lake on RED markers. You'll have the mountains in front of you across the lake as you hike. The trail around the S side of the lake is higher up and farther from the shore, screening views. Regardless of direction, the trail takes you through a deciduous forest with shrubs, ferns, berry bushes, and spring wildflowers. YELLOW DEC markers designate undeveloped campsites around the lake.

The trail crosses streams in multiple places, intersecting Alder Creek at 0.7 mi on the lake's E end (N42° 02.948′, W74° 40.336′). A YELLOW-marked trail leads to Mill Brook Ridge, offering the opportunity to extend your hike. It's only 0.8 mi along the trail to the Beaver Meadow Lean-to, a wonderful birding and wildlife area. You may want to join your dog for a swim in the cool, clear water of Alder Lake after the hike.

Andes Rail Trail and Bullet Hole Spur

HIGHLIGHTS AND SUMMARY: This interesting hike combines history, a railbed, and the Bullet Hole spur. The trail was designed by the Catskill Mountain Club with the cooperation of landowners and the New York City Department of Environment Protection (DEP). Enjoy views of the surrounding mountains, a red pine plantation, and a chance to see beaver activity. The Bullet Hole was reportedly named after a nineteenth-century get-together where an entire bull was consumed by attendees, the name being a corruption of "bull eaten whole."

MILEAGE: *3.8 mi r/t. 1.7 mi r/t for railbed.*

ELEVATION GAIN: *575 ft.*

DIFFICULTY: *2*

VIEW RATING: *2*

LEASH: *Required by landowners and DEP.*

DOG SAFETY AND HAZARDS: *None.*

WATER: *Small streams may have water.*

HIKER TRAFFIC: *Light*

TRAIL CONDITIONS: *Very good*

BEST TIME TO HIKE: *Spring through fall, but excellent cross-country skiing.*

GETTING THERE: *The trailhead (N42° 11.206', W74° 47.381') is on CR 2 at the outskirts of Andes at "The Andes Rail Trail and Train Depot" sign. Drive along the side of the depot building, circle around back, and park facing the woods.*

The beginning of the grassy railbed starts beyond the restored train station. Sections of wildflowers and ferns border the rail trail on and off throughout its length. There are historic markers and views of Grays Mt. and Ford and Dingle Hills across open meadows as you walk. Early in the morning or in late evening, quiet observers may look down and see beavers hard at work where they have dammed the Tremper Kill. Otters have also been seen there.

A sign at 0.85 mi marks the end of the railbed (N42° 10.561', W74° 47.493') and the beginning of the trail toward the Bullet Hole spur. YELLOW markers lead along the switchbacking trail uphill through sections of stone fences and ferns, and along interesting ledges and an

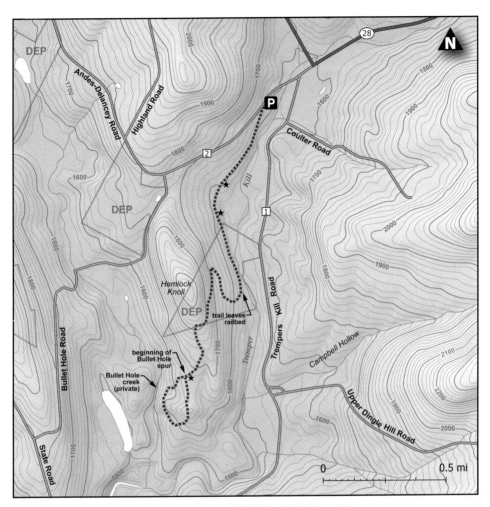

Andes Rail Trail and Bullet Hole Spur Map

ancient piece of Catskill sandstone. The trail climbs along the shoulder of Hemlock Knoll, below its viewless and pricker-laden summit. As it crosses Hemlock Knoll's S ridge, it reenters private land, descending 125 ft through hemlocks, large maples, and a sea of ferns to a small clearing (N42° 10.280', W74° 47.728') with views of the surrounding hills across a meadow.

The trail crosses a stone fence at 1.6 mi into a red pine plantation, the start of the Bullet Hole spur. Hiking the spur in either direction returns you here. Turning LEFT on the spur, the trail passes just inside the striking red pines on the spur's E side, climbs negligibly, then descends through a spectacular hemlock grove. As the trail turns N, enjoy a glimpse of private Bullet Hole Creek. Please respect the land-owner's privacy and stay on the trail. Continue along the spur's W side, returning to its beginning. Climb back toward Hemlock Knoll and descend to the railbed for the stroll back to the trailhead. The hike can take as long as you'd like, but this well-designed and scenic trail is usually a half-day outing.

Ashokan High Point

HIGHLIGHTS AND SUMMARY: Also known as High Point or Shokan High Point, this is one of the best hikes in the Catskills, with showy mountain laurel, small oaks, Kanape Brook, acres of blueberries, and summit views.

MILEAGE: *7 mi r/t.*

ELEVATION GAIN: *2000 ft.*

DIFFICULTY: *5*

VIEW RATING: *4*

LEASH: *Not required but keep dogs away from campsites.*

DOG SAFETY AND HAZARDS: *Trailhead traffic and crossing Peekamoose Rd.*

WATER: *Kanape Brook and tributaries.*

HIKER TRAFFIC: *Light during the week, busier on weekends.*

TRAIL CONDITIONS: *Much of the trail to the saddle is on a rocky woods road.*

BEST TIME TO HIKE: *Spring and autumn.*

GETTING THERE: *Turn onto NY 28A from NY 28 (N42° 00.276', W74° 15.963') in Boiceville. Drive 3 mi, turning onto CR 42 (N41° 58.156', W74° 16.618'), Peekamoose Rd. Continue to the 1125 ft Kanape Brook ("Ka-Nape") trailhead (N41° 56.106', W74° 19.721').*

Begin hiking on the opposite side of the road from the trailhead. Cross the Kanape Brook bridge following RED markers on what was formerly an Olive town road. The trail is rocky for much of the way to the Ashokan High Point (AHP)–Mombaccus Mt. col. It passes a number of camping areas, and follows or stays within sight of Kanape Brook for much of the distance to the col. The small waterfalls and wildflower-covered banks of Kanape Brook are enjoyable in spring-time and dogs will enjoy the stream and a number of its tributaries.

There are sections of conifers, but most of the hike is through wide-open oak, maple, and birch forest. The conifer plantations and

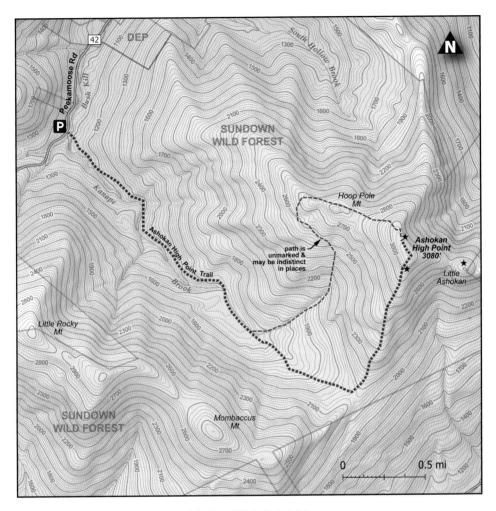

Ashokan High Point Map

hand-laid stone retaining walls through which the trail passes are the handiwork of the Civilian Conservation Corps from the 1930s. When ferns gain height in June, mountain laurel bejewels and perfumes the trail. The laurel is particularly prevalent from 1350 ft to 1600 ft.

   After 2.75 mi of gradual ascent, the trail reaches a grassy clearing, the 2060 ft AHP- Mombaccus col (N41° 54.757', W74° 17.663') where a sign points LEFT toward the summit. The climb up its SSW ridge begins gradually with intermittent steeper sections. Much of the trail is bordered by laurel. See if you can spot some of the American chestnut trees mingling with the ferns, wildflowers, and blueberries. The oaks seen in the col are shorter along the ridge and combined with the steep terrain you can look over their tops, allowing views of Mombaccus Mt. and Little Rocky.

As the ascent eases an open area provides your first views. There's a herd path (N41° 55.408', W74° 16.850') on the RIGHT that descends 400 ft to Little Ashokan. Its blueberry-laden, open summit offers a great view of the AHP summit and Ashokan Reservoir. Continuing on the trail, pass a pair of viewpoints, descending slightly to a large blueberry meadow created by old fires, said to have been set to increase the berry crop. It's an excellent place to bring out containers while savoring views of Cornell, Slide, Wittenberg, Rocky, Lone, Friday, and Balsam Cap. A short side path leads to a view of the reservoir.

If you're ready for more, continue to the back of the meadow where an unmarked path descends then climbs over Hoop Pole Mt., the name bestowed to commemorate the use of wooden barrel staves in an era when metal was hard to come by. The lesser-used Hoop Pole path has laurel and stunted oaks, and passes the wreckage of a plane crash on the way down to its intersection with the AHP trail. The beginning of the unmaintained path may be difficult to find and you should be comfortable with off-trail travel. Its intersection with the main trail is indistinct.

Balsam Lake Mt.

> HIGHLIGHTS AND SUMMARY: The trail follows a jeep road, offering spring wildflowers, autumn foliage, trailside water, and great views from the summit fire tower. There's an optional loop trail on the way back. With the high trailhead elevation, it's a relatively easy way to climb one of the premier Catskill High Peaks with a modest amount of effort.

MILEAGE: *6 mi r/t. 7 mi r/t loop.*

ELEVATION GAIN: *1140 ft. 1625 ft loop.*

DIFFICULTY: *3*

VIEW RATING: *4*

LEASH: *Not required but suggested at the summit.*

DOG SAFETY AND HAZARDS: *None.*

WATER: *Springs, small streams, and puddles.*

HIKER TRAFFIC: *Can be very busy, especially on weekends.*

TRAIL CONDITIONS: *Jeep road, rocky trail in places, a few muddy areas.*

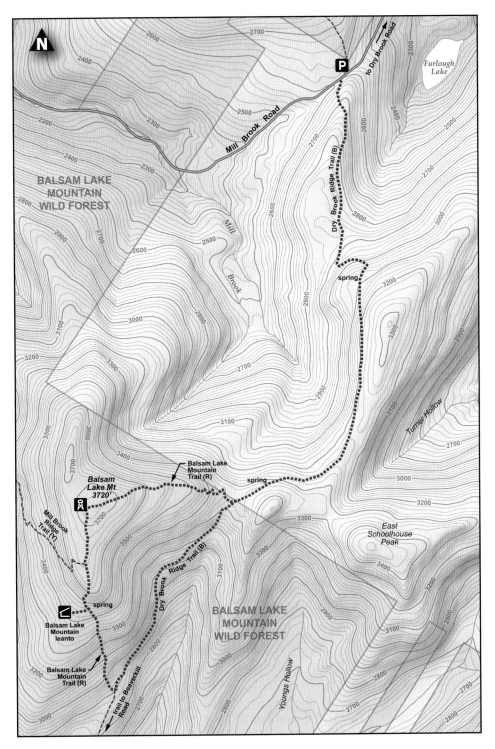

Balsam Lake Mt. Map

BEST TIME TO HIKE: *Spring and autumn. Midweek has less traffic. Great snowshoe hike.*

GETTING THERE: *Turn onto Dry Brook Rd. (N42° 08.797', W74° 37.414') from NY 28 in Arkville. Continue to Mill Brook Rd. (N42° 05.593', W74° 33.613'). The road gains 660 ft in 2.3 mi to the 2585 ft Dry Brook Ridge trailhead (N42° 04.220', W74° 34.426').*

Cross the road from the parking lot onto BLUE markers leading up the jeep road/trail on the other side. The road climbs steeply for the first 200 ft. Where the dense forest canopy opens, the road becomes grassy, lined with shrubs, ferns, and berry bushes. You reach the trail register at 0.35 mi. Beyond, the trail gains only an additional 300 ft in the next 0.5 mi.

There's a sharp uphill turn through a large patch of ferns at 1 mi. Dogs will find a spring a short distance ahead and another at 1.8 mi. There's little additional elevation gain until 2 mi as the trail passes alongside a section of rocks bands on one side, and large black cherry and birch trees mixed into the deciduous forest on the other. Look for a spring (N42° 02.826', W74° 34.633') coming out from a rock a short distance ahead.

You'll reach a trail junction (N42° 02.751', W74° 34.968') near 3330 ft, with the RED summit trail on the RIGHT. BLUE markers continue ahead toward the Beaverkill Rd. trailhead, offering an optional loop trail to or from the summit. Continuing on the RED summit trail, pass a metal gate beyond which the road becomes more trail-like and rockier, with switchbacks in the steep sections.

The sweet smell of balsam greets hikers in the final 0.25 mi. The lack of views from the 3720 ft wooded summit is more than made up for by the scenery from the 48 ft fire tower. Graham, Doubletop, East Schoolhouse, Beaver Kill Range, Woodpecker, Mill Brook, and Dry Brook Ridges are prominent. More distantly, countless summits circle the horizon.

For variety on the hike back to the trailhead, descend the RED trail down the mountain's S ridge. It's more lightly traveled, the first 0.3 mi losing a little more than 100 ft through wildflowers, ferns, birch, and black cherry trees. A very steep section follows to a reliable spring at 3450 ft and an intersection with the 0.15 mi spur trail to the Balsam Lake Mt. lean-to (N42° 02.378', W74° 35.779'). Below the spring, the trail descends a gradual 0.1 mi before dropping 550 ft in under 0.4 mi to a trail intersection at 2940 ft (N42° 02.100', W74° 35.555'). Trail signs point in two directions. Be certain to turn LEFT on BLUE markers.

Ferns on Millbrook Ridge, as described by John Burroughs.
—Joanne Hihn

This trail leads 0.9 mi with 460 ft of climbing to the intersection with the RED summit trail, and the route back your vehicle.

Belleayre Mt.

HIGHLIGHTS AND SUMMARY: The ski trails and access road offer out-in-the-open views that established hiking trails don't provide. Wildflowers, berry picking, and bird and animal sightings are a normal part of ski area hikes.

MILEAGE: *Overlook Lodge, 3.5 mi r/t. Base Lodge, 5.5 mi r/t.*

ELEVATION GAIN: *Overlook Lodge, 900 ft. Base Lodge, 1400 ft.*

DIFFICULTY: *2*

VIEW RATING: *4*

LEASH: *Not required.*

DOG SAFETY AND HAZARDS: *None.*

WATER: *Completely dry, carry water for dogs.*

HIKER TRAFFIC: *Almost nonexistent.*

TRAIL CONDITIONS: *Very good.*

BEST TIME TO HIKE: *Spring and autumn. No hiking on ski trails during winter.*

GETTING THERE: *Turn onto CR 49A (Galli Curci Rd.) from NY 28 (N42° 08.678', W74° 29.441') in Highmount. Pass the main entrance to Belleayre Ski Center, continuing uphill to a LEFT onto the Overlook Lodge Rd. (N42° 08.534', W74° 30.639') to lodge parking area.*

Though you can hike from the base lodge at the main entrance on Galli Curci Rd., a shorter trip for families and doghikers starts from

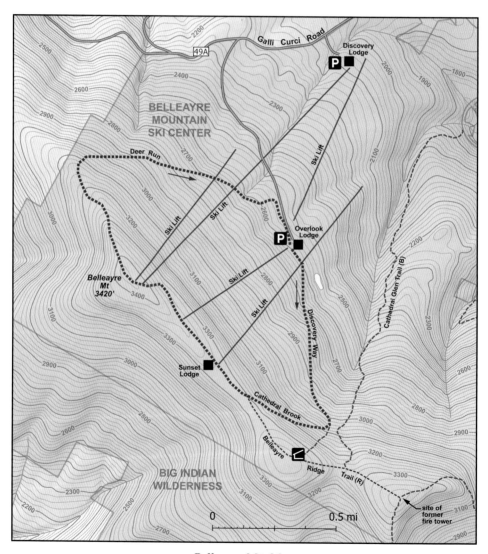

Belleayre Mt. Map

the 2500 ft Overlook Lodge located at the base of one of the ski lifts. The summit access road (Discovery Way and Cathedral Brook ski trails) begins uphill and LEFT of Overlook Lodge. In summer, this grass and dirt service road climbs Belleayre's E side.

You can hike any of the ski trails; they're more direct and steeper. Since they are designed to be used when covered by snow, they're often overgrown with grass and shrubs, and you may run into hay bales or low-lying branches. The ski trails are more difficult than the gently graded summit access road, which serves as an easy ski trail during winter. The service road is often out in the open, providing frequent N-facing views as well as having wildflowers and flowering shrubs nearby.

Look around as you climb. Deer and the occasional bear might have their young grazing on the slopes below. As the road (Discover Way Trail) ascends it becomes the Cathedral Brook Trail. As it reaches the ridgeline, it levels and turns NW, grassy and tree-lined, to become the Ridge Trail. Look for an opening in the trees a short distance ahead on the LEFT. If you turn LEFT here, there's a 0.8 mi trail that climbs over an intermediate bump, passes a lean-to, then continues to the viewless site of the former Belleayre fire tower. Other hiking trails converge here, but this is not the Belleayre high point.

Backtracking to where you reached the summit ridge, continue 0.8 mi NW to the open meadow and the small Sunset Lodge. It's located at the top of one of the chairlifts and not open after ski season. It's a good place for a break while you enjoy a pan-orama that includes Vly, Halcott, Rose, Sherrill, North Dome, and other mountains. The Ridge Trail doesn't cross the 3420 ft summit (N42° 07.719′, W74° 31.155′). To tag the top, go a few minutes up the grassy ridge, continuing until there's no higher point.

You can hike back to Overlook Lodge in a number of ways. Any one of the steep ski trails will give you an "elevator

Old friends.
—Barbara Via

ride" back down. A more enjoyable hike is to follow the Ridge Trail NW until it turns, descending, and becomes the Deer Run ski trail. The scenic, slightly roundabout trail is easy on the knees with views around every turn. Turn W at the base of another lift and follow a sign pointing to Overlook Lodge. The mountain is dry and hot for dogs. Carry water for them.

Bramley Mt.

HIGHLIGHTS AND SUMMARY: The hike loop combines a trail and woods road to the site of a former fire tower. Along the way, explore an old bluestone quarry and long sections of stone walls set in a beautiful forest. You'll love the raspberries and views along the SW ridge. In 2019, DEP and the Delhi town board approved the reinstallation of a fire tower on the summit. When built, it won't be a stretch to call Bramley Mt. the Queen of Delaware County.

MILEAGE: *3.9 mi r/t.*

ELEVATION GAIN: *875 ft.*

DIFFICULTY: *3*

VIEW RATING: *3*

LEASH: *Leashes required on DEP land.*

DOG SAFETY AND HAZARDS: *Porcupines. Big game hunting season.*

WATER: *Two streams along the Quarry Trail, otherwise dry.*

HIKER TRAFFIC: *Light, especially during the week.*

TRAIL CONDITIONS: *A little damp in places on the Quarry Trail, otherwise very good.*

BEST TIME TO HIKE: *Autumn foliage and berry seasons.*

GETTING THERE: *The trailhead is located NE of Delhi. Turn onto Glen Burnie Rd. at the intersection (N42° 18.461', W74° 50.578') with CR 18 for a steep, 500 ft of road in 0.8 mi to the trailhead (N42° 17.910', W74° 50.273'). For a safer winter alternative, drive N onto Glen Burnie Rd. from the intersection (N42° 15.461', W74° 51.711') with NY 28.*

You can hike Bramley by either the Quarry or Summit Trails. I recommend a loop, up the Quarry Trail and returning on the Summit Trail. The BLUE Quarry Trail begins on a woods road beyond the register

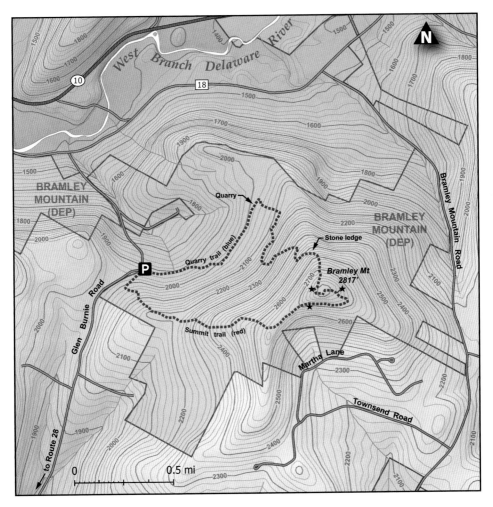

Bramley Mt. Map

and DEP metal gate at the rear of the trailhead. The trail is in good condition and easy to follow with a few wet places.

The trail traverses a deciduous forest and crosses two small streams. Remnant fruit trees and sugar maples may bring to mind the old farmstead that must have previously occupied the area. Ignore an overgrown woods road that intersects (N42° 18.148′, W74° 49.517′) the trail on the RIGHT. At 0.9 mi, pass through a former bluestone quarry where there may be water for dogs.

The road becomes a trail on the other side of the quarry. It begins with a gradual climb on Bramley's NW side for a short distance,

Catskill porky.
—Heather Rolland

then ascends more steeply. The trail switchbacks its way upward past stone walls through an open deciduous forest. It passes through a long stone ledge at 2380 ft that's worth the time to examine. Some of the ledges on this side of Bramley have small caves that porcupines occupy.

There's a gorgeous open area just under the wooded summit that has views of Mt. Pisgah and a sea of other Catskill 100 Highest summits. Bramley's 2817 ft top is encircled by a grassy path around the remains of the fire tower supports, where the new fire tower will be situated. A sign points 2.1 mi back to the trailhead along the BLUE Quarry Trail and 1.8 mi ahead on the RED Summit Trail.

There's another view on the RED trail E of the summit before the trail turns W then SW for a 0.2 mi stroll on a grassy portion of the trail. Courtesy of a destroyed forest canopy, this sunny section of trail is flanked by tall, sun-craving raspberry bushes that provide continual views over their tops that include Moon Mt., Scutt, and the Warren Range. Go during berry season and enjoy the vista while stuffing your face with ripe berries. The trail transitions from a grassy path to a woods road as it reenters the deciduous forest, descending Bramley's W ridge through a parade of stone fences and pole stands back to the trailhead.

Catskill Scenic Trail— Hobart to Bloomville

HIGHLIGHTS AND SUMMARY: The 26 mi Catskill Scenic Trail (CST) runs between Hubbell Corners (outside of Roxbury) and Bloomville. The old railbed is a wonderful place for hiking, skiing, trail running, or snowshoeing with dogs. There are lovely wooded sections, water crossings, corn field corridors, and almost continual views of the surrounding hills and mountains. This 9 mi segment can be done with a car spot, or as a long round-trip.

MILEAGE: *8.9 mi one way.*

ELEVATION GAIN: *-200 ft from Hobart to Bloomville.*

DIFFICULTY: *3*

VIEW RATING: *3*

LEASH: *Keep dogs leashed at road crossing and where the trail nears dwellings.*

DOG SAFETY AND HAZARDS: *Road crossings.*

WATER: *Streams, but the trail is exposed and dry in sections.*

HIKER TRAFFIC: *Very light.*

TRAIL CONDITIONS: *Excellent. Packed dirt, grass, or stone ballast.*

BEST TIME TO HIKE: *Spring or autumn.*

GETTING THERE: *For the Hobart trailhead: Turn onto Cornell Ave. (N42° 22.396', W74° 40.061') from NY 10 in Hobart, continuing 100 yd to the trailhead (N42° 22.360', W74° 39.989'). For the Bloomville trailhead: The Bloomville trailhead (N42° 19.910', W74° 48.185') is E of the village on the S side of NY 10.*

Dogs should be leashed in Hobart where the CST passes through backyards. Once beyond the village, other than passing through South Kortright, the CST is out in the country. At 1.1 mi from Hobart, the CST crosses CR 18. It crosses again a short distance ahead as it

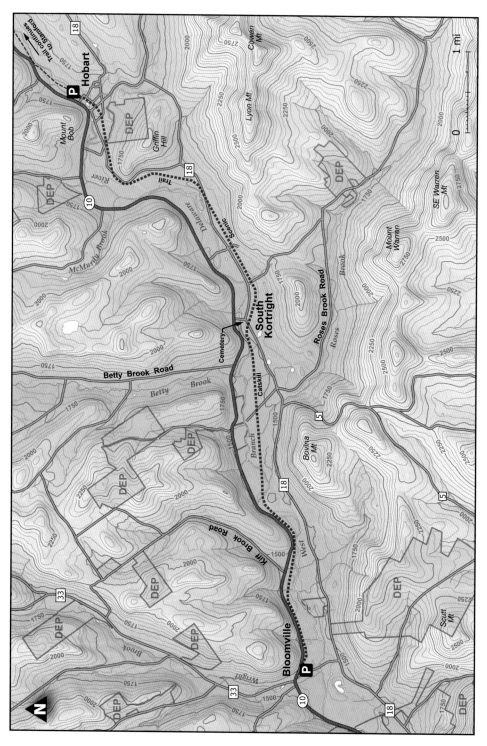

Catskill Scenic Trail Map—Hobart to Bloomville

passes the nose of Griffin Hill. The CST crosses a small tributary of the Delaware River's West Branch at 2.2 mi. After emerging from a wooded section, the trail again crosses CR 18 at 2.5 mi.

Passing Madison Hill Rd., you'll see an old church, stone buildings, and rock fences of South Kortright. Take a short detour to explore the historic graveyard N of the trail. Throughout these first few miles, scenery includes Cowan and Bovina Mts. and the Warren Range. Hiking W out of South Kortright, there's a bench overlooking the West Branch Delaware River that calls for a short break.

As you continue, the trail setting alternates between shady trees and open fields for much of the next 1.5 mi. The section through large cornfields is hot and dry on sunny days and has no water for dogs. At 5.75 mi, the CST parallels a section of Roses Brook (N42° 20.400', W74° 44.982'), the first reliable place since South Kortright where dogs can cool off and hydrate. At 6.25 mi, the trail crosses a 50 ft bridge where Roses Brook meets the Delaware River, the first of three bridges over deep, dog-friendly water in the last section toward Bloomville. The bridges have their original metal sides and supports with updated wooded decking and railings, which are impressive pieces of design. The 1465 ft trailhead in Bloomville isn't far ahead. Since the Hobart trailhead is at 1625 ft, other than some unnoticeable ups and downs, you've walked downhill along the trail!

Delhi Trails

HIGHLIGHTS AND SUMMARY: This trail system was designed and is maintained by the Catskill Mountain Club. Mix and match three trails, two of which are whimsically named after characters in *My Side of the Mountain* by Jean Craighead George, with the third named after the Delaware Academy Bulldogs. There are steep trails, and easier ones that include woods roads. This unexpected gem is outside of Delhi and It's not often you find as nice a hike as this so close to a small city.

MILEAGE: *3.1 mi r/t. Over 4 mi if you link them all.*

ELEVATION GAIN: *900 ft.*

DIFFICULTY: *3*

VIEW RATING: *2*

LEASH: *Leashes required on DEP land.*

DOG SAFETY AND HAZARDS: *None.*

WATER: *None.*

HIKER TRAFFIC: *Light.*

TRAIL CONDITIONS: *Woods roads and trails are in good condition.*

BEST TIME TO HIKE: *Spring or autumn.*

GETTING THERE: *The Sheldon Dr. trailhead (N42° 16.402', W74° 54.882') is adjacent to the Delaware Academy, located off of Delaware Ave. (CR18) at the Sheldon Drive Park. There's a second trailhead at the Lutheran church (N42° 16.023', W74° 54.970') on NY 28. You can spot a car or walk the easy 0.5 between trailheads.*

The Gribley Trail begins with a 200 yd walk through vegetation from Sheldon Dr. As it enters the forest, the trail joins a woods road that climbs a steep 600 ft to the ridge. The forest is wide open hardwoods with a profusion of spring flowers and sections of ferns. Hiking S along the ridge, there are filtered views. You can leave the trail (N42° 16.285', W74° 54.515') to the ridge's N high point for more views. This two minute off-trail detour has views W from an open forest and acres of ferns.

Back on the Gribley, it descends a short distance off the ridge to a viewpoint. Beyond is the 1860 ft intersection (N42° 16.099', W74° 54.519') with the Frightful's Falls Trail. You can descend Frightful's Falls, but Gribley begins climbing back to the ridge for a view of Delhi and the surrounding hills at 0.5 mi ahead. The Gribley Trail stays with the ridge, skirting the second high point, then descending to follow a power line with NW and SE views. Trail markers may be difficult to spot here, but simply follow the grassy path 0.1 mi down-hill under the power line to where the trail reenters the forest (N42° 15.574', W74° 55.018') at a YELLOW "Gribley Trail" arrow that points uphill.

Back in the woods, the trail descends steadily down the SW ridge amid acres of ferns as it skirts the top edge of a gorgeous section of hemlocks. It intersects (N42° 15.441', W74° 55.204') the Bulldog Run Trail at 1670 ft and, immediately ahead, an arrow points toward the continuation of Gribley and the Lutheran church trailhead. Gribley descends further, then turns N paralleling NY 28 for a short distance through a screen of trees before the trail climbs away from it.

Gribley intersects the other end of the Frightful's Falls Trail (N42°
15.878', W74° 54.893') where you can reclimb the ridge and hike back
to Sheldon Dr. or follow the end of Gribley to the Lutheran church
trailhead.

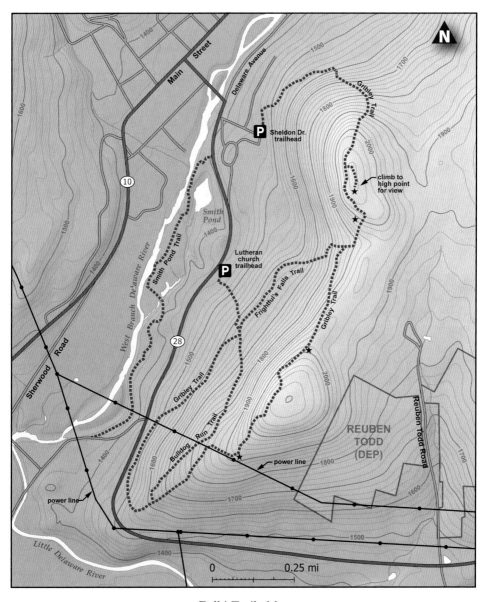

Delhi Trails Map

Cornell Crack.
—Joanne Hihn

Huckleberry Point

HIGHLIGHTS AND SUMMARY: The trailhead and the first half of the trail are shared with hikers heading to Kaaterskill High Peak (KHP). The spur trail to Huckleberry Point passes an untrailed peak by that name then descends to a clifftop referred to as Huckleberry Point. The trail passes a unique pitch pine forest and showy mountain laurel. Hell's Hole Brook is the only reliable dog water and may be difficult to cross after heavy rain. The views from the Huckleberry Point are spectacular.

MILEAGE: *4.5 mi r/t.*

ELEVATION GAIN: *1165 ft.*

DIFFICULTY: *3*

VIEW RATING: *4*

LEASH: *Not required.*

DOG SAFETY AND HAZARDS: *Large, busy trailhead and Huckleberry Point cliffs.*

WATER: *Hell's Hole Brook and seasonal water.*

Platte Clove—cascade and rocks.
—Katherine Varn Hawkins

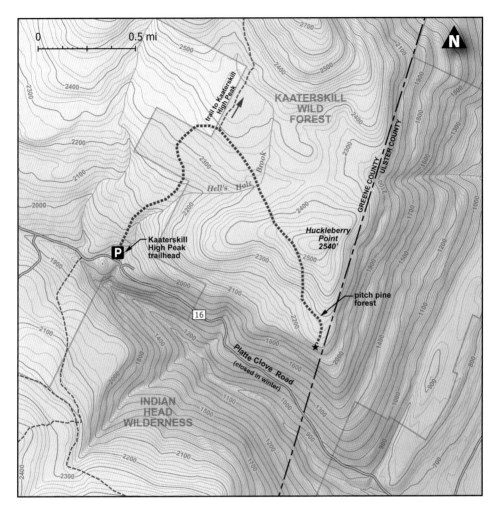

Huckleberry Point Map

HIKER TRAFFIC: *KHP portion of trail is busy, more so on weekends.*

TRAIL CONDITIONS: *The woods road is rocky, but the trail to Huckleberry Point is a typical trail.*

BEST TIME TO HIKE: *Autumn.*

GETTING THERE: *Drive E on CR 16 (N42° 11.494', W74° 10.043') from Tannersville to the 1900 ft trailhead (N42° 07.995', W75° 04.959') on Platte Clove Rd. Alternatively, from West Saugerties (N42° 06.763', W74° 02.843') on CR 33, which turns into spectacular and seasonally maintained Platte Clove Rd.*

The BLUE-marked KHP trail is shared with snowmobiles and is a woods road leading to both KHP and Huckleberry Point. Constructed by the Civilian Conservation Corps, the road is in good condition and climbs steadily. Bear RIGHT on YELLOW markers onto the Huckleberry Point trail at 2400 ft. The trail descends a gradual 100 ft over 0.35 mi to the only certain water source, Hell's Hole Brook. The stream becomes Plattekill Creek below the interestingly named Devil's Kitchen farther down the mountain.

It's an excellent place for a break while your favorite pooch swims, drinks, and cools off. Crossing can sometimes be a challenge after snowmelt or periods of heavy rain. The trail begins to ascend on the other side of the stream, climbing at an easy grade and passing through short ledges. While autumn is the best time for this hike, June is grand as the mountain laurel are at their most fragrant and showiest here.

Cross the trail's 2500 ft high point before descending 300 ft to the cliffs. On the way, look for an unmarked path on the LEFT near 2300 ft. It leads into a grove of short pitch pines, a remarkably small forest within a forest. Continue to descend another 100 ft on the trail to the spectacular Huckleberry Point cliffs. Dogs should be leashed for their safety and around other hikers. The Hudson River is visible from the precipice as are Overlook, Plattekill, Indian Head, Twin, and Plateau Mts. Massachusetts and Connecticut can be seen across Platte Clove. The close-up view of Plattekill Mt. is particularly impressive in autumn.

Hunter Mt.—Spruceton Trail

HIGHLIGHTS AND SUMMARY: At 4040 ft, Hunter Mt. is the second highest summit in the Catskills, and the Spruceton Trail is the nicest route for doghikers. The trail is a jeep road. It follows a stream and passes a high-elevation spring and a lean-to. The fire tower cab is open on weekends from Memorial Day through Columbus Day. Views from the tower are gorgeous and the alidade map in the tower cab was designed by Liz Cruz, map creator for *Doghiker*.

MILEAGE: *6.9 mi r/t.*

ELEVATION GAIN: *1940 ft.*

DIFFICULTY: *5*

VIEW RATING: *5*

LEASH: *At the trailhead, John Robb Lean-to, and on the summit.*

DOG SAFETY AND HAZARDS: *Busy trailhead and occasional horses along the trail.*

WATER: *Hunter Brook, spring, and seasonal water.*

HIKER TRAFFIC: *Busy, very busy on weekends.*

TRAIL CONDITIONS: *Excellent.*

BEST TIME TO HIKE: *Summer and autumn.*

GETTING THERE: *Turn onto Spruceton Rd. (CR 6) at the intersection (N42° 12.540′, W74° 23.309′) with NY 42 in Westkill. Follow CR 6 past side roads for almost 7 mi to the large 2090 ft trailhead (N42° 11.077′, W74° 16.337′).*

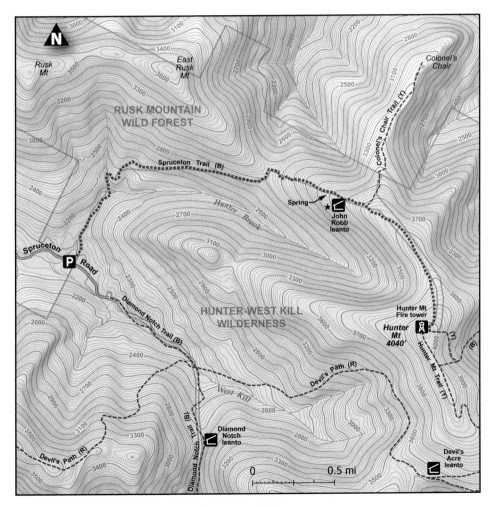

Hunter Mt. Map

Moochers—Bookah and Shiloh.
—Bill Chriswell

Follow BLUE markers along what was formerly the tower observer's jeep road. The road was originally constructed by the Civilian Conservation Corps for fire control. Hikers will occasionally share the trail with horses. The road slowly ascends through a deciduous forest along Hunter Brook for the first 0.5 mi, allowing dogs frequent opportunities for wading and hydration. Cross a wide foot bridge at a sharp turn at 0.7 mi (N42° 11.514′, W74° 16.065′) near where the Rusk Mt. herd path originates. The wide road surface gets steeper from here to the 2940 ft East Rusk–Hunter col (N42° 11.525′, W74° 14.910′), where a trail sign notes the remaining 1.7 mi and 1110 ft ascent to the summit of Hunter. For the next 0.75 mi, the trail grade again steepens, with switchbacks easing the effort.

The road was regraded and gravel added in 2014, which improved its already good surface above the col. The forest character changes here. Where beech, oak, and maple predominated below, the woodland is now mixed forest with occasional birches.

Turning around from time to time gets you views of East Rusk and Rusk Mts. At 3360 ft, a trail on the RIGHT leads to a spring, a usually reliable source of water. A little farther ahead on the RIGHT there's a short trail (N42° 11.367′, W74° 14.417′) to the relocated John Robb Lean-to. The views are among the best from any Catskill lean-to. It's worth the short detour, but leash dogs to avoid disturbing occupants.

At 3650 ft, the Colonel's Chair Trail intersects on the LEFT. It originates from the top of a ski lift; expect to see sightseers on the trail from here to the summit. The trail gradient eases significantly in the remaining distance but it is wet in places in all but the driest times of year.

The fire tower stands in a grassy clearing surrounded by trees. While there are no longer views from the ground, that's not the case from the tower. It's well situated in the NE Catskills with peaks in every direction. Weekends from Memorial Day through Labor Day will find volunteers staffing the tower. In addition to the mesmerizing views, be amazed at the gorgeous alidade map created by cartographer Liz Cruz, who designed the maps for this guidebook.

Huntersfield Mt.

HIGHLIGHTS AND SUMMARY: Seen from a distance, this large Catskill 100 Highest peak in northern Greene County resembles a giant starfish, with its ridges pointing in many directions. Located outside of the heart of the Catskills, it's mostly overlooked by hikers not familiar with its many attractions. At 2800 ft, the W ridge trailhead is the highest in the Catskills. Hike the loop to sample all the mountain has to offer.

MILEAGE: *4 mi r/t loop. 3.2 mi r/t W ridge.*

ELEVATION GAIN: *1000 ft loop. 675 ft W ridge.*

DIFFICULTY: *3*

VIEW RATING: *2*

LEASH: *Not required.*

DOG SAFETY AND HAZARDS: *None.*

WATER: *Only seasonal water for almost all of the hike.*

HIKER TRAFFIC: *Very light.*

TRAIL CONDITIONS: *Excellent.*

BEST TIME TO HIKE: *Spring or autumn.*

GETTING THERE: *Turn N onto Schrader Rd. (N42° 19.954', W74° 22.178') from CR 10 in West Settlement. Bear R in 0.15 mi onto Jim Cleveland Rd.*

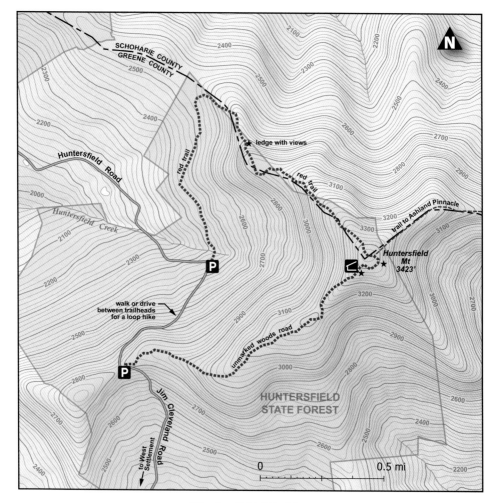

Huntersfield Mt. Map

Buckle your seatbelts for the steep drive up to the 2800 ft trailhead (N42°
20.948', W74° 21.925') You can also hike from the Huntersfield Rd. trailhead (N42° 21.323', W74° 21.534'). Jim Cleveland Rd. is steep, unmaintained in winter, and may be treacherous when other trailhead roads are
snow or ice free. The W ridge trail begins from a shale pit at the crest of the
ridge. You can hike an out-and-back to Huntersfield, do a loop, or spot a car
between trailheads. Note the 350+ ft elevation differential between them.

From the shale pit, follow an unmarked woods road along the ridge.
The road was constructed in order to ferry supplies for construction

Bookah and her posse.
—Joanne Hihn

of the lean-to. It's a little overgrown in sunny places during summer, easy to follow, but with no dog water. The surrounding forest is deciduous, with spring beauties, trout lilies, ferns, and summer flowers. The first trail markers appear near 3325 ft, leftovers from when a DEC trail intersected here. The lean-to is another 100 ft higher and has S-facing views of Patterson Ridge, East and West Cave, Bearpen, Vly, Rusk, Westkill, North Dome, and Sherrill.

There's another view a bit ahead where the trail makes the last, easy ascent to the summit, passing the intersection with the Ashland Pinnacle trail. "Pinnacle" would only describe its appearance from a distance as views from this wooded summit are scarce. Continue uphill on RED markers to Huntersfield's fern-blanketed top. There's a 1942 U.S. Geological Survey (USGS) benchmark set in a flat rock and a black cherry tree with a metal pole that may have once flown a flag.

To see more of the mountain, continue ahead 50 ft to RED markers that lead down the NW ridge to the Huntersfield Rd. trailhead. This section of trail sees light traffic, is well-marked, and coincides with the Long Path, marked with AQUA blazes. There are screened views from both sides of the ridge. Watch for an unmarked path near 2820 ft that leads to ledges with views of two reservoirs and Bearpen Mt. As the ridge descends it narrows, providing more peeks at the surrounding mountains. The forest does a makeover from deciduous to coniferous at 2670 ft. There are some striped maple and beech, but as the trail turns into a woods road the surrounding forest is a red pine plantation, the footing softened by conifer needles. It's shady and peaceful, the best location on the mountain to see or hear barred owls. In the last 0.25 mi to the Huntersfield Rd. trailhead, there's usually seasonal water, a treat for dogs after a long, dry day.

Cross Huntersfield Creek three minutes from the parking area. If you've left a car near the gate, you're spared the climb up Huntersfield Rd. to the upper trailhead.

Huyck Preserve

HIGHLIGHTS AND SUMMARY: With a visitor center, 12 mi of trails, and paddling on scenic Lake Myosotis, the botanical name for "forget-me-not," most of the hiker traffic is concentrated in the southern section of the preserve. The three interconnected Partridge Path loops are located in the remote northern section of the preserve. They are lightly visited and provide solitude for excellent hiking, snowshoeing, trail running, or cross-country skiing with your doghiker.

MILEAGE: *5.7 mi r/t all three loops.*

ELEVATION GAIN: *750 ft.*

DIFFICULTY: *3*

VIEW RATING: *2*

LEASH: *Required.*

DOG SAFETY AND HAZARDS: *None.*

WATER: *Trails intercept and parallel Ten Mile Creek and tributaries.*

HIKER TRAFFIC: *Very light.*

TRAIL CONDITIONS: *Excellent and well-maintained.*

BEST TIME TO HIKE: *Autumn is spectacular. Park on Peasley Rd. in winter.*

GETTING THERE: *Turn W onto Peasley Rd. from CR 6 (N42° 32.851′, W74° 08.876′) then S on Wood Rd. (N42° 33.039′, W74° 10.782′), past the old cemetery. Continue 0.2 mi to the 1800 ft trailhead (N42° 32.901′, W74° 10.754′). The kiosk is immediately beyond a culvert and marsh on the LEFT. Park on the side of the lightly traveled Wood Rd.*

The three Partridge Path loops resemble links of a chain. Begin hiking LEFT from the kiosk, clockwise, onto Loop 3, following the preserve's

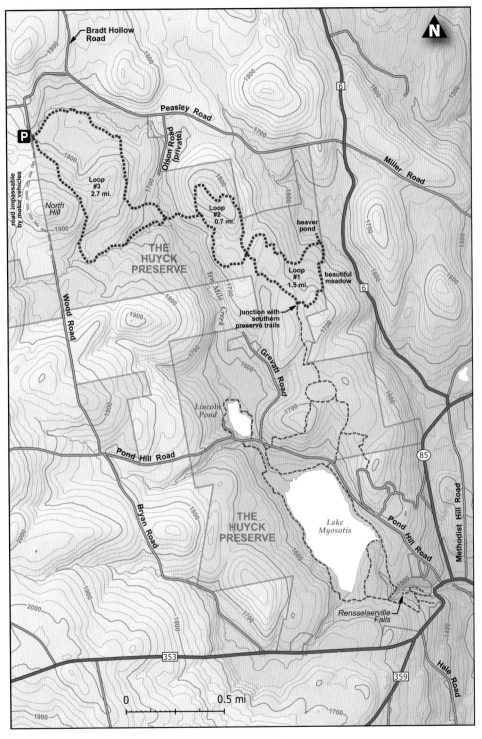

Huyck Preserve Map

large YELLOW and RED diamond markers. There're plentiful and easy to follow in any season on the well-designed and maintained trails. Hike through hemlocks and past stone fences along scenic Ten Mile Creek, which is photogenic, particularly at high water. You'll want to linger where the creek widens into a large waterfall-fed pool.

As the trail leads away from the stream, it turns S, passes a marsh, and crosses the NE ridge of North Hill. The trail takes you past a beaver pond and through a section of forest with large maples and crisscrossed by stone fences. At N42° 32.542', W74° 09.950', the trail reaches a junction at the easternmost part of Loop 3. You can return to the trailhead or cross Ten Mile Creek, following a 0.25 mi uphill spur to Loop 2.

Partridge Path Loop 2 is the shortest of the three loops. It passes through a mixed forest where sections of the trail are delightfully cushioned by conifer needles. Near N42° 32.518', W74° 09.489', you'll see one of the star attractions of the hike: long skeins of stone fences interlaced through a mature pole stand. The intersection with Loop 1 is a short distance beyond.

Turn LEFT onto Loop 1, descending 200 ft where gnawed tree stumps tip off the presence of a beaver pond visible from the trail. Continue ahead, following a stone fence alongside a large meadow, an excellent location for wildlife or autumn leaf-peeping at the surrounding hills. The trail starts to climb, attaining the high point of Loop 1 before descending to the intersection (N42° 32.160', W74° 09.169') of the 0.5 mi connector trail leading S toward Lake Myosotis. Head that way to add additional miles or explore the lake.

Otherwise, continuing N along the W sections of Loops 1, 2, and 3, look for an elderly white pine ahead. The photogenic, twin-trunked old-timer has seen better days and now presides over younger progeny. You're soon back to the intersection with Loop 2. Turn LEFT for an undulating 0.5 mi to the spur trail to Loop 3. A short, steep descent reaches Loop 3. Turn LEFT for more stone fences and another section of Ten Mile Creek on the way back to the trailhead.

Options in the Huyck Preserve are many. You can hike any or all of the loops, continue S toward more trails, or hike the loops in opposite directions.

Jennie Notch

HIGHLIGHTS AND SUMMARY: The jeep road/trail has wildflowers, a large beaver pond reflecting mountain views, a scenic stream flowing through a rocky ravine, and tall

Murphy.
—Bryan Robert

ledges just below the notch. You can extend the hike along the ridge on the Long Path.

MILEAGE: *2 mi r/t.*

ELEVATION GAIN: *400 ft.*

DIFFICULTY: *1*

VIEW RATING: *2*

LEASH: *Leashes required on DEP land.*

DOG SAFETY AND HAZARDS: *Active big game hunting area, avoid after mid-November.*

WATER: *Pond and a few streams.*

HIKER TRAFFIC: *Very light.*

TRAIL CONDITIONS: *Jeep road.*

BEST TIME TO HIKE: *Spring and early autumn, when you can see into the trailside forest.*

GETTING THERE: *Turn onto Old Rd. at the intersection (N42° 19.596', W74° 10.479') with NY 23. Turn onto Jennie Notch Rd. (N42° 19.224', W74° 11.252') and continue to the DEP parking area.*

Begin hiking from the 2050 ft DEP parking area. Walk around the gate following Long Path AQUA blazes on the hard-packed jeep road that gets grassy in summer. When leaves are on trees, portions of the road will make you feel as if you're hiking through a green tunnel. Be

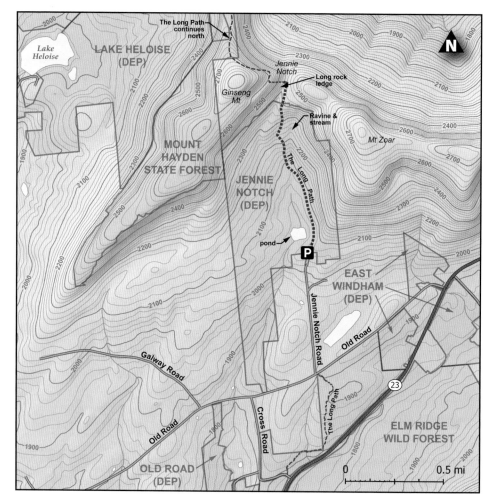

Jennie Notch Map

certain to visit the large pond two minutes from the parking area on the LEFT. Walk downhill through the woods where you'll be greeted by the reflection of Jennie Notch and Ginseng Mt. in its still surface. The area around the pond is a good place for birding and seeing wildlife. Your dog can drink and swim while you enjoy the views.

The trail to Jennie Notch has spring wildflowers, areas of summer ferns, and berry bushes in sunny sections. It's a gorgeous hike in autumn, with leaves afire before the hunting season begins. Dogs will find water in the trailside ditches and small streams. There's a larger stream midway to the notch that passes under the road through a large culvert.

The forest on both sides of the road is mostly hidden during summer, but when the trees are bare, you're treated to stone walls climbing the slopes, areas of rocky ledges, and a mixed forest that includes sections of hemlock. Don't miss the rocky ravine off the trail on the RIGHT near 2180 ft. A stream flows through a small gorge, another place for dogs to cool off and get a drink.

Just before the notch there's a long section of 25 ft tall ledges on the LEFT. Some scattered stone near the trail gives the impression that a quarry might have operated there at one time. The Long Path turns W from Jennie Notch, climbing steeply over Ginseng Mt.'s E ridge. See the Lake Heloise trip description for details about the trail between Jennie Notch and Barlow Notch. Part of the trail between the two gets a little "shaggy" in midsummer.

Kelly Hollow

HIGHLIGHTS AND SUMMARY: There are almost too many Kelly Hollow "gotta-sees" to adequately summarize. Hikers will enjoy the nice trails, large variety of flora, and old beaver pond with an adjacent lean-to. There is a spectacular Norway spruce plantation, "hemlock heaven," giant ash trees, and a forest laced with streams and stone fences.

MILEAGE: *4 mi r/t.*

ELEVATION GAIN: *500 ft.*

DIFFICULTY: *2*

VIEW RATING: *2*

LEASH: *Not required.*

DOG SAFETY AND HAZARDS: *None.*

WATER: *Throughout the hike.*

HIKER TRAFFIC: *Usually light.*

TRAIL CONDITIONS: *Excellent.*

BEST TIME TO HIKE: *Spring and autumn.*

GETTING THERE: *Turn onto Dry Brook Rd. (N42° 08.797', W74° 37.414') from NY 28 in Arkville, then onto Mill Brook Rd. (N42° 05.593', W74°*

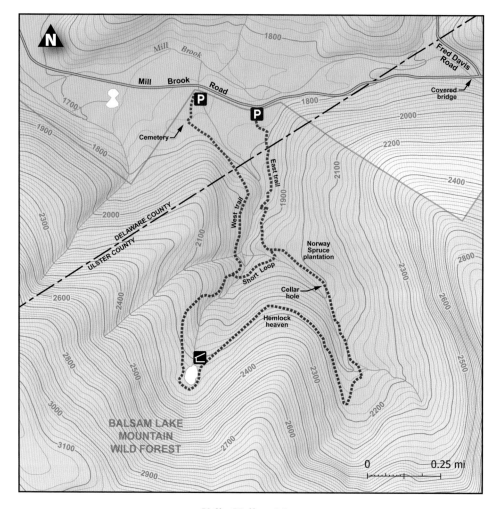

Kelly Hollow Map

33.613'). Follow Mill Brook Rd. 8 mi to the E trailhead (N42° 04.740', W74° 39.044') driveway.

The trail system is a Y-shaped loop with a short, middle connector. The E trail begins on a woods road at 1780 ft on YELLOW cross-country ski markers. Follow the markers through a mixed forest on a path softened by conifer needles. Pass a stream just beyond the trailhead. The trail is bordered by a stone wall and is ideal terrain for snowshoeing or cross-country skiing.

    There's a hemlock-shaded stream at 0.3 mi that has small

Are we there yet? Sheridan Mt.
—Alan Via

waterfalls. The trail continues gradually ascending, reaching an intersection with the "Short Loop." This 0.25 mi trail connects the E and
W trails, crossing one of the most photogenic locations on the hike,
a wooden bridge with stone supports on each end. There's another
bridge a short distance ahead on the Short Loop. In a few minutes,
the trail intersects the W side of the hollow.

Returning to the E trail, the leisurely ascent resumes through a
1930s Norway spruce plantation courtesy of the Civilian Conservation
Corps (CCC). A friend described this section of trail as "fern-lined
and moss-paved." Kelly Hollow must support a large population of
red squirrels. The tall piles of pine seed shells in the plantation cer-
tainly lead you to that conclusion. Look for a bluestone cellar foundation 30 ft off the trail at N42° 04.223', W74° 38.790' and, immediately
ahead, another stream crossing.

There are screened views of Dry Brook Ridge in an area with
huge ash trees on the upper E trail. As you hike along the top of the
"Y" that connects the E and W trails, there's a hemlock forest (N42°
04.145', W74° 39.027') I think of as "hemlock heaven," emblematic of
this gorgeous but threatened tree. The Kelly Hollow lean-to is ahead,

a good place for a break, adjacent to a pond constructed by the CCC at the top of the W trail. The trail loops around the pond, which is situated in the middle of a grown-over meadow and was once a home for a beaver colony. Flower sprays, flowering shrubs, and autumn foliage make this one of the most scenic locales in the hollow from early September through mid-October.

Sunny and grassy, the trail is overgrown where it circles the pond then it reassumes its shady character where it reenters the forest at the top of the W trail. The W trail is mostly deciduous with sections of hemlock along the ravine that the trail follows for much of the way. From the pond to the W parking area, the trail is a little steeper than on the E side, but still very gradual. At 1920 ft, the trail crosses a bridge (N42° 04.311', W74° 39.140') over a stream that feeds the main Kelly Hollow brook, one of many other areas for dogs to hydrate along the trail. The W parking area (N42° 04.799', W74° 39.283') has a stone fence and a nearby old cemetery and completes the loop for this extraordinary hike.

Lake Heloise to Jennie Notch

HIGHLIGHTS AND SUMMARY: There's lots to see in this lightly hiked area: old roads, a quarry, the Long Path, a high meadow, and a string of beaver ponds. It's a great hike with dogs.

MILEAGE: *5.5 mi r/t.*

ELEVATION GAIN: *1250 ft.*

DIFFICULTY: *3*

VIEW RATING: *2*

LEASH: *Leashes required on DEP land.*

DOG SAFETY AND HAZARDS: *Active deer hunting area.*

WATER: *Small stream near beginning, on side trail past beaver ponds, and near Barlow Notch. Otherwise dry.*

HIKER TRAFFIC: *Very light.*

TRAIL CONDITIONS: *Easily followed woods roads. No trail markers other than along the Long Path.*

BEST TIME TO HIKE: *Spring through early November.*

GETTING THERE: *Turn onto Old Rd. (N42° 18.543', W74° 13.989') from*

NY 23, E of Windham. Bear LEFT onto Nauvoo Rd. in 0.25 mi. Continue 2.25 mi, bearing LEFT at a fork with a "Dead End" sign, to the parking area (N42° 20.487', W74° 13.109').

Begin hiking from the 2000 ft parking area on the LEFT of a pair of dirt roads. Go through a gate. The road follows a small stream for a short distance, and in 0.3 mi intersects a road (N42° 20.758', W74° 13.125') on the LEFT. This side road is 1.4 mi r/t and leads over rolling terrain under Mt. Hayden's SSW ridge, passing a necklace of beaver ponds and ending at a private property gate. Returning to the trail,

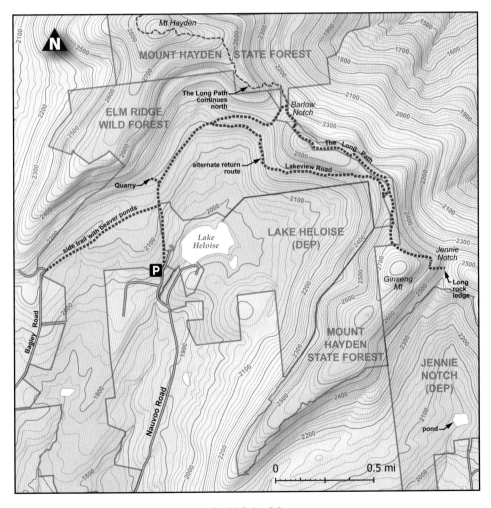

Lake Heloise Map

turn LEFT, passing a short path to a small quarry (N42° 20.857', W74° 13.122') at 0.45 mi.

The trail to Barlow Notch continues, a very gradual uphill through hardwoods and multiple stone walls. It gains little elevation, generally following the contour along the SE side of Mt. Hayden. There are screened views of Ginseng, Cave, and West Cave Mts., and an obstructed look at Lake Heloise. You won't see trail markers until reaching the notch, but the road is easy to follow. Note a key intersection (N42° 21.112', W74° 12.795') at 2200 ft, with Lakeview Rd. This is actually another woods road, an excellent route to or from Jennie Notch.

Just before Barlow Notch, there's a wet section where a stream runs over the road and dogs can cool off and hydrate. The road reaches 2300 ft Barlow Notch (N42° 21.174', W74° 12.390') at 1.5 mi where the Long Path crosses. Barlow Notch is mostly unremarkable but has NE and SW tree-filtered views. Turn RIGHT toward Jennie Notch on AQUA markers. The trail switchbacks, climbing 225 ft up "What Hump?," the 2560 ft grass and sedge meadow with SW views of Cave and West Cave Mts. across Lake Heloise.

The Long Path meanders SE along the ridge before a short descent, followed by a climb up Ginseng Mt.'s N ridge, bypassing the viewless summit. The first 100 ft of descent to Jennie Notch is moderate, but then it's steep the rest of the way. You can reverse your route back to Lake Heloise or bypass it. To intercept Lakeview Rd., leave the Long Path near 2550 ft on Ginseng's N ridge, walking 75 yd W through the woods to intercept it. Lakeview Rd. is in good condition and a gradual downhill through a deciduous forest. The compensation for leaving the Long Path is a section of spectacular ledges that the road passes before meeting the Lake Heloise trail S of Barlow Notch.

Leonard Hill

HIGHLIGHTS AND SUMMARY: The trail is a jeep road through an interesting and changing forest with a variety of flora. Although the decommissioned fire tower is inaccessible, there are views of the northern Catskills from a ledge immediately before the summit clearing. In winter, Leonard Hill is a terrific ski or snowshoe with dogs from the unmaintained section of Leonard Mt. Rd. There are plans to restore the fire tower in the future.

MILEAGE: *3.4 mi r/t. Additional 2.3 mi r/t in winter.*

ELEVATION GAIN: *545 ft. Additional 200 ft winter.*

DIFFICULTY: *2*

VIEW RATING: *2*

LEASH: *Not required.*

DOG SAFETY AND HAZARDS: *Avoid during big game season.*

WATER: *Small stream near trailhead, otherwise seasonal water. Carry extra water.*

HIKER TRAFFIC: *Very light.*

TRAIL CONDITIONS: *Excellent hard-packed jeep road.*

BEST TIME TO HIKE: *Spring or autumn. Excellent snowshoe or cross-country ski.*

GETTING THERE: *Leonard Mt. Rd. is located 0.1 mi E of the intersection (N42° 27.789', W74° 21.077') of CR 17 and CR 61 in Broome Center. Drive 1.35 mi to the trailhead (N42° 27.148', W74° 19.896'). Leonard Mt. Rd. is unmaintained in winter beyond the residences near its beginning.*

Begin hiking at the 2230 ft parking area adjacent to the Leonard Hill State Forest sign. The trail is a jeep road that was originally constructed for tower maintenance. It starts with a gradual uphill through a mixed forest, alternatively sunny or shady. Other than a small stream near the beginning, the only reliable dog water is puddles or seasonally wet areas.

Hiking the road is a treat. There are seasonal wildflowers, an interesting variety of bushes and shrubs, and summer ferns. It's as quiet and peaceful a trail as you've ever hiked. With the light hiker traffic, you shouldn't be surprised by the appearance of birds and animals on this sparsely traveled road. It gets a little steeper as it approaches the ridgeline (N42° 26.813', W74° 20.371') at 2500 ft, where Northwest Hubbard Hill blocks views of Leonard Hill.

Along the ridge, the road gains a paltry 75 ft, then gives back the elevation as it passes around the side of Northwest Hubbard Hill. As you hike past a photogenic red pine plantation, see if you can glimpse Leonard Hill's tower cab through an opening in the treetops.

Just before reaching the tower clearing there's a ledge on the RIGHT. It provides a sweeping view that takes in two reservoirs, Utsayantha, Moresville Range, Irish, and smaller mountains and hills. Though you can't climb the tower, walk into the woods near

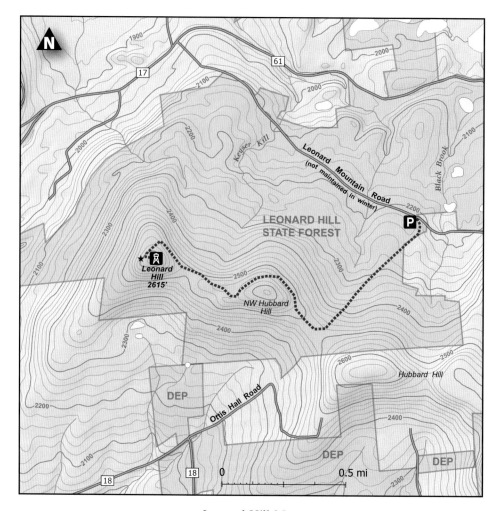

Leonard Hill Map

its base for views of Windham High Peak and the Blackhead Range, imagining what you could see were the tower to be restored someday. It would offer a completely unique perspective on the northern Catskills.

As you return to your vehicle, consider a short bushwhack to Northwest Hubbard Hill. Leave the road where the trail passes a large ledge and whack through open forest and red pines to a peek-a-boo view of the Leonard tower. There's a photogenic section of white birch screening views on Northwest Hubbard's SW side.

Overlook Mt.

HIGHLIGHTS AND SUMMARY: Spectacular views, American chestnut tree remnants, showy mountain laurel, the spooky remains of an old hotel, and unequaled people watching. What more could you want? Hike the old carriage road to this fire tower summit. Afraid of heights? Enjoy four-state views from a rocky ledge for which the mountain is named. This is timber rattlesnake habitat. Hike in cold weather or keep dogs on a close leash at all times. Stay on the woods road/trail and you'll never get close to one.

MILEAGE: *5 mi r/t.*

ELEVATION GAIN: *1400 ft.*

DIFFICULTY: *3*

VIEW RATING: *5*

LEASH: *Strongly suggested around hikers, dogs, hotel ruins, or on summit. Keep dogs leashed on the trail if they tend to wander away from your side.*

DOG SAFETY AND HAZARDS: *Very busy parking lot, precipitous cliff, and timber rattlers.*

WATER: *Seasonal brooks dry up.*

HIKER TRAFFIC: *Very busy, extremely busy on weekends and holidays.*

TRAIL CONDITIONS: *Rocky woods road, but dry.*

BEST TIME TO HIKE: *Late autumn through March. Great winter hike.*

GETTING THERE: *The main trailhead (N42° 04.264', W74° 07.351') is located at the height of land on Meads Mt. Rd. outside Woodstock. Overflow parking area for thirty cars is 0.25 mi beyond, on MacDaniel Rd. Arrive early for parking spot at Meads. Roadside parking is discouraged by ticketing.*

Begin hiking from the Meads trailhead on the other side of a gate where the 0.5 mi trail from the MacDaniel Rd. trailhead intersects. Hike a woods jeep road/trail on a steady uphill, gaining 800 ft in the first 1 mi. The few small brooks usually dry up. There's no other water for dogs on the mountain.

Observant hikers can spot one of the American chestnut tree remnants along the road, their leaves looking like elongated beech leaves. Look closely at the scratched wood on the poles bordering the trail. Bears use them as territorial markers, and hikers can find fur under

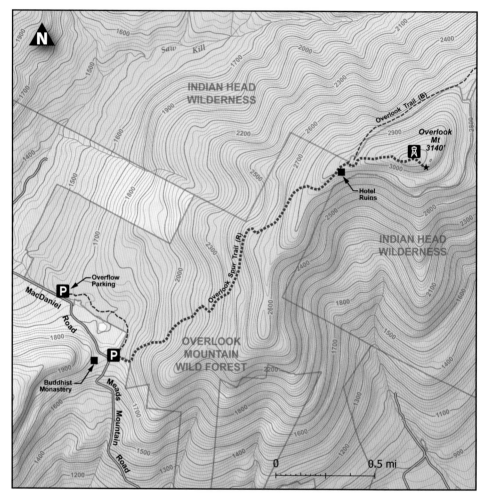

Overlook Mt. Map

the slivers. Fragrant white and pink mountain laurel line sections of the trail in June, turning it into a woodland florist shop.

The gradient eases above 2550 ft, with views appearing through the trees on the RIGHT side of the road. Following herd paths to them is discouraged for the safety of dogs after rattlesnakes have emerged from their winter dens. At 2900 ft, the road reaches the iconic and sometimes spooky-looking ruins of the old Overlook Hotel, its skeletal ruins a sight in any season.

The concrete walls are photogenic in winter, gorgeous when surrounded by fall foliage, and eerie when tendrils of fog partially hide the windowless walls and stone staircases leading nowhere. Take

Nancy and Denali—Overlook Mt. summit.
—Alan Via

a moment to imagine when carriages dropped off passengers who walked up the stone steps past the circular fountain. Back to modernity, there's a cell phone antenna and infrastructure a little ahead on the trail.

The road meets a trail sign and gate an easy 0.5 mi before the summit. Bear RIGHT as a LEFT takes you to Echo Lake and Platte Clove. You can see the fire tower as you approach the summit. Avoid a herd path through the summit ledges that saves three extra minutes of hiking.

Climb the tower for the stupendous views but be certain to take the 0.1 mi stroll along the trail that leads to the rocky overlook for which the mountain was named. On a clear day, enjoy views of the Hudson River, Shawangunks, Massachusetts, Connecticut, Vermont, and the southern Adirondacks. Tower stewards open the summit cabin and fire tower cab on weekends and holidays from Memorial Day to Labor Day.

Although shy and retiring, timber rattlesnakes can be a hazard to unleashed doghikers that venture into trailside rocks and vegetation. For their protection, keep dogs leashed at all times or visit Overlook during colder weather months when dogs aren't at risk. Carry extra water for dogs.

It's over there—the overlook on Overlook Mt.
—Neal Hirsch

Duke and Jenna—Overlook Mt.
—Juliet Lofaro

Pakatakan Mt.

HIGHLIGHTS AND SUMMARY: Hovering over Margaretville, Pakatakan Mt. is a great hike with dogs up the Dry Brook Ridge Trail. You'll likely have the trail to yourself and there's the option to lengthen the day by continuing to the summit of Dry Brook Ridge. You can hike to the trailhead from the heart of Margaretville.

MILEAGE: *3.5 mi r/t.*

ELEVATION GAIN: *1100 ft.*

DIFFICULTY: *3*

VIEW RATING: *2*

LEASH: *Not required other than near road.*

DOG SAFETY AND HAZARDS: *Traffic at trailhead and municipal parking lot.*

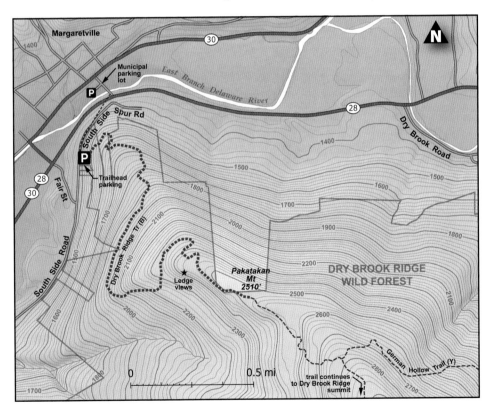

Pakatakan Mt. Map

WATER: *Seasonal spring, no other water.*

HIKER TRAFFIC: *Very light.*

TRAIL CONDITIONS: *Good.*

BEST TIME TO HIKE: *Great hike in foliage season.*

GETTING THERE: *The 1400 ft trailhead (N42° 08.657', W74° 38.959') is located on South Side Spur Rd. outside of Margaretville. See the end of the hike description for starting the hike from Margaretville municipal parking lot.*

Begin hiking up a logging road from the DEC trailhead on BLUE markers. There's little time to warm up as it's a steady 600 ft of ascent in the first 0.6 mi. Hikers can catch a breather where the trail levels for 0.25 mi near 1940 ft, before it resumes a steady switchbacking climb toward the Pakatakan's NW ridge. The lack of conifer in the surrounding forest means hikers can more easily keep their dogs in sight in the open deciduous forest. It also allows for a better look at the many sandstone ledges, profusion of wildflowers, and occasional fern patches.

The blowdown gang—Linda and Rob complete the Catskill 100 on Richmond Mt.
—Alan Via

Pakatakan Mt. is a named point on Dry Brook Ridge. Although not a standalone peak, this doesn't diminish its excellence as a trip for doghikers. Views are scarce, so be on the lookout for a herd path (N42° 08.291', W74° 38.430') at 1.6 mi on the S side of the trail near 2440 ft. The 0.15 mi path leads to an open ledge with views of the surrounding hills, mountains, and Pepacton Reservoir.

The "top" (N42° 08.194', W74° 38.324') of Pakatakan is around 1.75 mi near 2500 ft. The term "around" is proper as there is no sign or cairn to mark its location. You'll know you're there when you reach a long flat section of trail before it resumes ascending. For the ambitious, the hike can be extended to the summit of Dry Brook Ridge, a Catskill 100 Highest peak, 2.3 mi farther up the ridge.

Pakatakan hikes can also start from the municipal parking lot (N42° 08.854', W74° 38.825') on Bridge St. in Margaretville. Walk out of the back of the lot and cross the Delaware River bridge to a grassy trail 50 ft away on the other side of NY 28. Follow the unmarked path up to South Side Spur Rd. and walk a few minutes to the trailhead. This adds 0.25 mi and 100 ft of ascent to the official trailhead. Isn't it nice to have your car waiting near restaurants and stores at the end of a hike? Pakatakan is a dry trail, so be certain to carry water for your dog.

Palmer Hill

HIGHLIGHTS AND SUMMARY: Hike, snowshoe, or cross-country ski with dogs on trails creatively designed by the Catskill Mountain Club on DEP land. The hike takes you in and out of meadows bordered by stone fences, wildflowers, and berry bushes. Old trees, some of them past the two-century mark, are scattered through the area. The views are almost continual, and the forest and meadows are a birder's delight. Bring water, since there is only one reliable water source.

MILEAGE: *3.7 mi r/t all trails.*

ELEVATION GAIN: *600 ft.*

DIFFICULTY: *2*

VIEW RATING: *2*

LEASH: *Leashes required on DEP land.*

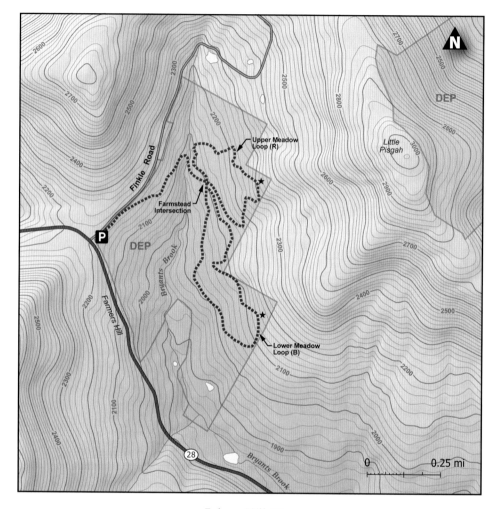

Palmer Hill Map

DOG SAFETY AND HAZARDS: *None.*

WATER: *A brook in the first part of the hike and seasonal wet areas.*

HIKER TRAFFIC: *Light.*

TRAIL CONDITIONS: *Excellent.*

BEST TIME TO HIKE: *Spring or autumn.*

GETTING THERE: *Turn off of NY 28 onto Finkle Rd. (N42° 11.704′, W74° 44.649′) between Margaretville and Andes. The Scenic Overlook trailhead is located within sight of NY 28. There's a large, interpretive plaque with peak names at the trailhead.*

BLUE markers lead downhill 0.1 mi through a meadow to the trail register. Continue descending through a line of trees to another meadow, then turn RIGHT at 0.35 mi onto an old farm road through a deciduous forest. Turn RIGHT over Bryant's Brook, the only reliable water for dogs on the hike. The trail emerges into another meadow, passing old homestead foundations, the site of the farm that formerly occupied the property. Poke around off the trail; lilacs, daylilies, and other domestic flowers are reminders of when the farm flourished.

An intricately laid stone barn bridge and what's left of the stone cow lane that directed cow traffic are all that remain of the old barn. The Farmstead Intersection (N42° 11.8567′, W74° 44.189′) is immediately ahead at 0.6 mi. Turn LEFT on RED markers for the 1 mi Upper Meadow Trail or RIGHT on BLUE markers for the 1.5 mi Lower Meadow Trail. Each loop returns to this intersection.

The Upper Meadow Trail enters a hardwood forest with old sugar maples and a seep whose moisture allows a large variety of plants and wildflowers to flourish. There's an interesting old stone wall with vertical coping stones set on top. This was designed to keep sheep from walking on the wall. The trail turns LEFT and uphill and passes a fern glade where thrushes serenade in springtime. Look for more sugar maples as the Upper Meadow Trail turns RIGHT, dips, then resumes ascending. It again enters a meadow at the loop's 2325 ft NE corner with views to the trailhead and the hills beyond. From the high point, begin descending through a meadow on a mowed trail, arriving at a large, flat rock, the perfect place for a break to contemplate the beautiful setting. The trail continues downhill, switchbacking to maximize views. Hawthorns are plentiful along the trail here, as is milkweed, a mainstay for monarch butterflies.

Continue downhill to the trail intersection and the beginning of the Lower Meadow Trail. Bear LEFT, descending as you hike through another meadow, and entering woods where the trail has you rock-hopping through a wet area. Continue ahead through a series of alternating woods and meadows, following a stone fence around the perimeter of the forest as the trail climbs. The trail turns LEFT through a stone fence, passing across a meadow with spring and summer wildflowers. Cross a woods line and turn LEFT to a large rock at 2160 ft, the highest point on the Lower Meadow Trail and another place to soak up the beautiful views. The trail alternates through more woods and meadows for 0.5 mi before arriving at the Farmstead intersection.

Mt. Pisgah

HIGHLIGHTS AND SUMMARY: A hidden treasure in the northern Catskills, with access roads that don't show on most other maps. Take an optional side trip to Northeast Richmond Mt., explore the site of the old Mt. Pisgah summit hotel, and follow the old hotel carriage road. Some of the old roads and trails in the area follow routes used by Native American Mohawks to pass through the mountains. See and hear barred owls in April.

MILEAGE: *3.5 mi r/t. 2.5 mi with car spot.*

ELEVATION GAIN: *950 ft r/t. 600 ft from Mt. Pisgah trailhead with car spot.*

DIFFICULTY: *3*

VIEW RATING: *2*

LEASH: *Not required.*

DOG SAFETY AND HAZARDS: *None.*

WATER: *Puddles and seasonal water. Carry water for dogs.*

HIKER TRAFFIC: *Extremely light.*

TRAIL CONDITIONS: *Generally dry, a few overgrown sections in summer.*

BEST TIME TO HIKE: *Spring and autumn.*

GETTING THERE: *Turn onto Mt. Pisgah Rd. (N42° 21.883', W74° 14.846') from CR 10. Continue 0.35 mi, turning RIGHT off of Mt Pisgah Rd. onto an unmarked service road (N42° 22.176', W74° 15.004'). The service road is hard-packed dirt and drivable, then becomes grassy and crowned farther ahead. Pull over to leave a vehicle or begin hiking where the service road intersects the carriage road (N42° 22.467', W74° 15.024') that leads to the Mt. Pisgah summit. For the 2740 ft Mt. Pisgah trailhead (N42° 22.408', W74° 15.779'), continue driving ahead on the service road almost 1 mi to a grassy circle. The roads are unmaintained in winter and lightly maintained the rest of the year.*

Follow YELLOW markers onto a woods road from the rear of the Mt. Pisgah trailhead. The road through the deciduous forest is sparingly marked and gets a little "shaggy," but it's easy to follow. Near 2820 ft, YELLOW markers lead RIGHT at a sharp uphill turn (N42° 22.332', W74° 15.887'), then LEFT 100 ft higher. Ignore another woods road that intersects straight ahead, continuing on YELLOW to the 2950 ft Northeast Richmond–Richtmyer col (N42° 22.488′, W74° 15.910′), where the trail intersects the Long Path's AQUA blazes.

You can take a short detour to the viewpoint on Richmond Mt.'s NE summit by turning LEFT in the col. It's an easy 170 ft ascent in 0.25 mi to 3120 ft Northeast Richmond, where an unmarked path leads to a S-facing ledge (N42° 22.320′, W74° 16.062′) with view of the Blackheads, Kaaterskill High Peak, Roundtop, Cave, West Cave, and part of the Devil's Path. The views are better when the trees are bare. You can continue SSW along the Long Path to where it leaves the ridge for a short bushwhack through deciduous forest to the summit of one of the Catskill 100 Highest, Richmond Mt.

Backtracking, follow the AQUA blazes from Northeast Richmond over the unnoticeable and viewless Richtmyer Peak where old stumps may have you wondering why loggers spared the larger hardwoods. The Long Path descends the E ridge, skirting private land in the Richtmyer-Pisgah col. Look for red columbine in late May where the trail passes a ledge.

Following the property line, the Long Path climbs steadily toward Pisgah, the forest transitioning from deciduous to widely spaced red pines and other conifers along a delightful section of soft trail cushioned by conifer needles. As the Long Path crosses from Schoharie to Greene County at 2880 ft, it passes what appears to be a neatly laid, short stone fence. It's actually the foundation of the summit hotel. *Beer's History of Greene County* notes that in 1880-1881, "a winding road nearly a mile in length made the peak accessible to carriages." By 1883, thirty-five hundred visitors and six hundred carriages had visited the completely cleared summit. The top is now forested. A benchmark sits in a small clearing 50 yd ahead where the Long Path turns LEFT and descends E.

Our route turns RIGHT, departing the Long Path, onto the unmarked old carriage road. The trail passes a rock-lined depression called Cold Spring on the LEFT in 75 ft. After a dowser was consulted, the spring was created by dynamite. It once served as the water supply for the hotel's guests and horses. Inscribed Rock is located opposite, on the other side of the carriage road. See if you can find the oldest initials and dates carved into the sandstone. Although the hotel burned down ten years after it was constructed, there are initials from decades later, after a large camp was built to accommodate guests.

There are no trail markers as you descend the carriage road trail. When trees are bare see if you can find the horse-racing track that

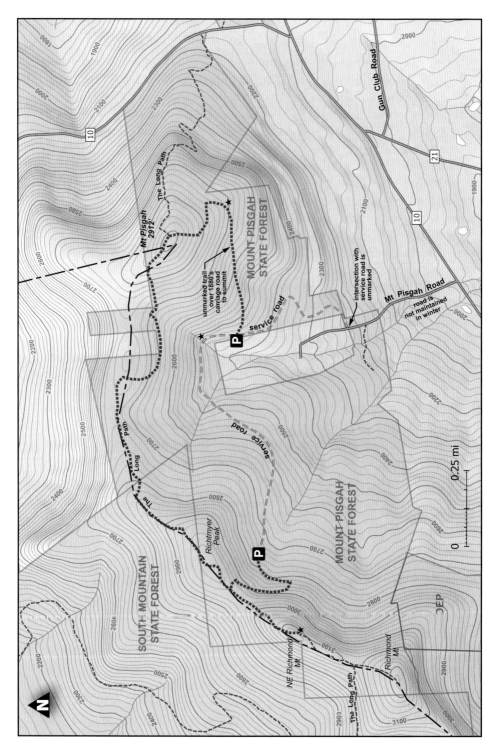

Mt. Pisgah Map

Paws-ing at Mt. Pisgah summit benchmark.
—Alan Via

circled the mountain below the summit. At 2700 ft, the road turns
RIGHT, emerging from under the dark canopy to more open skies;
deciduous trees and screened views on the LEFT and conifers on the
uphill side. The road is wider here, plunging back under darker forest canopy in 100 yd.

The road continues to descend, intersecting the service road at
2450 ft. If you haven't left a vehicle here, turn RIGHT and walk 1 mi
to the Mt. Pisgah trailhead observing the view of the Richmond ridge
as you walk.

Plattekills

HIGHLIGHTS AND SUMMARY: Hike a pair of summits from the Plattekill ski area. Service roads and ski trails lead to a ridgeline traverse with great views along the grassy trail. You'll seldom encounter others on this exceptional doghiker trek.

MILEAGE: *3.7 mi.*

ELEVATION GAIN: *1250 ft r/t.*

DIFFICULTY: *3*

VIEW RATING: *4*

LEASH: *Not required but advised near parking area and around cyclists.*

DOG SAFETY AND HAZARDS: *Mountain bike trails cross the ski trails.*

WATER: *None.*

HIKER TRAFFIC: *Very light.*

TRAIL CONDITIONS: *Grass and dirt ski trails and access roads.*

BEST TIME TO HIKE: *Spring or autumn. Little activity during the week. No hiking during ski season.*

GETTING THERE: *Turn onto Bridge St. (CR 41) from NY 30 (N42° 17.030', W74° 33.917') in Roxbury, bearing LEFT on CR 41. Cross West Settlement Rd. in 3 mi, after which it becomes Lower Meeker Hollow Rd. Continue on Lower Meeker Hollow Rd. to the Plattekill Mt. Ski center (N42° 17.354', W74° 39.131'). Park in the large lot.*

Looking up from the parking lot, you can see both summits and the connecting ridge in its entirety. Begin hiking up the Lower Powder Puff Trail that starts on the RIGHT. The trail is a grass and dirt service road. Part of it is out in the open, providing views as you climb. Hikers and dogs should provide the right-of-way to cyclists crossing on the mountain bike trail.

The Powder Puff Trails switchback their way to the first summit at the top of one of the chairlifts. You can look down the slope to the ski center buildings and likely spot your vehicle. There are excellent views across the valley toward a number of smaller peaks that serve as a foreground for the taller Slide, Westkill, and other higher summits in the distance.

Follow the Buckle Up Trail toward North Plattekill, descending into a shallow col, enjoying spectacular views across the ferny

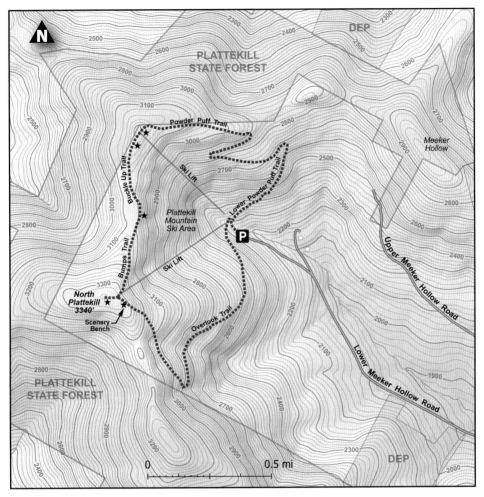

Plattekills Map

clearing. It's an easy 240 ft climb to North Plattekill's summit. The trail is a grassy woods road here, curbed by wildflowers and ferns, one of the nicest sections of trail on the mountain. In sunny areas, autumn foliage is further accentuated by blazing sections of goldenrod.

On North Plattekill's 3340 ft summit, stop to gawk at a view of Delaware County peaks stretching to the horizon. After lounging around near the other chairlift terminus, look for the Easiest Way Down Trail sign and follow the Overlook Trail back to your vehicle.

One minute beyond the summit there's a large deck with benches set in a grassy clearing that provides what I consider the best view on the mountain. It's the perfect place for a break to soak up the vista

Best seat in the house—North Plattekill.
—Alan Via

that includes a horizon of Catskill 100 Highest summits. After another pair of viewpoints, the Overlook Trail is swallowed up by a deciduous forest for the remainder of the descent on this remarkable hike. There's no water on the mountain. Carry water for dogs.

Red Hill

HIGHLIGHTS AND SUMMARY: This out-of-the-way hike leads to a 60 ft fire tower with extensive views of the southern Catskills. Along the way, hikers will enjoy the open deciduous forest and dogs will appreciate the spring situated in a rocky grotto a short distance off the trail. This easy outing is one families with dogs will enjoy.

MILEAGE: *2.6 mi r/t.*

ELEVATION GAIN: *815 ft.*

DIFFICULTY: *2*

VIEW RATING: *5*

LEASH: *Not required.*

DOG SAFETY AND HAZARDS: *None*

WATER: *Steam near trailhead and a spring 1 mi farther along.*

HIKER TRAFFIC: *Light.*

TRAIL CONDITIONS: *Worn with roots and scattered rocks, but in very good condition.*

BEST TIME TO HIKE: *Summer or autumn. Winter parking is 0.5 mi uphill from summer trailhead.*

GETTING THERE: *Turn onto Sugarloaf Rd. (N41° 51.830', W74° 30.392') at Lowe's Corners, to a LEFT onto Red Hill Rd. (N41° 55.001', W74° 29.749'). Make an immediate RIGHT onto Dinch Rd., climbing 200 ft uphill in 0.35 mi to a "Dead End" sign, which is the winter parking area (N41° 55.284', W74° 30.294'). The road continues ahead, descending 350 ft in 0.5 mi to the*

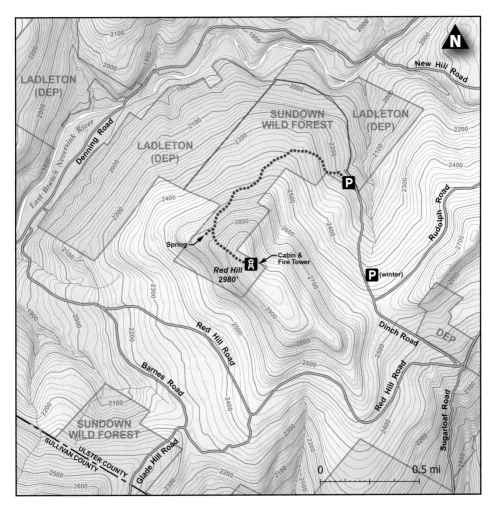

Red Hill Map

2180 ft trailhead (N41° 55.783', W74° 30.417'). Don't try to drive down to the summer trailhead in winter unless you're willing to risk a very expensive towing bill.

Follow YELLOW markers, quickly reaching the trail register and crossing two branches of a small brook. The well-worn trail begins ascending through a beech forest with scattered cherry and birch. The footing is dry, rocky in many places, with areas of avoidable, exposed tree roots. The first part of the hike is at a steady, but moderate, grade with three almost flat "breathers."

Near 2720 ft, there's a sign pointing to the summit. Look for an unmarked path here. It leads to a spring (N41° 55.560', W74° 31.274') with a pipe emerging from a rock, water that's cold, clean, and reliable for dogs. The mossy rock ledge surrounding the spring creates a peaceful setting resembling a shady grotto. Resuming the hike, there's a short, steep section after which the grade eases for the remaining 200 ft to the 2980 ft summit. Light through the thinning forest canopy heralds the tower clearing ahead.

The cabin is situated on one end of a grassy, sunlit clearing that's bordered by wood ferns. There's a pair of picnic tables at one end of the "lawn" and the tower at the other. Select a clear day for the hike and carry a good map up the tower for identifying peaks. The spectacular views include the Wildcat Range, Woodhull, Van Wyck, Table, and Peekamoose Mts. scattered across the N. Denman is prominent in the SW, and Beaver Kill Range, Millbrook, and Balsam Lake Mt. stand out in the distance.

Rip's Ledge

HIGHLIGHTS AND SUMMARY: The Rip's Ledge trail is one of a number originating from the Winter Clove Resort that continue onto New York State land. Stop by the resort's office to let them know you're hiking, say thanks on your way home, and consider returning as a guest. Please park away from guest areas, and avoid littering or asking to use resort facilities. Other than Rip's Ledge, dogs are not allowed on Winter Clove property. Keep dogs leashed on the Rip's trail until reaching public land. Resort trails don't appear on public maps and the trail to Rip's Ledge and intersecting trails require your attention.

MILEAGE: *5.3 mi r/t.*

ELEVATION GAIN: *950 ft.*

DIFFICULTY: *3*

VIEW RATING: *4*

LEASH: *Required on Winter Clove property, around other hikers, and at Rip's Ledge.*

DOG SAFETY AND HAZARDS: *Rip's Ledge cliff top.*

WATER: *Stream at the beginning and a couple of others on the hike.*

HIKER TRAFFIC: *Light.*

TRAIL CONDITIONS: *Excellent, other than one wet section.*

BEST TIME TO HIKE: *Autumn.*

GETTING THERE: *Turn off of CR 31 onto Winter Clove Rd. (N42° 15.534', W74° 01.276'), turning LEFT at the T intersection (N42° 14.801', W74° 01.809'). Make the first RIGHT onto Winter Clove Rd. (N42° 14.737', W74 01.699'). Drive past the main building and turn LEFT. Park next to a field across from the building with a red metal roof.*

Follow a path across the field adjacent to where you parked. A sign in the field points to "The Ledges, Indian Lookout, and Rip's Rock." Follow the path through the field onto a woods road. Continue over a bridge to a large tree where a YELLOW arrow points to "Hiking Trails." At the next intersection, there's another "Hiking Trails" sign leading to another woods road. Continue to a field (N42° 14.361', W74° 01.721') with a sign reading "The Daisy Field" and "Hiking Trails." Turn LEFT to stay on the official trail. A 40 yd shortcut across the field intercepts the trail near the 1030 ft border with the New York State Forest Preserve (N42° 14.267', W74° 01.629').

The trail is level here for a short distance on an excellent woods road, passing a side trail and sign on the LEFT toward Lost Pond. The trail continues climbing at an easy grade and flattens for a short distance near 1240 ft where the forest is notable for the mix of laurel, azalea, short oaks, and small red pines.

You are now following ORANGE blazes, nearing a stream and passing an impressive rocky gorge (N42° 13.840', W74° 01.485'). Just above, there's a trail intersection with a sign that points in one direction to "Indian Lookout and Upper Rip's Trail," and in the other direction to "Rip's Rock Lower Trail." Both lead to Rip's Ledge, but the Lower Trail is better maintained. Bear LEFT following ORANGE and

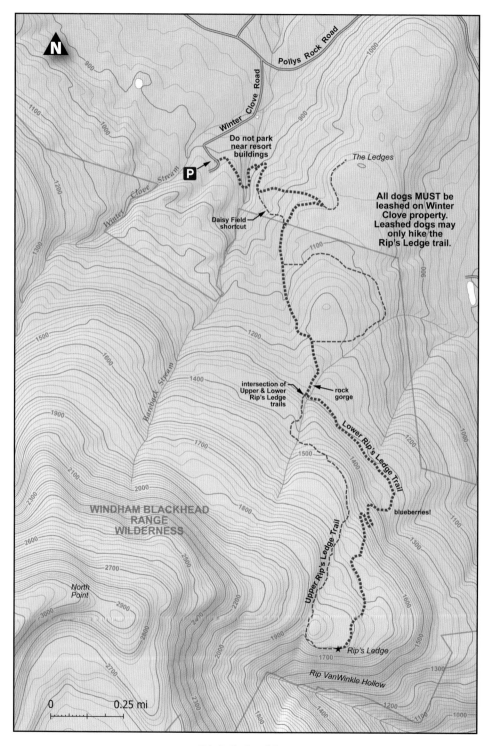

Rip's Ledge Map

RED blazes across a stream, through a 100 ft section of wet, muddy trail to a "gotta go in June" section of laurel in 0.3 mi.

Above 1300 ft, the trail bisects one of the largest sections of blueberries you'll ever see. They extend deep into the forest on both sides of the trail. This has to be a favorite bear foraging area. The trail makes a sharp RIGHT turn (N42° 13.484', W74° 01.191') at 1330 ft, passing a descending woods road that leads to private property. Begin a 250 ft switchbacking climb on an excellent woods road that's banked with bluestone as you hike through hemlocks. At its top, the trail traverses another section of laurel, climbing along the base of rock bands.

A RED arrow at 1570 ft points toward Rip's Ledge. After 200 ft of easier ascent, the last 0.1 mi to the ledge crosses a plateau through a forest of short conifers, oaks, laurel, and azalea. Walk out onto Rip's Ledge (N42° 13.047', W74° 01.416') at 1800 ft for great views across Rip Van Winkle Hollow toward North Mt., southern Massachusetts, and northern Connecticut over an expanse of the Hudson River. Safeguard dogs near the cliff top. Interestingly, the trees on your return to Winter Clove have BLUE markers on the opposite side of the trees you followed to the ledge.

Rochester Hollow

HIGHLIGHTS AND SUMMARY: A wonderful hike, trail run, ski, or snowshoe with dogs. Scenic and showy in all seasons with spectacular stone walls, a beautiful stream, the Burroughs monument, and a perfectly situated lean-to. This one-of-a-kind Catskills gem is a personal favorite.

MILEAGE: *6.5 mi r/t all trails.*

ELEVATION GAIN: *1200 ft.*

DIFFICULTY: *3*

VIEW RATING: *2*

LEASH: *Not required.*

DOG SAFETY AND HAZARDS: *Avoid during hunting season.*

WATER: *Rochester Hollow Brook, seasonal water, and a pond near Rochester estate.*

HIKER TRAFFIC: *Busy, but never crowded.*

TRAIL CONDITIONS: *Excellent.*

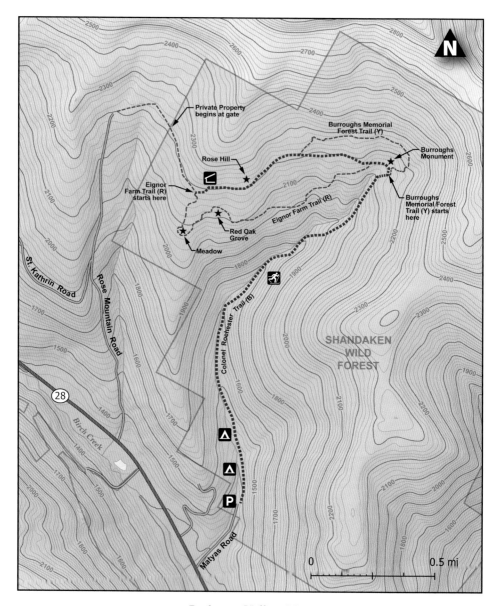

Rochester Hollow Map

BEST TIME TO HIKE: *Spring and autumn.*

GETTING THERE: *Turn onto Matyas Rd. (N42° 06.863', W74° 27.297') from NY 28 near Big Indian. Drive 0.3 mi to the 1375 ft trailhead (N42° 07.080', W74° 27.112') in the Shandaken Wild Forest.*

The BLUE Colonel Rochester Trail is a woods road that gains a bit over 800 ft to the height of land where two additional trails originate. The road has stone retaining walls and drainage channels and is in superb condition. Sections of hemlock mingle, but the forest is predominantly deciduous. According to botanist and historian Mike Kudish, shagbark hickories near the trail's beginning suggest a Native American presence in the hollow's pre-farming days. The profusion of stone fences show the hollow was settled with homes and pastures, in addition to the Rochester estate. Rochester Hollow Brook follows the road for much of its distance, providing opportunities for canine frolicking and hydration. The steam has small cataracts and its banks and the trail are speckled with trillium, trout lilies, columbine, mayflowers, and spring beauties.

Long stretches of the road are shady in summer and provide foliage fireworks in autumn. Just before the height of land, contemplate the legacy of naturalist John Burroughs at the stone fence enclosing the historic Burroughs monument (N42° 08.226′, 74° 26.422′), placed by the Riordan School in 1921. The E end of the 0.75 mi Burroughs Memorial Trail begins on YELLOW markers S of the monument.

On the memorial trail, hike through a mostly deciduous forest with a section of dying conifers planted in the 1920s by the Riordan School. Dr. Kudish observes that the trees couldn't compete with the faster-growing deciduous trees surrounding them. The highlight of

Rochester Hollow.
—Katherine Varn Hawkins

this short trail is one of the most spectacular sections of stone walls (N42° 08.303', W74° 26.320') you'll see anywhere in the Catskills.

The other end of the trail meets the road 0.5 mi E of Rose Hill, the remains of the late nineteenth-century home site (N42° 08.203', W74° 27.017') of Colonel William Rochester, veteran of the Spanish-American War and World War I. Retaining walls, garage remains, and a small pond are reminders of the era. Stone steps on the N side of the road lead to the foundation of Rochester's home. Daffodil clumps, iris, vinca, and other domesticated flora not native to mountains hang on, living signs of man's past occupation here.

An ancient paper birch on the N side of the road has been dated to nearly 1900. Planted as a decorative seedling, it's now one of the oldest examples of its species. Nearby, an impounded pond is a good place for dogs to drink and cool off; it's the only reliable water in the vicinity. Continue E along the road to the James Smith Lean-to (N42° 08.206', W74° 27.127'), situated in a pole stand that was likely a pasture at one time.

The Eignor Farm Trail begins 0.2 mi W of the lean-to. Follow RED markers as they lead downhill, turning sharply LEFT at a meadow (N42° 07.998', W74° 27.268') and a large sugar maple. Along its 1.15 mi length, the trail passes through a large grove of northern red oaks and stone foundations before ascending 200 ft to rejoin the road (N42° 08.247', W74° 26.467') W of the Burroughs monument. Rochester Hollow is one of the best non-mountain hikes in the Catskills.

Rock Rift

HIGHLIGHTS AND SUMMARY: The trail was created in 2014 by the Catskill Mountain Club in conjunction with DEP and the Finger Lakes Trail Conference. The fire tower is inaccessible until its eventual restoration. Enjoy delightful open woods with interesting trail features overlooking the Cannonsville Reservoir. The WHITE trail markers can be difficult to notice in winter and the top half of the S ridge has steep sections.

MILEAGE: *5.5 mi through hike.*

ELEVATION GAIN: *1450 ft.*

DIFFICULTY: *3*

VIEW RATING: *1*

LEASH: *Leashes required on DEP land.*

DOG SAFETY AND HAZARDS: *Highway traffic.*

WATER: *A few small streams, seeps, and wet areas, otherwise mostly dry. Carry dog water.*

HIKER TRAFFIC: *Light.*

TRAIL CONDITIONS: *Good, mostly woods roads. The S ridge is steep and slippery when covered by leaves and acorns.*

BEST TIME TO HIKE: *Spring and early autumn. Trail closed mid-November to mid-December during deer season.*

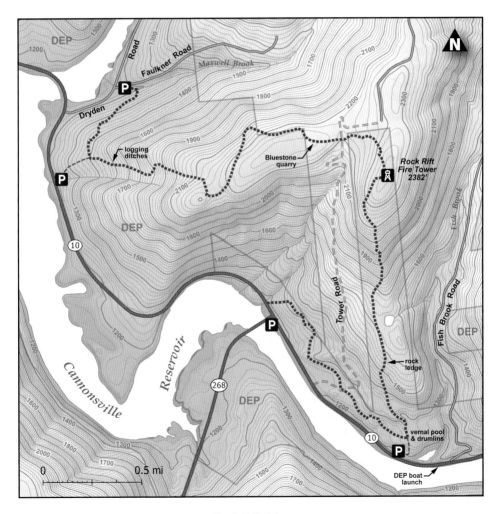

Rock Rift Map

GETTING THERE: *The Faulkner Rd. trailhead (N42° 06.608', W75° 15.152') is located adjacent to the intersection with Dryden Rd. The other end of the trail is 50 yd NW of the parking area at the NY 10 and NY 268 intersection (N4°2 05.637', W75° 14.294'). There is roadside parking on NY 10 for the two spur trails (N42° 05.021', W75° 13.529' and N42° 05.030', W75° 13.533').*

Begin hiking on WHITE blazes from the Faulkner Rd. kiosk, soon crossing Maxwell Brook. The trail quarters uphill through hardwoods, intersecting (N42° 06.292', W75° 15.350') the BLUE spur trail at 1400 ft. Continuing on WHITE, follow a woods road through patches of hemlocks, taking notice of a series of downhill-facing ditches that begin near 1500 ft. These are logging remnants created by draglines that pulled logs downhill, the blunt ends plowing soil and scraping narrow troughs 15 to 20 ft in length. Soil build-up allowed the tree trunks to slide up and over, leaving dirt mounds in their wakes.

The hemlocks disappear near 1800 ft, the forest now predominately beech and oak. The trail grade begins to ease above 2000 ft and passes through areas of grass and brush with filtered views of the surrounding hills when trees are bare. The trail skirts (N42° 06.153', W75° 14.641') a viewless 2217 ft knob, dips slightly, then descends 120 ft before quickly regaining the elevation. It passes a bluestone quarry near 2250 ft where a sign reminds hikers they are on private property and must remain on the trail.

The trail is again a woods road beyond the quarry where it descends and crosses what was called Tower Rd. It resumes being a trail and climbs 180 ft in the last 0.3 mi to the summit. The fire tower was constructed by the Civilian Conservation Corps in 1934 and is being turned over to the town of Tompkins. A volunteer group plans to restore the tower, which will create unsurpassed views of the area.

The wooded summit is viewless, but there are screened views as you follow WHITE markers down the S ridge. At 2200 ft, the gradual descent gets sharply steeper as the ridge sheds 500 ft in the next 0.4 mi. Fallen leaves covering roots, rocks, acorns, and cut-off saplings demand attention when descending the ridge in autumn. Look for remnants of the old telephone poles that carried service to the tower. Bears scratch and bite them, using them as ursine scratching posts and territorial markers.

There's a large, overhanging rock off the trail near 1560 ft with room to sit underneath and look up at the upside-down pothole in its ceiling. Just before the trail turns NW, there's a vernal pool set back from the trail on the LEFT, and a number of drumlins, leftovers from the ice age. The trail arrives at the intersection with another spur trail at 1275 ft at the bottom of the S ridge. If you've left a car on the road or at the nearby DEP boat launch, follow BLUE markers downhill to NY 10. Otherwise, turn RIGHT and follow the roller coaster ups and downs 1.25 mi to the NY 268 bridge parking area.

Shavertown Trail

HIGHLIGHTS AND SUMMARY: The Shavertown Trail was designed and constructed on DEP property in 2013 by the Catskill Mountain Club. The original trail was closed in 2018 to allow removal of ash trees infected by the emerald ash borer. The new trail to Snake Pond is a delight with a cold-water pond, scenic overlook, ferns, wildflowers, and benches with views. A new trail will be constructed when the logging has concluded. In the meantime, the shorter hike to Snake Pond is an interesting hike all by itself.

MILEAGE: *2 mi r/t to Snake Pond.*

ELEVATION GAIN: *520 ft to Snake Pond.*

DIFFICULTY: *1*

VIEW RATING: *3*

LEASH: *Leashes required on DEP land.*

DOG SAFETY AND HAZARDS: *Trailhead and parking are right on the road. Hunting is allowed here.*

WATER: *Small streams and Snake Pond.*

HIKER TRAFFIC: *Light, busier on weekends.*

TRAIL CONDITIONS: *Very good.*

BEST TIME TO HIKE: *Spring and early autumn.*

GETTING THERE: *Trailhead parking (N42° 05.379', W74° 49.122') is located at the DEP boat launch site near the NW end of the Shavertown Bridge on CR 1 (BWS 4 Rd.). Walk 0.1 mi along the road to the 1300 ft trailhead. Guardrails prevent closer parking.*

The trail register is located just inside of the woods. The hike begins with a gradual ascent through a mixed hardwood and conifer forest on the lower SSW slope of Perch Lake Mt. The forest becomes

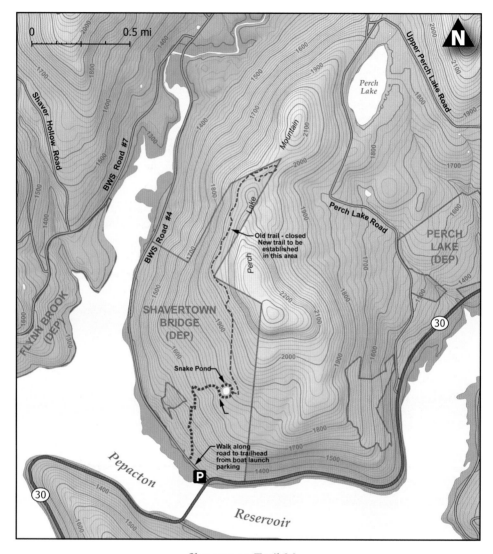

Shavertown Trail Map

deciduous as you climb, with ferns and seasonal flowers. The trail crosses a brook near 1480 ft and another a few minutes ahead.

Near 1550 ft, the trail intersects a gravel woods road (N42° 05.669′, W74° 49.188′) at 0.4 mi. Cross the road and immediately reenter the forest, switchbacking uphill through Norway and white spruce. You cross a pair of small streams 100 ft higher, another canine watering hole. As you continue, be on the lookout for a tall mountain laurel near 1700 ft. Botanist Mike Kudish believes this fifty-year-old specimen may be a record for height.

The woodland is a delightfully open hardwood forest below Snake Pond and you'll cross a seep coming from it. Walk across a good stream that emerges from the pond. Snake Pond is a wonder, as picturesque a water and mountains composition as exists in the Catskills. In addition to a view of the Pepacton Reservoir from its shore, Brock, Little Spring, East Mary Smith, Middle, Cabot, and Barkaboom Mts. are visible from the "contemplation" benches.

The cold, clear water is a fantastic place for dogs. After soaking up the scenery, be certain to hike the 0.3 mi loop around the pond, passing its crystal-clear inlet on the NE side.

Prior to the trail beyond the pond being closed for logging, the original trail continued N below the cliffs of Perch Lake Mt. through a mixed forest with sections of hemlock to a high point N of the mountain's summit. There are areas of layered sandstone ledges beyond which seas of ferns compete with seasonal wildflowers for attention. When the logging is completed, the Catskill Mountain Club will design a new trail along Perch Lake Mt.

Pepacton Reservoir from Shavertown — Snake Pond overlook.
—Eileen Catasus-Chapman

Silver Hollow Mt.

HIGHLIGHTS AND SUMMARY: Also called Edgewood Mt., this is one of the Catskill 100 Highest peaks. The hike begins on a rough woods road and ends on a multi-summit trail through a gorgeous forest, passing a high-elevation bog.

MILEAGE: *4.5 mi r/t.*

ELEVATION GAIN: *1200 ft.*

DIFFICULTY: *3*

VIEW RATING: *2*

LEASH: *Near the residence, otherwise not required.*

DOG SAFETY AND HAZARDS: *None.*

WATER: *A couple of springs, seeps, and a bog. Carry water.*

HIKER TRAFFIC: *Light.*

TRAIL CONDITIONS: *Washed-out dirt for the first 0.5 mi.*

BEST TIME TO HIKE: *When leaves are missing.*

GETTING THERE: *Turn onto Notch Inn Rd. (Silver Hollow Rd.) from the intersection with NY 214 near Edgewood (N42° 08.470', W74° 12.747'). Continue 30 yd from NY 214 and park on the shoulder. Do not park farther up the road or near the residence at the beginning of the trail.*

Begin hiking 0.3 mi up Notch Inn Rd., passing a stream and old railroad stonework. The trail begins opposite a driveway at the top of Notch Inn Rd. Although there's no sign indicating the beginning of the trail, step into the woods across a berm onto a woods road. You cross a small brook and see the first YELLOW trail marker just ahead. The woods road is rocky and eroded, after being beat up from Tropical Storm Irene.

The road takes you through a deciduous forest bordered by nettles, ferns, shin hobble, and wildflowers. At 2170 ft, there's a small spring (N42° 08.078', W74° 12.709') and seep. The trail leaves the woods road for a short distance before rejoining it 100 yd ahead. At 0.5 mi, there's a DEC trail sign (N42° 07.942', W74° 12.814') at 2370 ft, just before Silver Hollow Notch. It points LEFT to Plateau Mt., but the trail to Silver Hollow Mt. is RIGHT on BLUE markers along the Warner Creek Trail. Before continuing, walk ahead a short distance to check out the notch.

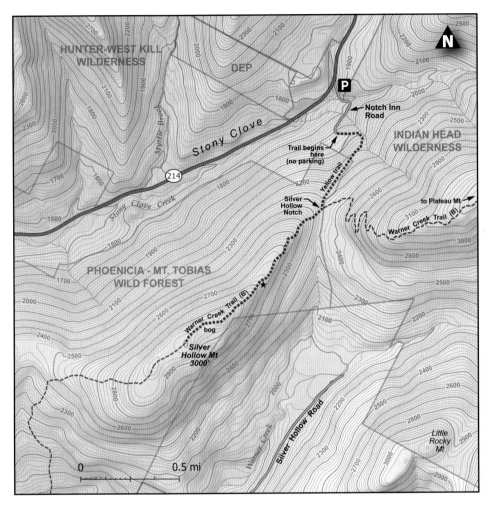

Silver Hollow Mt. Map

The BLUE trail leads on a steady ascent up Silver Hollow's NE ridge. Depending on the season, noticeable are ferns, wildflowers, nettles, and an occasional patch of shin hobble. The trail can get a little overgrown in summer. The grade lessens near 2675 ft at the first of a few screened views. Another 100 ft higher, the trail again nears the edge of the escarpment where there are views of Olderbark, Little Rocky, and Plateau Mts. This is the best viewpoint on the mountain, screened unless the trees are bare.

Continue along the ridge toward the first of Silver Hollow's three summits with a 100 ft section of ascent through moss-covered

Jim and Molly—Six legs stream crossing.
—Heather Kolland

boulders. Although many hikers visit all three indistinguishable summits, the middle, at 3000 ft, is the highest. Be sure to look for a large bog off the SE side of the trail between the first two summits, the first real place along the ridge where dogs might get a drink. Other than seasonal water, most of the hike is dry, so carry extra water for your doghiker.

Slide Mt.

HIGHLIGHTS AND SUMMARY: The tallest peak in the Catskills, Slide attracts a lot of hiker traffic. Rather than the standard route, the nicer, and less-busy, Curtis-Ormsbee (C-O) Trail is a better alternative for doghikers. The trail was built to commemorate Allan Ormsbee and the Reverend Henry Curtis who pioneered the route. They perished on Mt. Washington in June 1900. There is a stone marker at the beginning of the trail. The C-O joins the Wittenberg-Cornell-Slide Mt. Trail shortly before the summit.

MILEAGE: *7.5 mi r/t.*

ELEVATION GAIN: *1750 ft.*

DIFFICULTY: *5*

VIEW RATING: *3*

LEASH: *At the trailhead, viewpoints, and summit.*

DOG SAFETY AND HAZARDS: *Crossing the Neversink River during periods of very high water.*

WATER: *Small streams and seasonal water. Carry extra during dry periods.*

HIKER TRAFFIC: *Very busy.*

TRAIL CONDITIONS: *Rocky in many places.*

BEST TIME TO HIKE: *Spring and autumn.*

GETTING THERE: *Turn onto CR 47 at the intersection (N42° 06.171', W74° 26.595') with NY 28 in Big Indian, continuing to the large 2400 ft trailhead (N42° 00.539', W74° 25.667').*

Follow YELLOW markers from behind the kiosk across the West Branch Neversink River. Depending on conditions, crossing can vary from dry, to rock-hopping, to impassible in very high water. Climb steadily on a rocky trail, across a small stream, to a trail sign at 2780 ft (N42° 00.417', W74° 25.225'). Turn RIGHT, crossing a series of small streams to the 2850 ft intersection (N42° 00.28', W74° 25.117') with the RED Wittenberg-Cornell-Slide Trail to the summit. A better alternative with dogs is to continue hiking another 0.8 mi on YELLOW markers, passing more small streams, toward the beginning of the C-O Trail (N41° 59.644', W74° 25.176'). It originates at 3075 ft in the East Wildcat–Slide col where BLUE markers lead 2.3 mi to Slide's summit.

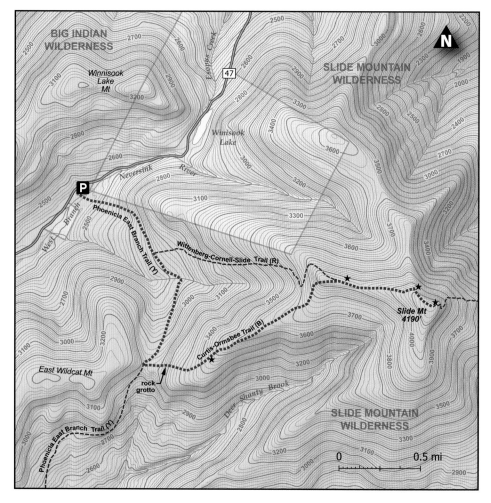

Slide Mt. Map

The bottom of the trail is marked by the stone marker, and the trail begins climbing through a deciduous forest that becomes more boreal as you ascend. At 3150 ft, stop to admire one of the most interesting features on the trail, a 50 ft deep rock grotto with tall, "pancake rock" sides. Imagine the people and animals that have sheltered here over the centuries. Near 3450 ft, there's a rock ledge with views and, just beyond, a section of trail garlanded by ferns with scattered birch and black cherry trees, a gorgeous place to linger.

Look for an unmarked 50 ft long path on the RIGHT side of the trail leading to views of Table, Lone, and Rocky Mts. Above 3600 ft,

Boo gets a snack—Slide Mt.
—Joanne Hihn

the now slowly ascending trail passes through conifers with a moss-decorated forest floor. After ascending another 200 ft, you reach 100 ft of steep trail, the last challenging bit of ascent. You soon intersect the main trail (N42° 00.073′, W74° 23.798′) at 3940 ft, now following RED markers to the summit.

The remaining distance along the E ridge gains only 225 ft, passing a ledge with a panoramic view. The only remnants of the former fire tower are concrete supports at Slide's 4190 ft wooded high point. Continue down to an open ledge with an historic John Burroughs memorial plaque. There are too many peaks to count over the ever-growing conifer tops.

South Escarpment

HIGHLIGHTS AND SUMMARY: After a quick peek at Kaaterskill Falls, hike past mountain laurel and American chestnuts to the remains of the historic Kaaterskill Hotel. Great views along the Escarpment Trail. There are many trails in the area; pay extra attention to map and trail description details.

MILEAGE: *6 mi r/t.*

ELEVATION GAIN: *900 ft.*

DIFFICULTY: *3*

VIEW RATING: *3*

LEASH: *At trailhead, near cliff tops, and around other hikers.*

DOG SAFETY AND HAZARDS: *Cliffs along the S escarpment.*

WATER: *Infrequent, carry water.*

HIKER TRAFFIC: *Very busy on weekends, especially the trails near Laurel House and Scutt trailheads.*

TRAIL CONDITIONS: *Excellent*

BEST TIME TO HIKE: *Spring or autumn. Avoid Escarpment Trail when icy or snow-covered.*

GETTING THERE: *Drive onto CR 18 (North-South Lake Rd.) from NY 23A (N42° 11.775', W74° 05.820') in Haines Falls. Turn RIGHT onto Laurel House Rd. (N42° 12.046', W74° 03.935') to the very busy DEC trailhead (N42° 12.748', W74° 03.804'). Parking beyond signs guarantees a ticket.*

Follow the trail from the parking lot to the Falls View Trail intersection for a 0.1 mi side trip to the usually crowded Kaaterskill Falls viewing platform. Back at the intersection, cross the Lake Creek bridge, turning LEFT toward the Scutt Road Trail intersection. Pass the backyard of a residence, then turn RIGHT on RED markers at the next intersection. In 0.25 mi, bear RIGHT on YELLOW markers that lead to the YELLOW Horse Trail (N42° 11.286', W74° 03.654').

The Horse Trail is lightly used, mostly level, with almost unnoticeable elevation changes. There are long sections of showy mountain laurel in June, but the treat for tree enthusiasts is the American chestnuts interspersed with oaks and maples. Continuing on the Horse Trail, turn LEFT at the next intersection. BLUE markers lead 0.5 mi with 200 ft ascent toward the summit of South Mt. If you continue to the RIGHT on the Horse Trail, there's an intersection with the Harding Road Trail 2 mi from the trailhead. It leads downhill to Palenville. It's a scenic hike if you spot a car in Palenville, a trip for another day.

Following BLUE markers, at 2440 ft, the trail meets an intersection (N42° 11.287', W74° 03.019') with the Scutt Road Trail. Turn RIGHT here onto the unmarked woods road that circles the remnants of the old Kaaterskill Hotel. Allow your imagination to envision a building with twelve hundred rooms, outbuildings, and a lawn where large

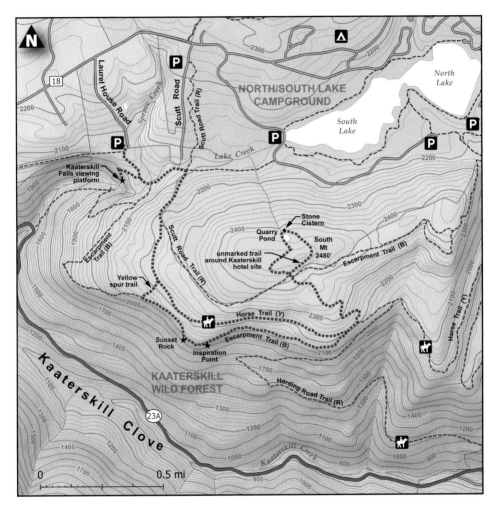

South Escarpment Map

trees now grow. A more "concrete" remnant is the 20 ft deep cistern (N42° 11.452', W74° 03.149') adjacent to the large pond from which the hotel drew water. Take care that your dog doesn't jump over the cistern wall. Other than a couple of seasonal streams, the pond is the only reliable place for dogs to drink and cool off on the hike.

The woods road circles the pond back to the intersection and descent to the Horse Trail. Turn RIGHT onto the Horse Trail, then turn onto the Escarpment Trail (N42° 11.098', W74° 02.764') in 0.2 mi. BLUE markers follow the S edge of the escarpment past a series of

Garter snake hunting on mountain laurel.
—Katherine Varn Hawkins

views across Kaaterskill Clove. Dogs should be leashed for their safety and that of hikers on this section of trail. The trail here is usually busy and is narrow. Courtesy requires stepping off the trail with your leashed dog on the uphill side when meeting approaching hikers.

Inspiration Point (N42° 11.064', W74° 03.426') and Sunset Ledge (N42° 11.092', W74° 03.542') are just a few places where leashes and photography are necessary. Follow the Escarpment Trail back to the trailhead or turn RIGHT on a 0.1 mi YELLOW spur trail (N42° 11.225', W74° 03.729'), then LEFT back along the way you came.

Twin Mt.

HIGHLIGHTS AND SUMMARY: Many consider the views from this double summit peak among the best in the Catskills. The ridge section of the trail is on the aptly named Devil's Path. The rocky, steep, and tricky sections make the hike more challenging than the mileage and ascent first seem.

MILEAGE: *5.8 mi r/t.*

ELEVATION GAIN: *1800 ft.*

DIFFICULTY: *5*

VIEW RATING: *5*

LEASH: *Not required but suggested on summits and near other hikers.*

DOG SAFETY AND HAZARDS: *Hazardous at the viewpoint before the first*

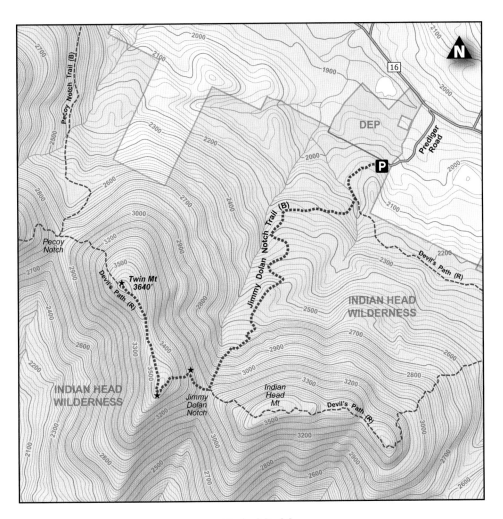

Twin Mt. Map

summit and on the actual summit.

WATER: *Small streams. Carry water.*

HIKER TRAFFIC: *Busy, especially on weekends.*

TRAIL CONDITIONS: *Well-marked. Hike along the ridge is challenging.*

BEST TIME TO HIKE: *Spring and autumn.*

GETTING THERE: *Turn off of CR 16 (Platte Clove Rd.) onto Prediger Rd. (N42° 08.273′, W74° 05.917′), continuing 0.5 mi to the large 2050 ft trail-head (N42° 08.047′, W74° 06.236′). Parking is not allowed on Prediger Rd. Platte Clove Rd. from West Saugerties is closed during winter.*

Lily on the Devil's Path.
—Heather Rolland

RED markers lead 0.2 mi from the trailhead following a dog-friendly stream for part of the way to the intersection with the Devil's Path. Turn RIGHT onto BLUE markers here for the remaining 1.6 mi to Jimmy Dolan Notch, the col between Indian Head and Twin Mts. The rocky trail ascends at a moderate gradient, gaining a bit under 400 ft in the first 1 mi.

Dogs can wet their whistles in some seasonally wet areas and where the trail crosses a small brook near 1.4 mi. The climbing gets steeper beyond and there are some filtered views of Twin's S summit as you gain 450 ft in the final 0.3 mi to Jimmy Dolan Notch. You again meet the RED markers of the Devil's Path as it crosses the 3125 ft notch, leading toward Twin. Turn RIGHT to follow the RED markers. The trail above the notch is rocky, boulder-strewn, and challenging for some doghikers. It's typical Devil's Path terrain.

You quickly gain elevation on the steep trail, reaching a boulder and rock step 0.15 mi above the col, where some dogs might need a boost. A couple of minutes ahead, turn around for a good look at

Ryder and Melissa on Twin's south summit.
—Melissa Bean McCutcheon

Indian Head Mt. A nice overlook at 0.35 mi has views of Huckleberry Point, Ashokan Reservoir, Overlook Mt., and Indian Head. Keep dogs close as it's a drop to the trees below.

The grade eases as you step out onto the open rock near Twin's first summit where a horizon of smaller peaks—Ticeteneyck, Tonshi, and Tobias—greet you. They're a bonus to the better-known higher summits all around. Hikers unfamiliar with Twin's topography sometimes think they've arrived at Twin's high point, mistaking the true summit ahead for Sugarloaf Mt.

After soaking in the views, it's an easy 0.2 mi stroll down to the flat and shady col between Twin's two summits. The trail is less rocky and is cushioned by conifer needles on the even easier 200 ft ascent to Twin's 3640 ft high point.

The view from the large summit ledge is unsurpassed. Sugarloaf, Plateau, Olderbark, Huntersfield, Richmond, and the Burroughs Range are on full display. Many believe the view may be the best in the Catskills. It's advisable to leash dogs to keep them away from the cliff and off fragile vegetation.

I recall a day on Twin Mt. when a hiker was so intent on passing us that he missed a bend in the trail and ended up in the woods.

Afterward, we laughed about the hiker's head-swiveling as he scampered to get ahead of my dog, Bookah, embarrassed she had shown him the trail.

West Cave—Cave Mts.

HIGHLIGHTS AND SUMMARY: Hike a pair of the Catskill 100 Highest summits that are part of the Windham Mt. ski resort. The grassy slopes have wildflowers and an absence of hiker traffic. It's is a great place to see deer and bears with their young on the slopes below you.

MILEAGE: *5.25 mi both peaks. 3.5 mi West Cave only.*

ELEVATION GAIN: *1700 ft both peaks. 1375 ft West Cave only.*

DIFFICULTY: *4*

VIEW RATING: *4*

LEASH: *Required around parking area, buildings, maintenance vehicles, and workers.*

DOG SAFETY AND HAZARDS: *Dogs and hikers should wear orange during hunting season as many local people hunt in the area.*

WATER: *Seasonal wet areas, but otherwise dry. Carry extra water.*

HIKER TRAFFIC: *Very light.*

TRAIL CONDITIONS: *Service roads and ski runs.*

BEST TIME TO HIKE: *Spring and "scenery" autumn.*

GETTING THERE: *Turn off of NY 23 onto CR 79 (N42° 18.426', W74° 15.123') in Windham. Continue to a RIGHT onto CR 12 (N42° 18.238', W74° 15.032') and follow the signs to the 1650 ft parking lot in front of the main building. Park on the RIGHT side of the lot for a shorter walk to the hike.*

You get your first look at the slopes of West Cave and Cave Mts. from the parking lot. Begin hiking on the RIGHT, on Wonderama, a trail that begins climbing West Cave along a row of trees separating the trail from condominiums. Wonderama ends near 2380 ft (N42° 17.481', W74° 15.983'), where you can select a number of ways to continue.

My recommendation is Wedel, but any of the ski runs on the W side of the mountain will land you on top. The view as you climb and those from West Cave's 3040 ft summit (N42° 17.074', W74° 15.861') encompass a NW to NE sweep that includes the Huntersfield Range, Windham High Peak, and a gaggle of smaller and taller mountains.

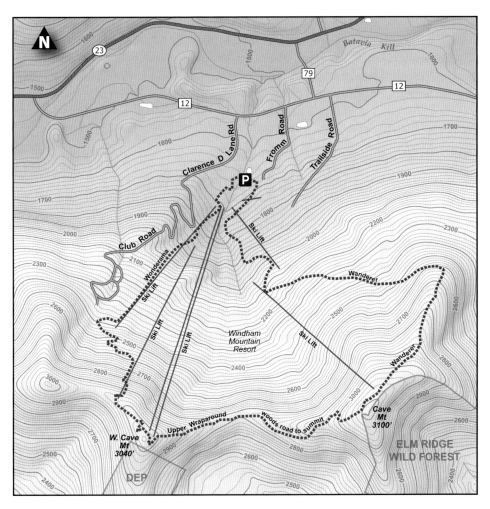

West Cave Mt. Map

You can head back from the summit but adding Cave Mt. is worth the extra effort. From West Cave, follow a trail called Upper Wraparound along the ridge line, descending to the 2800 ft col between the summits. Where the trail leaves the col, look for a grassy and sometimes overgrown woods road/trail that climbs 300 ft in 0.8 mi to Cave's 3100 ft summit clearing and chairlift terminus.

You'll want to take a break on the carpeted platform underneath the summit tram station. It's shady, breezy, and the perfect perch for lunch while you soak up the wonderful views. If you're a stickler for getting to the highest point, head S into the woods for a short bushwhack to the glacial erratic that marks Cave Mt.'s tip top. The nicest way back to your vehicle is Wanderer, an inviting trail that eases its way down Cave Mt.'s N ridge before turning W into the forest.

Hiking the Caves is always a treat. The almost continual views are something you don't often get on hiking trails. Although dogs are oblivious to the views and wildflowers lining the slopes, you'll savor them and the sightings of animals, birds, and butterflies. Bring water for your dog as the hike is dry.

Windham High Peak

HIGHLIGHTS AND SUMMARY: The hike from Peck Rd. has an abundance of water along its first mile and avoids crossing busy NY 23. The "spooky forest," spring wildflowers, pole stand, and great views from three summit viewpoints are just some of Windham's superlatives. Look for eagles in the last couple of miles to the trailhead.

MILEAGE: *6 mi r/t.*

ELEVATION GAIN: *1550 ft.*

DIFFICULTY: *4*

VIEW RATING: *3*

LEASH: *Not required.*

DOG SAFETY AND HAZARDS: *None.*

WATER: *Lots of water in the first mile with a stream and seasonal water.*

HIKER TRAFFIC: *Very busy on weekends.*

TRAIL CONDITIONS: *Wet areas in the first mile, mostly dry the rest of the way.*

BEST TIME TO HIKE: *Early spring and autumn.*

GETTING THERE: *Turn onto CR 56 in Maplecrest (N42° 16.520', W74° 11.241') and continue to Peck Rd. (N42° 17.426', W74° 09.627'). Follow Peck Rd. to the 2040 ft trailhead (N42° 17.795', W74° 10.156').*

YELLOW markers lead past the trail register that is located within sight of the trailhead. Keep dogs close for the first few minutes until you're past the backyards of a couple of homes. The first mile follows a woods road that has sections of bedrock, and wet areas and streams that dogs will enjoy. In spring, it's an excellent section of trail for wildflowers.

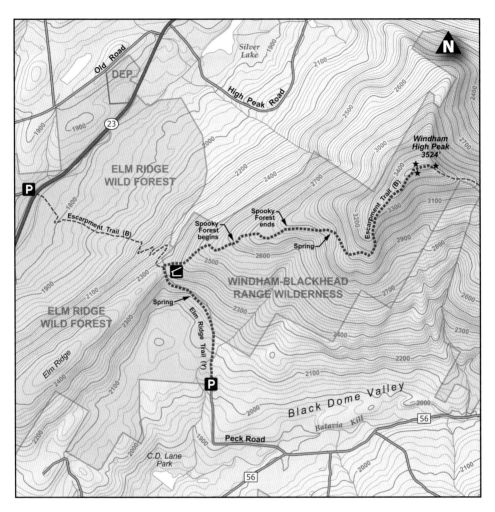

Windham High Peak Map

Pass the YELLOW Cranberry Bog mountain bike trail on the LEFT at 0.3 mi and look for a good spring coming from a pipe at 0.6 mi. Pass a long cliff set back on the RIGHT just before intersecting (N42° 18.396′, W74° 10.476′) the BLUE trail that comes from NY 23 at 2315 ft, where a sign points to the summit 2.2 mi ahead. Turn RIGHT on BLUE markers and soon pass a spur trail that leads to the Elm Ridge lean-to. It sits on the cliff you previously passed.

The trail ascending Windham's W ridge climbs at a steady, but moderate, grade through a mostly deciduous forest that's shady in summer and showy in autumn. Old sugar maples indicate the forest was previously farmed, with much of the surrounding reforestation formerly pasture. The trail enters what many call the "enchanted" or "spooky forest" at 2620 ft, a large area of Norway spruce planted by the Civilian Conservation Corps in the 1930s. On any but the drabbest of days, hikers go from bright daylight into a dark and shady conifer forest, walking over exposed tree roots for much of this 0.4 mi section. On hot, humid days, this refreshing section of trail feels like standing in front of an open refrigerator.

Popping out of the spooky forest into bright woodland near 2800 ft is a startling contrast. The trail becomes rockier as it begins climbing in the next 0.25 mi through a pole stand suggestive of a former meadow. When trees are bare there are screened views of the Blackheads. From late April until mid-May, the area is an excellent location to see wildflowers. Above 2850 ft, the woods transition from former agriculture to first growth. It's a rarity in the Catskills where there's no intervening section of second growth.

The trail climbs little in the next 0.2 mi and may have seasonal wet areas. The only reliable water source for dogs between the Elm Ridge intersection and the summit is a stream near an ancient sugar maple at 2860 ft. The trail turns S then E getting onto Windham's S ridge. After a couple of hundred feet of steeper trail, it's an easy grade to the top. There are screened views of the Blackheads, Hunter, and Westkill in the last 200 ft of climbing, better when the trees are barren. The summit ridge has three viewpoints.

The first is a ledge on the RIGHT that hikers often use as a lunch spot while gazing at the Blackheads. The next is 25 ft ahead on the opposite side of the trail where the NE and E views have, unfortunately, been "improved" by hikers wanting to add to what Mother Nature provided.

The summit benchmark is two or three minutes ahead and encircled by low trees. The best view is 50 ft farther down the trail, from a ledge with 270-degree views. I'm indebted to Dr. Michael Kudish, professor emeritus of botany, for sharing his insights on the forest.

Trail training starts early—Windham High Peak.
—Nancy Swete

Watching.
—Joanne Hihn

Glossary

When it snows I like to listen to the quiet.

—Bill Keane

Asian longhorned beetle: This invasive insect likely hitchhiked into the U.S. in a wooden pallet. Scientists believe the 0.75-inch to 1.50-inch beetle has the potential to be one of the most devastating insects that has ever threatened our woodlands. Its hosts of choice are sugar maple, birch, and ash, but other deciduous trees are also in jeopardy. Millions of trees have already been killed in the eastern U.S. and the potential damage to the forest is almost unimaginable. Transportation of firewood accelerates the threat.

ATVs (all-terrain vehicles): These vehicles are useful farming, logging, and property maintenance tools. They do little damage to hard dirt roads and trails designated for them. You're likely to encounter illegal ATV use on some trails in *Doghiker*. These illegal trails slashed across public property damage the land that belongs to all of us. If you see an ATV where they're forbidden, note its plate number and that of the truck hauling it and report it to the local ranger.

black bears: The Catskills have an estimated population of between 2500 and 3000 black bears, a sharp increase from the less than 250 estimates of the 1970s. When numbers were low, DEC delayed the opening date of the hunting season to allow pregnant females to den before hunters entered the woods. The start of the hunting season has recently been readjusted in order to control the now-large population. The bear population in the Adirondacks is much smaller and issues are mostly confined to places where hikers camp or backpack.

Bear attacks are extremely rare, but any interaction should be from a distance. Be careful your dog doesn't approach a cub or decide to investigate the "big furry dog" or its "puppy." See the "Safeguarding Your Dog" chapter for advice on dog bells.

blowdown: Used to describe blown-over trees, fallen treetops, or branches, blowdown can make an easily travelled route more difficult. Severe wind or ice storms can wreak havoc on the mountains and trails.

bogs: Botanist Dr. Mike Kudish discovered that tree fossils preserved in high elevation peat bogs could be used to reconstruct forest history. The age of the peat and seeds in core samples can be determined by radiocarbon dating. His research has pushed the date of Catskill forest history back by 14,000 years.

boreal forest: A wet or boggy forest with conifer trees, mostly spruce or pine.

bushwhacking: Departing a marked trail, striking out with a map, compass, and perhaps accompanied by a GPS unit. Experienced hikers often refer to this as "whacking." See "herd paths."

cairn: A pile of rocks, small or large, marking a route, usually where trail markers aren't practical. Thought to be of Scottish origin, cairns were originally used to mark routes above tree line for travelers in bad weather. They often mark wooded summits that lack a readily identifiable high point. The proliferation of "decorative" cairns is seen as an issue that impacts the wilderness feel of the backcountry. See "Leave No Trace."

canopy: Forest canopy refers to the treetops under which hikers pass. The canopy provides shade for flora and fauna that live under its umbrella. It's a home, refuge, and hunting territory for a variety of birds and fauna. A damaged or missing canopy allows sunlight to penetrate, affecting plants and animals on the forest floor or in the trees.

Catskill Scenic Trail (CST): A twenty-six-mile unpaved railbed used by hikers, cyclists, and runners. It was formerly the railroad tracks used by the Ulster and Delaware Railroad. This trail connects Hubbell Corners and Bloomville.

Civilian Conservation Corps (CCC): The CCC was established by the New Deal and operated from 1933 until 1942. The projects they are best known for by hikers are the trails, woods roads, impoundments, campgrounds, and large red or white pine plantations seen throughout the Adirondacks and Catskills.

col: A low point between two mountains or sections of mountains.

DEC (Department of Environmental Conservation): This New York State agency controls and regulates state public property that is not regulated by the New York City Department of Environmental Protection (DEP).

DEP (Department of Environmental Protection): This New York City agency was originally set up to protect the watershed and reservoirs for the New York City metropolitan area. The DEP purchases land and protective easements. DEP has allowed the Catskill Mountain Club to design trails on its property. Dogs hiking on DEP property are required to be "under control" of the owner. DEP regulations state that this mean leashing.

dogleg: A term used by hikers or bushwhackers to describe an L-shaped mountain ridge or a trail. Viewed on a topographic map, the turn it describes will resemble a dog's rear leg. Look at a dog's rear leg and you'll instantly see what "follow the ridge until it dog-legs" means.

eastern tent caterpillar: The silky tents seen during spring are homes for tent caterpillar larvae. The emerging caterpillars attack the leaves of deciduous trees, with cherries and apples being their favorites. Periodic infestations result in forest canopy loss and the growth of sun-loving vegetation such as berry bushes.

emerald ash borer (EAB): This metallic green insect invader measures in at just under 0.4 inches. It snuck into Michigan from Asia in 2002, making its appearance in New York State in the summer of 2009. It wreaked havoc in the Midwest, and is beginning to endanger the large ash forests of the Northeast, as well. Purple plastic rectangular objects seen hanging in trees, nicknamed "Barney Boxes," are EAB traps. They contain a natural plant oil to attract the insects and an ecologically safe glue traps them, allowing scientists to see if the EAB has invaded a new territory.

erratics: Glacial erratics are large rocks and boulders that were transported by glaciers and left in place as the glaciers retreated at the end of the last ice age. Wikipedia describes them as pieces of rock that differ in size and type from the rock native to the area and explains that their name comes from the Latin "errare," to wander.

ferns: *Doghiker* readers will notice the frequent references to ferns along the trails. Most hikers can readily identify common wild-flowers, but their beauty is ephemeral. Ferns don't fiddle (sorry,

Glacial erratics.
—Alan Via

I couldn't pass it up) around. Their shade helps keep small brooks cool and prevents weeds and briars from overtaking trails. Lush fern glades are trail adornments and a natural complement to wildflower identification.

first growth forest: Defined by botanist Dr. Michael Kudish as forest that has not been commercially used. Dr. Kudish has discovered over one hundred square miles of first growth forest still surviving in the Catskills, in nearly fifty separate parcels. Logging, tanbark peeling, quarrying, agriculture, and forest fires have each contributed to their disappearance. Ridgetop and second home "development" is their latest threat. (I do not consider the replacement of pastures, ridge-lines, and mountainous terrain with houses or second homes a good thing for future generations or the animals that live there.)

forest tent caterpillar: These caterpillars don't actually make tents, but rather silken covers. Ash, oak, and maples are their targets, but sugar maples are their food of choice. Their appearance is cyclical, and hikers are aware when they are plentiful. See "eastern tent caterpillar."

GPS (Global Positioning System): GPS was originally developed by the U.S. Defense Department to identify the precise position of military targets and personnel adversaries. GPS marries satellite and information technology hardware and software and has been adapted for civilian use.

Nonmilitary GPS receivers had a built-in one-hundred-meter error, called "selective availability" (SA). SA was developed to prevent the technology from being used by military adversaries. In 2000, the Clinton administration turned off SA, leading to highly accurate units and an explosion of recreational and commercial use.

grid: A term in use by the Rip Van Winkle hiking club in recognizing hikers who have climbed each of the thirty-five Catskill High Peaks in every month. "Completing the Grid" means you've done 420 ascents. The term is also used to describe the goal of climbing the High Peaks of the Adirondack and White Mountains in each month. Hiking the Grid in the Adirondacks means hiking each of the forty-six Adirondack High Peaks in every month, or 552 ascents. Due to the above-tree-line summits, different soil makeup, and length of the mud season in the Adirondacks, conservationists and DEC see completing the Grid here as environmentally unsound and ask hikers to avoid hiking the higher summits during the mud season.

hemlock woolly adelgid (HWA): These small, aphid-like invaders from Asia threaten the health and sustainability of eastern and Carolina hemlocks. They were first seen in the western U.S. in 1924, and near Richmond, Virginia, in 1951. By 2005, the adelgid was established in portions of sixteen states from Maine to Georgia, where infestations covered about half of the range of hemlock. In the north, hemlock decline and mortality occurs within six to ten years of infestation. The adelgid is now found in the Catskills and Adirondacks, presenting a severe threat to the survival of iconic hemlocks.

herd paths: These unmarked paths develop as a result of hikers taking the same, often easier route to a summit, viewpoint, or campsite. Those leading to popular, untrailed summits are often so well-used that they look like marked trails without trail markers. *Doghiker* readers are cautioned to remain on established trails unless they are comfortable with off-trail travel.

hiking clubs: Adirondack Mountain Club (ADK), Catskill Mountain Club (CMC), Appalachian Mountain Club (AMC), Catskill 3500 Club, Taconic Hiking Club, and Rip Van Winkle Hikers all schedule hikes led by experienced leaders. This is a great way to meet like-minded hikers and learn about new areas.

hunting seasons: These include the month-long turkey hunting

Three's a crowd.
–Joanne Hihn

seasons in spring and autumn, and big game hunting seasons in autumn. Check with DEC for dates and locations in New York State. Avoid bushwhacking during hunting season, particularly during the autumn deer and bear seasons. Hikers should wear blaze orange clothing and dogs a blaze orange vest and large bell.

ice storms: Deciduous forests are particularly susceptible to ice damage. At high elevations, precipitation is often in the form of snow when it's raining in the valleys. Where temperatures are in between, tree branches can ice up and break from the extra weight of snow and ice, or when the wind picks up. Trails can be cleared, but blowdown and damaged canopy can impact the forest for years.

leave no trace (LNT): A series of techniques that emphasizes ways to lessen human and canine impact on trails, summits, and in forests. When hiking with dogs, prevent them from damaging fragile summit vegetation and pack-out or bury their waste well away from trails and water.

ledges: These are the cliff bands trails pass through or follow. *Doghiker* identifies hikes and locations where some dogs or hikers may have difficulty or where trails lead past cliff tops. Dogs have good survival instincts, but icy rocks or being startled by another dog can be dangerous. Be careful where you throw sticks when accompanied by dogs with strong retrieve drive.

maps: Referred to as "topos" by hikers, topographic maps show contour lines, elevations, and bodies of water, as well as roads and other man-made features. Topo maps for the Catskills are published by the New York-New Jersey Trail Conference and National Geographic. The Adirondack Mountain Club (ADK) has an excellent topographic map series for the Adirondacks done in partnership with National Geographic. ADK has developed its own map to the Adirondack High Peaks that is simply the best map of its kind. Large-scale topographic maps with coverage of the entire state of New York are produced by the United States Geographic Survey (USGS) and are available in digital form from the online USGS Map Store (store.usgs.gov/map-locator). Some book and outdoor stores still carry USGS paper maps, but they are out of print and getting hard to find. *Doghiker* has the best maps available for the trails in this book. They were specifically created for each hike by Liz Cruz of Cruz Cartography using Geographic Information System (GIS) data and GPS tracks provided by the author.

microchip: This small implant the size of a rice grain is injected into the loose skin on a dog's nape by a veterinarian. A hand scanner allows vets, animal control personnel, or dog shelters to quickly read your contact information from the chip. This is one of the best ways of being reunited with a lost dog.

MICROspikes®: Kahtoola revolutionized winter hiking by filling the niche between boot crampons and bare booting with this product. MICROspikes® are attached by a heavy rubber rand that fits around the bottom edge of your boots. They have triangular spikes attached by small chains and a wire bail that fits over the front of your boot. Though they don't have the bite or grip of boot crampons, they go on and come off in seconds and perform well on moderately icy terrain. They are not a substitute in conditions requiring crampons.

mixed forest: A mixed forest is a forest with both conifers and deciduous trees.

perched wetland: Bodies of water, usually small, that collect water from drainage or precipitation, not from streams.

peak lists: I refer to three groups of peaks throughout *Doghiker*. In the Adirondacks, there is the list called the Adirondack 46. This refers to a group of peaks first thought to all be 4000 ft in elevation or higher. Mountains on this list are generally referred to as the Adirondack High Peaks. The Catskills have two lists. The Catskill 35 refers to a group of 35 summits, each 3500 ft or higher. These are generally referred to as the Catskill High Peaks. A third group of summits is a list called the Catskill 100 Highest. The 100 Highest consist of the Catskill 35 plus an additional 67 peaks. There are 102 peaks on this list because some are tied in elevation. You can read more about this list in "Suggested Reading."

pole stand: A forest where deciduous trees, generally of the same height, diameter, and age, predominate. Pole stands are usually seen colonizing the site of a former pasture or meadow, before other tree varieties can take root. They are very often beech or maple trees.

poopsickles: This term describes frozen "deposits" of dog waste left by inconsiderate dog owners for others to step on, carry out, or bury.

posted signs: Signs by property owners to denote boundaries and private property. There are also DEC and DEP posters. Posted signs should contain the name and address of the landowner. Recording contact information may lead to permission on a future hike.

retractor leash: Although convenient so dogs can extend their distance, these leashes allow dogs to run into traffic, get into mischief, be involved in a fight, or bother other hikers. Dogs can get a running start that jerks the handle out of your hand. See comments in the gear chapter.

Ruffwear: Makers of great collars, leashes, and harnesses. They have an excellent selection of well-made gear.

seep: Botanist Dr. Mike Kudish explains that this hydrological term describes sheets of water of higher pH and oxygenation. Seeps serve as a water source for local fauna and flora and are often home to a wide variety of plant life that Dr. Kudish refers to as "seepers." The presence of a seep often leads to an otherwise unlikely concentration of plant life in a small area. A seep differs from a spring as springs come from a point source and a seep from a broader area.

Bushwhack summit celebration.
—Mike Kalin

side hilling: When a trail passes across a slope instead of uphill or down. Long sections of side hill hiking can be tiring.

sling leash: At a convenient four feet, a sling leash is long enough to fit most hikers, but short enough to avoid snagging on branches. When the leash handle is clipped into the leash buckle, it can be slung, bandolier style, across your chest and over pack straps, allowing quick deployment.

stone fences: The mountains and hills over which *Doghiker* leads were settled long ago. Beautiful stone fences mark old farmsteads and property lines. Settlers cleared woodlands for agriculture and livestock and the stones ended up as fences. Though the old farms are gone, the walls remain, a scenic reminder of different times.

switchbacks: On steep terrain, trails and woods roads often zigzag up slopes. Switchbacked roads allowed tractors, log skidders, and quarry loads to climb and descend safely. Switchbacks allow hikers to gain elevation with longer distance but easier climbing.

training commands: "Recall," "stay/wait," and "leave it" are essential dog-training behaviors that can save a dog's life. These are covered in detail in the training chapter.

woods roads: Constructed for logging, agriculture, fire control, quarrying, or access to fire towers, woods roads may be unpaved dirt, grass, or clay. Their surface can vary from drivable to rough and washed-out, overgrown, or rocky. Trails that follow woods road in this guide are generally easy hiking. Bushwhackers who find one heading in the direction they're traveling look at them as a gift from the bushwhacking gods.

Hitchhiker — Holt Preserve.
— Alan Via

Suggested Reading

Dogs are our link to paradise. They don't know evil or jealousy or discontent. To sit with a dog on a hillside on a glorious afternoon is to be back in Eden, where doing nothing was not boring—it was peace.

—Milan Kundera

Suggested Nonfiction

The Catskill 67: A Hiker's Guide to the Catskill 100 Peaks under 3500', Alan Via. Adirondack Mountain Club. 2012.

Not a book about hiking with dogs, but my Lab Bookah hiked all the peaks with me, sometimes over and over again. Our Lab Toby is following Bookah's pawprints on the Catskill 100. This is another good source of places to hike with or without your dog.

Merle's Door: Lessons from a Freethinking Dog, Ted Kerasote. Harcourt, Inc. 2007.

A bestseller that earns the right to be described as such. The book chronicles the life of the author's dog, Merle, and their relationship at their cabin in Wyoming. Merle lives an enviable life, joining Ted on all of his outdoor adventures. To read this book is to open your eyes and heart to the canine-human relationship in the Wyoming outdoors.

Pukka's Promise: The Quest for Longer-Lived Dogs, Ted Kerasote. Houghton, Mifflin, Harcourt. 2013.

Kerasote's follow up to *Merle's Door*. Much more science and information about selecting and raising a healthy dog. A wonderful book about nutrition, avoiding environmental problems, genetics, dog rescue, and much more in a very readable format.

The Book of the Dog, Angus Hyland and Kendra Wilson. Lawrence King Publishing, Ltd. 2015.

Describing this dog art book as spectacular would be an understatement. Dogs depicted in historic and contemporary oil, watercolor, and drawing.

1000 Dog Portraits: From the People Who Love Them, Robynne Raye. Rockport Publishers. 2014.

The dog portraits are drawn and painted by amateur and professional artists and range from creatively interesting to spectacular. Open the book and plan to get lost in its pages for a few hours. The settings and poses will bring to mind your dogs or those of friends.

How to Look After Your Human: A Dog's Guide, Maggie Mayhem and Kim Sears. Frances Lincoln Children's Books. 2016.

A delightful and whimsical guide for training humans from a dog's point of view. Often hilarious, with great illustrations. This is a fun look at selecting and training dogs, and a light-touch look at both sides of the canine-human relationship. There's a chapter on "How to Dress Your Human" and another on a dog's Ten Commandments.

The Art of Raising a Puppy, The Monks of New Skete. Little, Brown and Co. 2011.

Considered somewhat dated by advocates of modern dog training techniques that disagree with coercive training, the book is nevertheless loaded with useful information, particularly about the early stages of puppyhood. I strongly disagree with some their harsher training methods.

Dogs Don't Bite When a Growl Will Do, Matt Weinstein and Luke Barber. Penguin 2003.

The subtitle, "What Your Dog Can Teach You About Living a Happy Life" is reflected in sixty-seven well-written essays that cover just about every eventuality or peculiarity of living with a dog. You'll smile through tears when reading the last essay, "Dogs Dance with Life and Death." The authors recall the last day of life for their dog, Blue, when he walked into the room with a ball in his mouth. They envisioned him thinking, "I'm not dead yet. Let's play."

Retriever Training of Spaniels, Pamela Owen Kadlec. Just Ducky Publishing. 2002.

Interesting training tips for any of the retriever breeds.

The 10 Minute Retriever: How to Make an Obedient and Enthusiastic Gun Dog in 10 Minutes a Day, John and Amy Dahl. Willow Creek Press. 2001.

Not just for gun dogs.

Water Dog: Revolutionary Rapid Training Method, Richard A. Wolters. Dutton. 1964.

The title describes interesting methods of retriever training.

Old Dogs Remembered, edited by Bud Johns. Synergistic Publications. 1999.

A wonderful and heartwarming collection of essays, poems, and stories about beloved dogs by the likes of James Thurber, John Cheever, Eugene O'Neill, E. B. White, John Burroughs, Raymond Carver, and Robinson Jeffers.

Never Cry Wolf, Farley Mowat. Dell Publishing, Co., Inc. 1963.

From the book jacket: "Mr. Mowat describes the captivating summer he spent in the Arctic with these long-misunderstood animals."

Best Hikes with Dogs: New Hampshire and Vermont, Lisa Densmore. The Mountaineers Books. 2005.

A terrific guide for dog hikes in our nearby New England states. The book deserves the praise given it by reviewers.

Hiking with Dogs: Becoming a Wilderness-Wise Dog Owner, Linda B. Mullally. Falcon Guides. 1999.

Good basics about hiking with dogs, not related to a specific geographic area.

Dog Hikes in the Adirondacks: 20 Trails to Enjoy with Your Best Friend, edited by Annie Stoltie and Elizabeth Ward. Shaggy Dog Press. 2009.

This sixty-three-page book describes twenty nice hikes in the Adirondacks.

Dog Is My Co-Pilot: Great Writing on the World's Oldest Friendship, from the editors of *The Bark*. Crown Publishers. 2003.

A reviewer in the *Kansas City Star* wrote, "In case you didn't know, *The Bark* is a magazine for dog lovers. It has been out there since 1999, and *Esquire* has called it 'the coolest dog magazine ever.' This anthology is cool, too, as it fetches intelligent but emotional writing on the bond between humans and canines. . . . Herein lies the skill and wit."

The Seattle Times notes, "From start to finish, this rich tapestry of stories takes the reader on a roller-coaster ride of emotions, soothing and benign in one selection, carousing and spirited in the next."

Inside of a Dog: What Dogs See, Smell, and Know, Alexandra Horowitz. Scribner. 2009.

From the book: "Horowitz introduces the reader to dogs' perceptual and cognitive abilities and then draws a picture of what it might be like to *be* a dog. What it's like to be able to smell not just every bit of open food in the house but also to smell sadness in humans, or even the passage of time." A wonderful and eye-opening read.

Good Dog. Stay, Anna Quindlen. Random House. 2007.

A wonderful, heartwarming love story summarized on the book jacket as, "Heartening and bittersweet . . . honors the life of a cherished and loyal friend and offers us a valuable lesson on our four-legged family members: sometimes an old dog can teach us new tricks."

Going Home: Finding Peace When Pets Die, Jon Katz. Villard. 2011.

By one of dogdom's most esteemed writers. The title says it all. Katz has written so many great dog books, you can't go wrong with any of them. This one helps dog owners cope with the inevitable loss of their pets.

Suggested Fiction

The Story of Edgar Sawtelle, David Wroblewski. Harper Collins. 2008.

This novel had a long run on *The New York Times* bestseller list. A wonderful story of a boy and his dogs, but so much more.

The Big New Yorker Book of Dogs, foreword by Malcolm Gladwell. Random House. 2012.

As the dust jacket says, "Only *The New Yorker* could fetch such an unbelievable roster of talent on the subject of man's best friends. Stories and essays by the likes of John Cheever, Susan Orlean, A. J. Liebling, Ogden Nash, Alexandra Fuller, Ian Frazer, T. Coraghessan Boyle, and too many other luminaries to list."

Dancing Dog: Stories, Jon Katz. Ballantine Books. 2012.

Sixteen heartwarming stories described thus on the dust jacket: "Whether sitting, staying or rolling over, in the barnyard, shelters,

Walking to a trailhead with Bookah.
—Joanne Hihn

or home sweet home, the creatures in *Dancing Dogs* are genuinely inspiring and utterly memorable."

The Art of Racing in the Rain: My Life as a Dog, Garth Stein. Harper. 2008.

The story of Enzo and his family is hard to describe, a classic and deservedly so. It's more than just a dog story. A grown-up fairy tale that draws you into its world.

The Dog Master: A Novel of the First Dog, W. Bruce Cameron. Forge Books (Reprint Edition). 2016.

Tells the story of man's first bond with a canid, how our long and storied history with dogs began in a long-ago time.

City, Clifford Simak. Ace. 1952.

Described in *The New York Times* thus: "Each of these [eight] stories is satisfying; taken together they have a good deal more depth than most science fiction." Set in the far future when humans have disappeared and dogs have evolved. "I can't go back," said Towser. "Nor I," said Fowler. "They would turn me back into a dog," said Towser. "And me," said Fowler, "back into a man."

MARY

How can this dog on the cushion
at my feet have passed me
in the continuum of age, a knot
in our hearts that never unwinds? This dog
is helplessly herself and cannot think otherwise.
When called she often conceals herself
behind a bush, a tree, or tall grass
pondering if she should obey. Now crippled
at twelve, bearing up under pain
on the morning run, perhaps wondering
remotely what this is all about, the slowness
that has invaded her bones. Splayed out
now in a prone running pose
she moves in sleep slowly into the future
that does not welcome us but is merely
our destiny in which we disappear
making room for others on the long march.
The question still is how did she pass me
happily ahead in this slow goodbye?

—Jim Harrison

Matt and Janie Gizmo.
—Alan Via

Bookah—the inspiration for Doghiker.
—Joanne Hihn

Index

Boldface indicates a hike description.

About the Author

All the best-laid plans in the world can be rewritten
into something better from the right perch.

—Hope Jahren

Alan Via grew up wandering the woods in upstate New York. He feels fortunate to have belonged to nine dogs during his lifetime. Alan discovered hiking in his early twenties when introduced to the sport by a coworker who was then the chairperson of the Outings Committee for the Albany Chapter of the Adirondack Mountain Club (ADK). His love affair with the mountains began with those first hikes in the Adirondack High Peaks.

It wasn't too long before Alan was a regular on ADK hikes and eventually he began leading trips himself. In just a few years, he succeeded his coworker to become chair of the Albany Chapter's Outings

Fern glade—Bookah and Alan.
—Joanne Hihn

Committee, a position he held for fourteen years. Since that time, he's had an unbroken tenure as a committee chair for the main ADK club and received the organization's Distinguished Volunteer Award in 2006. Alan has been a hike leader for the ADK, Catskill Mountain Club, Taconic Hiking Club, and the Catskill 3500 Club. He founded and led the Bethlehem YMCA's hiking group for several years.

Alan's hiking achievements include the completion of the Adirondack 46 High Peaks and repeating them in winter. He's also hiked the Catskill 35 High Peaks with winter repeats. Alan completed the Adirondack 100 Highest and New England 111, and led end-to-end hikes on the Taconic Crest Trail five times. One of his most memorable days in the mountains was completing the Catskill 100 Highest with his Labrador retriever Bookah, the first dog to achieve that milestone. His most recent project was climbing the Catskill 200 highest summits.

Alan's greatest joy comes from his children, Gillian and Matt, and amazing grandkids, Rob, Holly, Thomas, and Jesse.

He is a frequent contributor of hiking-related articles for numerous outdoor publications. *Doghiker* is his second hiking guide. *The Catskill 67: A Hiker's Guide to the Catskill 100 Highest Peaks under 3500'* was published by the Adirondack Mountain Club in 2012.

Alan and Bookah complete the Catskill Hundred Highest.
—Joanne Hihn